The
DIRECTOR'S & OFFICER'S
Guide to Advisory Boards

Recent Titles from Quorum Books

The
DIRECTOR'S & OFFICER'S
Guide to Advisory Boards

Robert K. Mueller

Q
QUORUM BOOKS
New York · Westport, Connecticut · London

Library of Congress Cataloging-in-Publication Data

Mueller, Robert Kirk.
The director's and officer's guide to advisory boards / Robert K.
Mueller.
  p. cm.
Bibliography: p.
Includes index.
ISBN 0-89930-467-2 (alk. paper)
  1. Corporate governance. 2. Directors of corporations.
3. Consultants. 4. Business consultants. 5. Executive advisory
bodies. I. Title.
HD2745.M834 1990
658.4'6—dc20   89-32858

British Library Cataloguing in Publication Data is available.

Library of Congress Catalog Card Number: 89-32858
ISBN: 0-89930-467-2

First published in 1990 by Quorum Books

Greenwood Press, Inc.
88 Post Road West, Westport, Connecticut 06881

Printed in the United States of America

The paper used in this book complies with the
Permanent Paper Standard issued by the National
Information Standards Organization (Z39.48-1984).

10 9 8 7 6 5 4 3 2 1

Copyright Acknowledgment

Portions of Chapter 5, "Activity and Societal Scan," are from Robert K. Mueller,
Board Compass: What It Means to be a Director in a Changing World (Lexington,
Mass.: D. C. Heath and Company, 1979) and have been updated and included herein.

CONTENTS

TABLES AND FIGURES

PREFACE

"No more effect than a sparrow's tears," quoth John E. Thayer III, Research Fellow, Peabody Museum, Salem, Massachusetts. The occasion was a symposium in Boston on March 15, 1986, on Japan in the United States, subtitled "Do we really understand each other?" Thayer was one of sixteen distinguished participants noting that despite heightened sensitivity to bilateral problems and realities of conflict resolution, the two countries still are not listening to each other.

The listening problem is one that boards of directors also have with respect to certain stakeholders' interests and the many forces at work in the environment. We can go as far back as Sophocles (*Antigone*, 442–441 B.C.) to hear, "It can be no dishonor to learn from others when they speak good sense." The more recent environmental turbulence in which corporations must now function has heightened sensitivity to the complexity of doing business worldwide. However, unless the advisors "speak good sense," and competitive or other perils are acute, boards of directors tend to entertain only limited advice from outsiders.

The recent director and officer (D&O) liability insurance availability and cost crisis causing some directors to defect from boardrooms is one such acute peril. Dr. John J. Arena, president and chief executive officer of Endowment Management & Research Corporation (Boston), points out that this trend is one "in which boards of directors are currently in a self-destruct mode." This trend, added to the chronic problem of business complexity, has forced many corporations to look to other means for getting expert advice. It is important to listen for early warning signals from forces potentially impacting future performance. This situation reminds me of Samuel Johnson's late eighteenth-century comment, "When a man knows he is to be hanged in a fortnight, it concentrates his mind wonderfully."

There is evidence that a new *governance geometry* is forming around the organization of expert groups engaged in sensing early warning signals from forces at work external to corporations. These adjunct groups normally report either to the chairman of the board or to the chief executive officer.

One view of an advisory board or council is that it is a prosthetic device, that is, an artificial organizational device to replace a missing part of the corporate body. The missing part may be inadequate resource persons on the statutory board or in top management. The prosthesis may be useful for a period of time until the expertise or counsel needed is available internally. Unlike some prosthetic devices that are permanently required, I believe an organizational prosthesis of an advisory council has a definite life cycle. Conditions and needs of the corporation change and more integral, permanent resources are often substituted for the outside councillors.

One of the important cautions about advisory groups is to avoid having those responsible—the board of directors or the chief executive officer—defer or abdicate to the advisors with regard to decision making. The advisors must be careful not to confuse accountability in the organization or de facto, assume authority without responsibility. Advisors are a resource and nothing more.

The structural addition of an advisory council attached to a corporation is, in my opinion, only a transitional resource model. In most instances the function of such a council or board of advisors is an enabling mechanism. The arrangement may accommodate a gradual restructuring of either the board or top management. Alternately, it can permit or provoke changing the actors in their present organizational roles in order to meet the new challenges facing the corporation better.

In this sense, an advisory adjunct group is often a dissipative structural device created to fill a special company need. When such function or purpose is fulfilled, a more permanent organizational solution is often institutionalized. Changing advisors as needs change may justify a continuing or standing outside advisory group. But the renewal of the advisor incumbents has a cycle of its own. This must be addressed; otherwise the value of the advice becomes obsolete and the advisory council assumes a life of its own, which may or may not be congruent with the host corporation.

The boundary and the external network relationships of key corporate actors need periodic reassessment in order for boards of directors and top management to be ready for the impact of acute future events. More effective conduct of business may be attained through some different organizational linkages and communications bridges to the outside world. Advisory councils of advisory boards can be useful in this regard.

There are at least six overlapping spheres or levels of external conditions that can be tapped by advisory board or advisory council members and their individual networks external to a corporation. These spheres are (1) the societal realm dealing with social accountability, values, institutional purpose, ethics, and ideology; (2) the political sphere concerned with power, communication, influence, linkages, and networks; conflicts and harmony of interests, regulatory, political, consumer and environmental issues; (3) the legal sphere, that is, the stakeholder interests and relevant fiduciary and statutory requirements; (4) the corporate sphere dealing with governance canons, articles of incorporation, identity, bylaws; corporate culture and communications; the corporate strategic objectives and boundary, its employees, hierarchy, command, control, and power flow; (5) the commercial or economic sphere involved with suppliers, customers, competition, innovation, economic and business development initiatives, diversification, pricing strategy, and last, but not least, (6) the professional sphere where individual net worth, peer respect, peer response, eliteness, and human networking relationships dominate. Integrity, professionalism, and expertise are key. Professional networks can be invaluable means of sensing what is going on in this sixth domain.

Advisory boards or councils can provide an early warning system at the directorate zone or the executive management zone of corporate enterprise. The former zone concerns matters of a purposeful nature, including values, philosophy, conduct, and goals of the enterprise. The executive management zone at a normative level deals with performance criteria and standards, what the corporation "should" do, its organization, systems, and plans.

A systems approach and construct is a useful concept on which to couple the notion of an advisory board or advisory council. These adjunct resources can help raise consciousness, facilitate multilevel decisions, and help crystalize a strategic decision or direction to be taken by the statutory board and management in responsible charge.

The key message of this book is that advisory councils can have an increasingly important role as corporations become more competitive and sensitive worldwide. However, such adjunct councils of experts must be engaged appropriately and often considered a transitional organizational device to respond to a particular need for outside advice and counsel.

Outside advisors can provide channels for sensing early warning signals, for communicating signals from stakeholder constituents, and for assessing external influences impacting the corporation. In theory, at least, such sensing systems and talents can be incorporated in top management or on the statutory board. However, the outside, independent perspective has a unique value that even the most sophisticated corporations may find only by a continually renewed and changing composition of advisory directors or councillors.

Advisory boards or councils can alert the board of directors and top management to defensive or innovative measures to cope with these potentially powerful external forces. This alert may also minimize the necessary damage control response when the impact of changes catches a corporation unaware.

The Director's and Officer's Guide to Advisory Boards pilots the selection, scoping, and "care and feeding" of advisory boards or councils. This is an old but evolving organizational device to help deal with uncertainty, ambiguity, complexity, and accountability of corporate conduct. I believe that outside advisors, properly engaged for an appropriate period, can be a valuable resource to those who are fiducially and statutorily responsible.

"Good counsel without good fortune is a windmill without wind," according to an old German proverb. I have the good fortune of getting advice on the subject of advice from a worldwide network of colleagues and fellow directors. I respect and acknowledge their counsel. My thanks goes to these many peers and friends, most of whom prefer to remain unidentified.

I also acknowledge English literary critic John Churton's nineteenth-century caveat: "To profit from good advice requires more wisdom than to give it." Such pith prompted *The Director's and Officer's Guide to Advisory Boards.*

The
DIRECTOR'S & OFFICER'S
Guide to Advisory Boards

INTRODUCTION

This introduction leads the discussion of what's new, what is an advisory board, how does it work, and why not stick with the statutory board or hire a consultant?

The concept of advisors to the person in responsible charge, the ruling monarch or head of state is, of course, not new. Richard II and Henry VI recognized the King's Privy Council as a selected body of men appointed by the crown, without any patent or grant to advise the crown in matters of state. Originally, the council had legislative, judicial, and administrative powers. Now most of these powers have been either abolished or delegated. The individuals, if any, provide official or private counseling on specific issues.

The corporate descendants of advisors-to-the-chief have existed informally or formally in business since the beginning of enterprise development. While not yet a common industrial organization tool, the historical use of advisory councils is perhaps more common with financial intermediary companies such as banks, insurance companies, and financial services. Chapter 1 identifies over one hundred large publicly owned corporations of all types around the world that publicize their advisory councils.

The advice comes from various sources: fellow entrepreneurial founders and directors, senior family members, or other shareowners in closely held corporations. Attorneys, accountants, bankers, scientists, friends, consultants, experts, and mentors of diverse sorts show up on advisory councils, depending on the business sector size, state of development of the firm, and nature of ownership.

What *is* new is the context in which business and other institutions must now function. Rate of change in economic, social, political, environmental, communications, and technological matters is increasing dramatically. Turbulence, discontinuities, and competition require new approaches and sensitivity to the dynamics of strategic governance and management. Hence the interest in obtaining the best advice available in order to cope with these new forces at work in the environment.

Chapter 1 introduces the new "advice age" and reviews what contract advice is all about. Chapter 2 presents the current and future forces at work on institutions that create new problems, issues, and challenges.

Chapter 3 provides comparative analysis of what advisors do that statutory boards, consultants, or mentors do not do. This is further positioned in Chapter 4. The next four chapters survey how advisory boards of different species work to carry out their special role or functions. Chapters 9 and 10 suggest practical guidelines for the contracting advisee organization, in order to optimize the value of an advisory board, council, or panel.

The final six chapters offer clinical experience from the advisor perspective. The way an effective advisory group normally views its role reinforces the contemporary value of the outside advisor concept. The special worth of expert resources and independent perspectives provided by a carefully selected council of advisors is particularly timely. This is topical because of the rapidly changing environmental uncertainties faced by corporate directors and officers.

The Appendix examines the position of a director or officer of a company, an independent, experienced individual from most any walk of life (e.g., education, public, or social service), or a professional person, seeking engagement as an advisory council member. I am constantly asked, "How do I get invited to be on a board of directors or an advisory board?" This is difficult to answer. The situations, opportunities, barriers, and criteria for qualifying as an independent advisor are person-specific, company-specific, and time- and need-specific. However, there are practical ways to increase the odds on being invited to serve as a corporate advisor.

But why an advisory board or council rather than a consulting firm or a clutch of independent consultants? The contemporary concept of an advisory board or council has unique and powerful bespoke characteristics. These distinguish the advisory council model from conventional consultancy, as generally practiced. Statutory directors, on the other hand, are guided by statutes and regulations and the duties of loyalty, care, and attention familiar to all directors of corporations (along with numerous normative governance conduct rules).

An advisory board or council has special differentiated (1) princi-

pals, (2) structure or nonstructure, (3) role and process, (4) cost benefits, (5) criteria for accountability, (6) networks, (7) identity and status, (8) individual versus group contractual relations and social rapport
with the advisee and fellow advisors, (9) flexibility, availability, agenda,
and priorities, and (10) rites and rituals.

Principals. No advisor looks to an advisory board as a source of
current daily living income. Advisors expect to be paid for their professional services but are not dependent on the engagement for income. When serving on a not-for-profit institutional advisory board,
expenses may or may not be reimbursed. Fees are not normally involved.

Advisors are experienced, trustworthy, peer-respected, innovative,
thoughtful persons who can preserve confidentiality and independence. They become "insiders" with regard to the advisee's affairs.
Advisors are individual experts or generalists in different domains of
activity relevant to the interests of the corporation served.

The "stranger factor" is a valuable notion in moderation, in the
sense that principals are outsiders usually with expertise in fields of
relevance to the corporation *other* than that of their fellow advisors.
Each principal offers a different background of education, culture, career, experience, perhaps geographical, ideological, or possibly some
social distinctions. Ethics, morals, value systems, beliefs, articles of
faith, and attitudes may differ but should not be acutely in opposition
or out of step with current societal or business norms. Congeniality,
collegiality, and mutual esteem should exist among advisors and advisee.

Advisors are primarily motivated by the service ethic. The attraction is the opportunity to make a meaningful contribution and new
associations—colleaguesmanship—with other special principals. The
advisee, in return, has an obligation to receive the advisory input
responsibly. Otherwise, the advisor may opt out of the relationship
rather than have his or her time, efforts, and identity neglected, used,
abused, or associated with a token role or involved superficially with
an elite "privy council."

Structure. An advisory board or council is a loose cluster of independent principals. The aggregate gets some sense of order in its deliberations through an informal chair or the advisee point-person with
regard to meeting agenda, schedule, scope, and pace of discussions.
Effective use of an advisory council is best achieved when the advisee
decides what subjects to put on the agenda and informs the advisors
well in advance. No legal structure is normally involved, except the
individual contractual agreements. Advisors remain independent contractors.

Role and process. Given the seniority, experience, and expertise of the principals, minimum learning-curve time and energy are required to get advisors in synch with the advisee situation and issues facing the corporation. Therefore, the advisee does not have to pay for the usual learning period required on most consultant engagements. Only dedicated principals are invited to serve on an advisory board with no alternates or substitutes permitted. Advisory boards or councils may serve their role for a period and be abandoned after having served their purpose.

Alternately, the incumbents may be replaced with a new set of experts offering different perspectives as the competitive position or business environment changes and different type advice is needed. The advisee contacts the group or individual principals at will. No attempt is made to force consensus at meetings. There is no political force at work between advisor members or the advisee. The advice and counsel is individual and independent. The group may agree but such consensus is not necessarily a product of an advisory board's contribution. An array of different perspectives and judgments are valuable.

No oath of office is required, as of statutory directors of a U.S. bank. Advisory directors have either a formal or an informal contractual understanding of their obligations, compensation, and other terms of engagement. However, these are usually general and broad in scope. Advisory boards normally have no "flight plan," target objective, or detailed specific tasks. They serve as a focus group and a sounding board for the proposed or existing policies and plans developed by the advisee. Principals may offer alternative approaches, concepts, viewpoints on assumptions, opportunities, or threats.

Advisors provide outreach in perspectives and early warning signals on externalities likely to impact the corporation. Advisory boards focus on early problem and issue sensing, on identification and definition as distinct from problem solving, issue resolution, or decision making. Once identified, the advisee may use the corporation's internal staff resources or employ a consultant on a specific assignment. Any "finder" role suggestions from advisors are followed up, usually by the advisee who has the resources in-house to do the staff work required. The advisor's role normally does not include follow-through, implementation, or monitoring unless specifically engaged to do so. An advisory board functions as a small, apolitical group of soloists—primadonnas perhaps—rather than as a symphony orchestra or chamber ensemble.

Cost benefits. Advisory boards normally have little impact on the overhead burden of a corporation other than the fees and travel expenses of the principals. Normally, these expenses are considerably less than a statutory board's budget, which includes director perquisites, higher retainer, meeting attendance fees, and committee service compensation, costs of ambassadorial activities, corporate representation expenses, and a more frequent meeting schedule. Advisory boards have no economic engine or drive inherent in a consultant's contract to produce a survey, a solution, a model, or a body of intellectual property specifically in accord with the terms of a consultant's engagement. Some senior consultants do operate with a retainer fee for general counseling. The character of such engagement is for purchased services. The meter runs depending on the request. Advisors usually do not require the advisee to provide staff support nor does the advisory board produce a specific product or formal report. Advisory boards commit no resources other than their own knowledge, perspectives, and contacts. Advisees get what they pay for. Therefore, they insist on highly qualified, experienced, mature, sophisticated principals who collectively know the territory, industry, technology, economics, dynamics, and the cultural and competitive environment.

Criteria for accountability. Corporate statutes and government regulations prescribe legal accountabilities of directors and officers. No such legal framework exists for advisory boards, councils, or panels. Consultants usually limit their liabilities specifically by agreement to value of the consulting contract involved. Malpractice liabilities, as a professional, set the probable extent of accountability for advisor principals. This is seldom an issue with advisory boards. Advisors are encouraged to have the advisee extend its company director and officer (D&O) liability insurance coverage and indemnification to cover the activities of the advisory board. An advisory board takes no "title" to the product or composite of its advice, other than risking the reputation of the principals as experts giving an opinion or judgment. This peer accountability is fuzzier than legal accountability, but it is powerful.

Networks. Experienced, distinguished advisors bring with them their personal, business, and professional network contacts. The advisee organization acquires the gatekeeper to these special networks by virtue of engaging the principal involved. Similar to a center or focus group in an academic environment, an advisory board acts as a knowledge center—without walls. Principals share, or do not share, access to their respective networks.

Identity and status. Like the medieval privy councils, a modern advisory board may be modeled as a private, confidential council, or may have a publicly identified organizational identity. Sometimes creation of an advisor group is perceived to signal distress or alternately "good form" because of the judgment to engage distinguished outside talent. Engagement of an elite advisory board solely for the prestige the members enjoy and bring to the advisee is discussed in Chapter 9.

I have served on advisory boards which were formed with publicity releases, including advisor pictures with the chairman. All public relations techniques, including listing in the annual report to share-owners, may be employed to display the talent and wisdom that the chairman has at his disposal, over and above his statutory board. Other advisory boards I have served on have kept the engagement confidential, except to the advisee's bankers to impress them with the company's efforts to obtain the best business advice available. Note that the identity of an adjunct group of advisors may be perceived as a threat to, or bypass of, the statutory board or top management. Depending on the political sensitivity of this reaction, advisors are often identified as members of a *council* or *panel* of advisors to the CEO or chairman, rather than as a competitive "board." From a legal liability perspective, there are reasons for an advisory group avoiding being treated as a board of directors. These reasons are discussed in Chapter 2.

Professional/social contract. Advisors enter into a professional, independent contractor relationship with the advisee. They also tend to develop some empathetic social contract with other advisors and the advisee over the time they work together. One of the benefits to the advisors is learning from each other and the advisee, plus sharing thoughts and experiences on a third-party situation, problem, or challenge.

Advisors contract with the advisee to devote a certain amount of time, thinking, and travel to their role. This is normally less than when engaged as a consultant on a specific project, which is clearly defined. The size, maturity and nature of the advisee company may suggest different advisory group structures or connections with the advisee. Not many would wish the advisory council to meet with the board of directors on a regular basis, if at all. I have been on a board where this was the practice despite the significance of keeping these groups apart for many reasons. It is best to keep these groups separate.

Rites and rituals. Advisory boards can be large or small in number. Large groups need some formality to their deliberations in order to give air time to all participants. Smaller boards, councils, or panels function without much meeting drill or structure. Robert's rules of order, minutes of meetings, voting, or propositions are not normally characteristic of the advisory board style. The advisee point-person usually chairs the meetings informally and manages the agenda, which has been communicated to advisors before their meeting.

The primary purpose of rites and rituals is to manifest cultural expressions for one event. The event is carried out through social interaction, usually for the benefit of an audience and to manage anxieties. Since an advisory board does not perform for only one event or for an audience, and members are anxiety-free by nature of their role, accountability, and independence, there is little reason for standardized sets of techniques and behaviors. Rites and rituals are replaced by collegial exchanges and informal behavior.

In contrast, consultants' meetings with their clients are carefully structured for clarity of presentation and scope, recitation of findings, and demonstration of the effort and research that precedes the consultant's recommendations. Advisory board members usually present their own opinions, informally and independently. There is a minimum of preparation, other than thinking about the issues on the agenda, if advisors have been alerted in advance.

In summary, advisory boards, councils or panels differ in important ways from statutory boards or consultants in nature, composition, structure, process, and role. There are no standards or fixed patterns for advisory boards, nor should there be. Advisory boards often are dissipative structures and are phased out after a period, or the composition of the group is changed. Advisory boards also incur almost no overhead other than fees and expenses, which are usually less than costs of statutory boards or consultants.

The principals are top quality persons normally with professionally diverse backgrounds. Advisory boards are informal, small, collegial, flexible, structureless, noninstitutionalized, nondecision making, and speedy in action. They are dedicated to being a valuable optional counseling resource to the advisee, fostering enterprise, corporate initiatives, and innovative strategy.

Advisory boards are, or should be, open-minded about risk rather than being risk adverse. Advisors are not integrated with the advisee or each other. Advisors invest their intellectual know-how, personal networks, and experience as independent contractors.

Advisors are accountable only for their own professional best effort, advice, and counsel. Last, and perhaps a prime distinction, while each principal expects to be economically rewarded for his or her role, no principal looks to an advisory board as a vocational source of income or for maintaining a professional career. There are a limited number of "professional directors" or senior consultants who make a business out of giving senior-level counsel, but these are not typical of the universe of talented persons serving on advisory boards.

1

ADVISORS UNLIMITED

Where no counsel is, the people fall: but in the multitude of counsellors there is safety.

—Proverbs 11:14

Thomas Fuller, the seventeenth-century clergyman, recaptured the proverb's essence with "Good counsels observed are chains to grace." These chains are now called networks—networks of knowledge and influence provided by people who really know. The advice and counsel may concern a trend, a threat, an opportunity, or just a sounding-board reaction. More "chains to grace" are forming around the higher echelons of institutions as complexity, uncertainty, and turbulence increase in the environment in which institutions pursue their corporate missions.

THE ADVICE AGE

The Scots say "Gude advice is ne'er out o'season." Seasonal formation and appointments are more common in the professions and the educational, publishing, and governmental fields. For example, the editors of the American Chemical Society publications in early 1986 announced its annual three-year appointments of 418 members of twenty-two advisory boards. These advisors serve without compensation and provide an expert resource to guide editorial policy. Editorial boards have been permanent fixtures in the publishing field for years.

In August 1977 President Carter, amid great fanfare, announced that the number of federal advisory committees would be reduced by 40 percent that year.[1] Criteria for the hit list of advisory groups were three: the lack of compelling need for their continuation, a lack of balance in their membership, and lack of openness in the way they conducted their business. From a political standpoint, a sacred criterion—lack of balance in membership—spawned a yearly index to advisory committee membership, which was formerly published by the Senate Subcommittee on Reports, Accounting and Management. The 1,340-page index for 1976 revealed that:

Representatives of 28 large companies held more than a thousand seats on the advisory committees. American Telephone and Telegraph led the list with 120 employees on advisory committees, RCA had 94 members on 24 panels advising eight federal agencies, and General Electric was third with 74 seats. . . .

Fourteen universities held more than 1,800 seats on committees. University of California led with 394 seats, University of Texas had 160 representatives, and Harvard University was third with 140 seats. . . .

Four labor unions held nearly 200 seats. . . .

One hundred seventy-three individuals, most of them from corporations, held between 4 and 12 seats each.

The president's objective was worthy, but early results from just one of the federal agencies, the National Science Foundation (NSF) reflected what a formidable and elusive task this zero-based review of advisory panels proved to be. *Science* magazine reported that although thirty-six NSF advisory committees were consolidated into fourteen, the overall membership would actually rise from 378 to 540.[2]

When Congress passed a law in 1972 reducing the number of federal advisory committees there was a temporary decrease in their number. Originally, the overall government total of advisory committees was 1,189. It grew to 1,242 at the end of 1974 and 1,341 in 1976. First efforts pared off 304 committees (25 percent) from a number of agencies. But committees are hard to extirpate. The Office of Management and Budget (OMB) has taken over the oversight function on federal advisory groups since 1976. The latest count on committees continues upward encyclopedically. Over 3,400 committees are described in the third edition of the *Gale Encyclopedia of Government Committees,* up 750 from the second edition. Interestingly, after five years' existence, the Subcommittee on Reports is no longer in existence, apparently a victim of its own mission. Their last report (in calendar year 1976) listed 23,375 members serving on federal advisory bodies.

The United States is not alone in its penchant for advisory committees. Most governments have them. The European Economic Community (EEC) has more than seventy consultative bodies aiding its work. Probably of most importance, is the 144-member Economic and Social Committee representing employers, organizations, trade unions, consumers, and others. Other key consultative committees are those for the coal, and iron and steel industries: The Monetary Committee, the Economic Policy Committee, the Committee of Central Bank Governors, the Committee of the European Social Fund, the Standing Committee on Employment.

The British government has used advisory groups for years and, in fact, publishes successive editions of a handbook on such bodies officially advising Her Majesty's government and its territorial interests. While in Hong Kong late in 1988, I reviewed the latest edition available there to find a list of eighty-five advisory entities (in existence in 1982): fifty-nine advisory committees, seventeen advisory councils, and nine advisory groups, working parties and panels.[3] This handbook provides information on a variety of bodies whose common factor is that they bring together, by invitation or appointment, a group of experts or representatives of bodies concerned with a particular subject for the purpose of: (1) advising a government department or public authority, (2) exercising certain regulatory or investigatory functions in the public interest, (3) exercising certain administrative or executive functions in the public interest, (4) reviewing a particular problem or problems of public concern and recommending actions to be taken, or (5) coordinating certain common interests of government departments, public agencies, trade or professional associations, or interest groups.

Creation and elimination of governmental advisory groups waxes and wanes with political shifts and the rise and fall of public issues. Efforts to reduce the number of advisory committees will undoubtedly continue, for, as Josh Billings observed long ago, "Advice is a drug on the market; the supply always exceeds the demand."

While other fields of endeavor draw heavily on standing groups of outside advisors, only relatively recently have business corporations begun to adopt the outside advisory council notion in any noticeable way. Some large multinational corporations, particularly banking institutions, have had advisory boards to assist them internationally, but only recently has the practice gained a more general interest. The reasons for this interest are discussed in the next chapter.

Growing Trend of Contract Governance Advice

Advice being more blessed to give than receive, it is understandable why persons are reluctant to lose their status as advisors. In my experience, this problem has arisen with certain advisors selected by corporations to keep management informed on various industrial, disciplinary, or geographical areas where an enterprise has interests. The rotation of membership or otherwise graceful means of retiring advisors who are no longer needed or qualified is important.

Conversely, unless a carefully planned scheme is developed to make service on such an advisory board meaningful, the advisors tend to become disenchanted, and their attitude may do more harm than good from a public relations standpoint. As the value of the advice proves to be limited, the management and the advisors become disenchanted, and the delicate problem of disbanding a group of distinguished outside advisory directors has to be managed properly.

The growing trend of contracting for governance advice is tapping a breed of self-employed free-lancers who hire themselves out to companies for long-term advisory assignments. This relationship is different from that of consultants who focus generally as problem-solvers, or mercenaries employed to fill in on a project need or to supplement existing staff. Of the eight million self-employed in the United States, it has been estimated that fewer than 1 or 2 percent of all professionals are "contract advisors."

The downsizing of corporate staff in the last few years in many U.S. industries has been caused by major economic swings, worldwide competition, technological changes, mergers and acquisitions, and fundamental industry restructuring. This has increased the pool of experienced executives and professionals who are redundant. Many of these early retired or decoupled executives and professionals have marketable skills. They have become interested in practicing these skills as consultants and advisors. Example: In a January 1986 workshop sponsored by Dow Chemical as part of its voluntary incentive retirement program, a group of six Dow executives laid out plans for a new consulting company, Omni Tech International (Midland, Michigan) to pool the talents of retirees. Three executives from American Cyanamid who accepted a voluntary retirement program formed a similar consulting group called the Chemists Group in Stamford, Connecticut.

More relevant to advising than to consulting, three retired executives of Monsanto teamed up April 1, 1986, in St. Louis to offer advisory board and management services to companies having sales under $1-2 billion per year. Retired Monsanto chairman, Louis Fernandez, Monte Throdahl, former Monsanto vice president for environmental affairs, and Francis Reese, former Monsanto vice president for facilities and materiel, offer their collective wisdom on a sustained basis to senior executives dealing with such issues as long-range planning, research and development programs, plant safety, quality and pro-

ductivity, environmental questions, and government and media inter-
facing. Dr. Fernandez explained the role of the three-person group as
serving as advisor to management of mainly medium-sized companies
in the chemical and related industries. According to Dr. Fernandez,
"we want to understand the culture of the company, its strengths and
weaknesses, as opposed to solving a problem and leaving." Undoubtedly, this model of contract advisors will increase for the reasons discussed in Chapter 2.[4]

One advantage to contracting for continuing advice is that good
advisors may tend to be more productive in the sense that they are
not involved in the socializing, the bureaucracy and politicking, that
exists in all corporate hierarchy. Further, the CEO, as contractor, does
not have to heed the advice given, certainly not to the same degree
as when advice is given by statutory board members who have the
power and responsibility for appointing the CEO.

Table 1-1 is a random list of companies that have publicly identified advisory boards or councils; that is, they contract for governance
or top management advice from outside experts. In some cases, the
advisory board consists of former directors of the corporation whose
experience and sense of corporate history are deemed valuable to access from time to time after they have retired or are no longer eligible
to serve on the board of directors.

The species of adjunct advisory groups, the rationale for membership, and the honorary and working roles involved are separate and
interesting dimensions of the growing trend of corporate contracting
for governance advice. My perspective on these dimensions is offered
in Chapter 6.

RECENT VARIATIONS IN ADVISORY RESOURCE GROUPS

The following items are a potpourri of advisory boards or councils.
The variations demonstrate the raison d'être and flexibility of this
organizational art form:

Item: *Planned Gifts Advisors*

Some progressive nonprofit organizations use advisory boards to increase the effectiveness of their planned gifts program. The advisory
board gives the hired staff better access to key financial professionals
through a resource bank of advisors. Cultivation of prospective board
members is enhanced. For example, the Overlake Hospital Foundation in Bellevue, Washington, established such an advisory board in
late 1985. The board consists of fifteen members drawn from fields of

Table 1-1
Some Public Companies Having Advisory Boards or Councils of Outside Experts

Industrial Companies Headquartered in Europe or Asia

ASEA (Stockholm)	Advisory council
BSN Group-Gervais Danone (Boussois Souchon Neuvesel)	Comité Consultatif International
Compagnie de Saint-Gobain-Pont-à-Mousson (France)	International advisory board
Esselte AB (Stockholm)	Advisory council
Foseco Minsep Limited (England)	Advisory Council
Imperial Chemical Industries (ICI)	North American advisory board
Incentive AB (Stockholm)	Scientific advisory council
Jardin Matheson & Co., Ltd. (Hong Kong)	International advisory board
Lafarge Coppee (France)	Global advisory council
Malaysian Rubber Research & Development	Quango board-level coordinating advisory committee drawn from eminent specialists from U.S., U.K., Italy, France, and Malaysia
Montedison (Italy)	International advisory board
Perstorp (Sweden)	Scientific council
Resistoflex GmbH (Germany)	Advisory board (Beirat)
Robeco N.V. (Netherlands)	Advisory board
Royal Dutch Petroleum Co.	International advisory council
Shell	International advisory council
John Swire & Sons (HK) Ltd. (Hong Kong)	International advisory board
Thyssen-Bornemisza N.V. (Netherlands)	International advisory council
Unilever (Britain and the Netherlands)	Global advisory council
A.B. Volvo	International advisory council

(A.B. Volvo North America also has U.S. advisory board)

Financial Intermediary Companies Headquartered Outside the United States

Allianz Versicherungs AG (West Germany)	Advisory board
Banca Nazionale del Lavoro (Rome)	International advisory board
Canadian Imperial Bank of Commerce	Global advisory council
Deutsche Bank (West Germany)	Advisory board and regional advisory councils
Dresdner Bank (West Germany)	Advisory management council
Bank of Israel (state bank)	Advisory board
Royal Bank of Canada	Global advisory council
Scandinaviska Enskilda (S-E) Banken (Stockholm)	Social and economic council
Swiss Bank Corporation	Council of international advisors
Touche, Remnant & Co. of Britain	Advisory council

Corporations Headquartered in U.S.

Albany International	Foreign advisory board
AMAX	Global advisory council
AMF Inc.	European and Asia/Pacific advisory council
AT&T International, Inc.	Asia/Pacific & European Advisory councils
Air Products & Chemicals	International advisory council
ALCOA	Advisory council
Allied Chemical	Scientific advisory councils
Allied Signal Corp.	Technical advisory council
American Can	Advisory councils (Asia-Pacific)
ARCO	Advisory council
Berol Chemical Corp.	Advisory council
Black & Decker	Foreign advisory board
Burroughs Corporation	International advisory board
Campbell Soup	European advisory council
Caterpillar Tractor Co.	Advisory councils (Brazil & Asia)
Celanese	Scientific advisory councils
Cetus Corp.	Technical advisory panel
Citicorp	International advisory board
Conference Board, Inc.	International advisory councils
Corning Glass	European advisory board

Table 1-1 (continued)

CPC International, Inc.	European advisory board
Data General Corporation	Scientific advisory board
Exxon	Foreign advisory board
Ford Motor Co.	European advisory council
General Electric	Brazil advisory council
General Motors Corp.	European advisory board (Europe, Australia)
B. F. Goodrich Corporation	Scientific advisory board
Gould, Inc.	Scientific advisory council
W. R. Grace	International advisory board
Gulf	International advisory board
Hercules, Inc.	Advisory council (1979-1984)
Honeywell Inc.	European advisory council
IBM	Advisory board (Europe, Latin America)
Jacobs Engineering Group, Inc.	Advisory board
Lord Corporation	Advisory panel
Merck	European advisory council
Mitre	Scientific advisory councils
Monsanto	Scientific advisory councils
Nova Pharmaceutical Corp.	Scientific advisory board
Owens-Illinois	Asia Pacific advisory council
Pan American Airways	Global advisory council
Reliance Electric Co.	Technology advisory board (1960-1972)
R. J. Reynolds Industries	International advisory board
Rockwell International	European advisory council
Rohm & Haas	Advisory Council
Sperry Corp.	International advisory panel
Sprague Electric	Technical advisory board
Tenneco Europe, Inc.	European advisory council
Texas Instruments, Inc.	Board advisory council
TRW	International Advisory Council
United Technologies Corp. (UTC)	European advisory council
Valmont Industries, Inc.	Advisory council
Westinghouse Electric	International advisory board
Whirlpool Corp.	Technology advisory panel

financial services, real estate, and professional areas. The board helps
the staff plan educational seminars for use in the community, provides a core of speakers to help in developing donor cultivation programs, and other elements of the planned gifts initiative.

Item: *Marketing via Celebrity Advisors*

United Sciences of America, Inc., was formed to provide an easy
way for people to take all the vitamins and nutrients doctors recommend as diet supplements. The entrepreneur, founder-chairman Robert Adler, devised his own nutritional supplement, then commis-
sioned research on the multilateral marketing system involved.
Following that, he assembled an impressive scientific advisory board
that includes two Nobel laureates to give distinction and guidance to
the enterprise.

Item: *Knights of the Roundtable*

In June 1983 a private group of seventeen European business leaders met in Paris to form the Roundtable of European Industrialists.
The Roundtable was dubbed G-17, giving it faintly official tones of
some International Monetary Fund (IMF) offshoot of finance minis-
ters. The membership now numbers twenty-seven (G-27) and represents a "roll of honor" of chairmen, vice chairmen, presidents, chief
executives and officers, managing directors and managing partners of
leading firms in Western Europe.

This powerful advisory group is positioned to influence the shaping
of modern Europe as a source of ideas and counsel for grappling with
Europe's deep-rooted impediments to unity. It is also an effective gen-
erator of venture capital for high-technology startups. In effect, the
Roundtable is a sounding board or advisory council for the Common
Market Commission.

Most of the membership was recruited by the EEC's former industry commissioner, Vicomte Etienne Davignon, a Belgian aristocrat
who for eight years presided in Brussels over EEC industrial policy.
Davignon pioneered "crisis cartels" in steel and chemicals to assist
restructuring during the darkest years of recession. Formation of the
Roundtable was a natural extension to tap the knowledge and influence in an advisory model, and to establish an ongoing dialogue with
people who could genuinely claim to be the voice of industry.

Volvo chairman Pehr Gyllenhammar was the sparkplug who translated Davignon's ideas into reality by creating the Roundtable's
structure. Gyllenhammar's term as chairman of the Roundtable ex-
pired in 1987. Wisse Dekker, chairman of the supervisory board of

Philips Gloeilampenfabrieken N.V., was elected chairman of the Roundtable in May 1988 for two years. This Roundtable advisory group has had some growing pains, but its achievements have been noteworthy to date. Each member company contributes 30,000 European Currency Units (ECUs) annually to fund studies on such topics as "Missing Links" (December 1984), which outlined the case for spending $60 billion over twenty years on projects such as the English Channel fixed link, a "Scanlink" to connect Scandinavia and northern Germany, and a new European high-speed rail network. Subsequent studies have included a survey of economies of scale, an assessment of the unemployment situtation, and a proposal for a European Institute of Technology.

As an independent group of knowledgeable industrial leaders, this group serves as a resource to the European Common Market Commission and other interested European organizations. The focus of the Roundtable is advice on strategies and actions to hasten the streamlining of Europe. The Roundtable is a major force shaping public opinion concerning the need to speed up European integration and restructuring.

Item: *Hotel Marketing Advisors*

Members of the Meeting Planner Advisory Board of Sonesta International Hotels (Boston) attend intensive, semiannual meetings where there is an open discussion on issues affecting their industries and on expectations from their suppliers. The board consists of representatives of Sonesta's customer base. Meetings are structured so that Sonesta executives can learn about industry trends and get advice on sales, marketing, and advertising of hotel operations.

The meetings are held at Sonesta hotels with a carefully planned and selected invitation list. Sonesta has created a close-knit, ongoing relationship with this important segment of its clientele who are honored to be asked to speak on what is transpiring in their industries, allowing Sonesta to understand and serve its customers more effectively.

Item: *Director-for-a-Night*

In 1978 the Massachusetts Institute of Technology created and sponsored a program called the Enterprise Forum. The one-night sessions offer young companies free management advice plus a chance to meet bankers, venture capitalists, prospective customers, suppliers, and other business professionals. The forum's role is to help companies grow and emerge successfully. The approach is to expose a willing entrepreneur to a panel of outsiders who listen to his or her explanation of the business concept, business plan, and general understanding of the business in which they are engaged. No punches are pulled in the forum from either the panel of four or five business professionals or from the audience, which may range from 100 to 150 interested persons, including other entrepreneurs faced with start-up problems.

The panel of businesspeople who react to the presentation volunteer their services. The "recruiting" of such an ad hoc "board of directors for a night" has been a successful initiative for those companies having some link to technology whose business problems may hold lessons for other entrepreneurs in the audience.

Item: *The Private Advisors to the Canadian IIC Group (Toronto)*

This maker of compressor valves has benefited greatly, according to its president Phil Soiffer, who engaged a Harvard Business School professor, a lawyer, a retired industry executive, a stockbroker, and an international banker to meet privately with him every three months. A dinner is followed by an open discussion of company problems and opportunities, personnel matters, market strategy, acquisitions, raising private equity, and possible expansion. Soiffer stresses the criterion that he must avoid persons with whom he is involved socially, discuss fees for their services candidly, and set forward meeting schedules and agenda.

Item: *Closely Held Corporation Advisory Boards*

John D. Foster, former Marcor executive and now president of his Chicago-based executive search firm, points out that many small and medium-sized firms with closely held ownership engage advisory boards to counsel with the chairman, CEO, and board of directors. For example, Foster is a member of the advisory boards of the following private companies in the Midwest: Land's End, Inc. (Wisconsin mail order house); Century 21 of Northern Illinois (real estate); Spring Green Lawn Care, Inc. (Chicago); and Teng Associates, Inc. (architect).

In 1984 Charles B. Larson, president of The Condor Group (St. Joseph, Missouri), formed an advisory board for this closely held CPA firm. Under state law, non-CPAs are not eligible to be official board members. The Condor advisory board is nonstatutory and consists of three outsiders and one insider, all having knowledge of the profession and either marketing or financial expertise. According to Larson, "The advisory board has made many and quite valuable contributions to the company . . . the advisory board has been a broad purpose board dealing with all aspects of company operation. While advisory in nature, it has, in fact, with the agreement of the key stockholder, 'made decisions.' "

Item: *Japanese-British Advisory Blend*

The Toshiba Consumer Products plant in Plymouth, England, has successfully blended Japanese business practices with British management traditions to become a model of harmonious industrial relations, according to its chief executive David Oates. A company advisory board (COAB) includes representatives from all levels of the company who meet monthly to discuss issues that threaten industrial harmony. Actions stemming from this advice include introduction of merit awards, elimination of a traditional half-day holiday, and adjusting policy on employee benefits.

Item: *Window-Dressing Advisors*

Burlington Industries' Burlington House Draperies Division undertook a $1 million redressment campaign in 1982 to fight the decline of the drapery industry by redesigning its showroom and promotion programs. An important element in broadening the image of the company was establishing a Design Advisory Board. Five leading interior designers from across the country offered upscale ideas for business development.

Item: *Social and Economic Advisors*

The Scandinaviska Enskilda (S-E) Banken of Sweden has a forty-person Social and Economic Council listed in its 1985 annual report. The members are from Swedish universities and academies, government, hospitals, fine arts museums, and financial and industrial companies. Three meetings are held annually with outside speakers. The council members are joined by the directors and deputy directors of the bank and the executive management. Typical agenda topics last year included Professor Mancur Olson, University of Maryland, speaking on "Economic Growth Stagflation and Social Rigidity"; a "Foreign Policy" journalist discussing European security problems from an American viewpoint; and three faculty members leading a seminar devoted to "Leadership and Knowledge of the World of Human Nature." The council serves as a sounding board for the bank on social and economic matters.

Item: *Presidential and Ministerial Decision Making*

Gerald Ford created an advisory board on economic policy in 1974. Ronald Reagan created a Foreign Intelligence Advisory Board in 1985 to improve the quality and effectiveness of intelligence available to the United States. The Department of Health, Education and Welfare (HEW), the U.S. Army Corps of Engineers environmental wing, as well as many other governmental departments, frequently resort to creation of advisory groups to assist them.

Item: *Retirement Vehicle Advisory Board*

In 1982, the twelfth party congress of China's Communist Party created a Central Advisory Commission. The purpose was to provide a vehicle to get old leaders to surrender their posts to younger men and "be promoted" into dignified semiretirement as a party elder. Deng Xiaoping, then seventy-eight years old, joined the commission almost immediately as chairman of the advisory commission. In the United States business world, this organizational process is called "percussive sublimation," in other words, "being drummed upstairs."

Item: *University Business Strategy: A Pop-Celebrity Board*

American University president Richard Berendzen introduced a startling new strategy for academia. He promotes American University and its location in the glittering locale of politics and diplomacy in the District of Columbia's Northwest by pushing into the world of pop celebrity. American University's ad hoc advisory board includes such luminaries as Walter Cronkite and Farah Fawcett. Such contacts have translated into donations and a higher profile for the university. According to *Fortune* (March 3, 1986), in the past five years endowment has gone from $5 million to $15 million. In 1984 and 1985, enrollment applications have been increasing by 15 percent annually.

Item: *Bank Customer Interest Advisors*

The Bank of Mid-Jersey touts its use of advisory boards as one of its competitive advantages. The bank has three permanent advisory boards all formed around the different interests of customers—farming, business and industry, and consumers. Members of these advisory boards are selected to bring background and expertise in their field of activity to the bank's marketing effort. They need not be customers of the bank. Six members are elected annually for three years by the bank's board of directors for each advisory board. An officer of the bank serves as secretary and a director is assigned as liaison.

Item: *Interdisciplinary Research Advisory Council*

IIASA, the International Institute for Applied Systems Analysis, Laxenburg, Austria, is a nongovernmental, interdisciplinary research institute founded in October 1972 on the initiative of the academies of sciences or equivalent institutions in twelve countries. The institute's member organizations now comprise scientific and professional bodies in sixteen countries. The governing body is the IIASA Council, which is composed of one representative from each of the National Member Organizations (NMOs), as of January 1989. The chairman of the Council and of its Executive Committee is Academician Vladmir S. Mikhalevich, director of the V.M. Glushkos Institute of Cybernetics of the Ukrainian Academy of Sciences. IIASA's director is Dr. Robert H. Pry, founding president of the Center for Innovative Technology and Adjunct Professor at the Massachusetts Institute of Technology.

IIASA's objectives are to initiate and support individual and collaborative research on problems associated with social, economic, technological, and environmental change, and thereby to assist scientific, industrial, and policy communities throughout the world in tackling such problems. The institute's nongovernmental and interdisciplinary nature has given it a unique ability to bridge gaps of understanding between scientific disciplines, between nations, and between the scientific, industrial and policy communities.

Collaborating networks and IIASA-sponsored or cosponsored scientific meetings provide a timely platform for discussions of topics that are being addressed in research at IIASA and collaborating institutions. In 1985, forty-five meetings were held at Laxenburg or in countries with National Member Organizations.

The IIASA Advisory Board was established in 1985. It serves as a vital link with potential users of IIASA research results and represents a new forum for an expanded East-West dialogue among scientists, industrialists, and members of the policy community. The board is currently composed of sixty-one leaders from twenty countries. The chairman is Donald Kendall, chairman and chief executive officer of Pepsico, USA. Vice chairmen are Professor Umberto Colombo, president of the Italian National Committee for Research on Nuclear and Alternative Energy (ENEA); Dr. Karlheinz Kaske, president and chief executive officer of Siemens AG, Federal Republic of Germany; Dr. Valeri A. Pekshev, deputy chairman of the State Bank of the Soviet Union; and George Pirinski, deputy minister for foreign trade, Bulgaria.

Item: *Management Education Advisory Councils*

The American Management Association (AMA) is a not-for-profit educational institution chartered by the Regents of the University of the State of New York. The broadly based membership of 78,367 in 1988 was served by 4,238 seminars, courses, meetings, conferences, plus a host of publications. AMA is guided by hundreds of business leaders who form their management advisory councils. Over 450 members make up fourteen councils focused primarily on functional areas: finance, general and administrative services; general management; growing enterprises; human resources; information systems and technology; insurance and risk management; marketing; manufacturing; packaging; purchasing; transportation and physical distribution; research and development; limited companies; and international business activities.

These advisory councils were instituted about 1935. The councils meet twice a year with AMA staff participating in roundtable discussions of the challenges and trends in their fields of expertise. The staff translates these vital exchanges of information into new programs, publications, and services that better serve the membership. Dr. Thomas R. Horton, president and chief executive officer, is an active participant in most council meetings and is a strong advocate of the advisory council role in providing special help and perspective in AMA's programming. Dr. Horton commented, "I am impressed by the sharing of ideas and the assistance constantly available to us."

Item: *Overseas Security Advisory Council (OSAC)*

The Reagan administration developed a counterterrorism strategy based on a good defense, good intelligence, and the threat of U.S. retaliation. Many private firms have asked the U.S. government for help as terrorism against U.S. targets has increased in the 1970s and 1980s. Thus, the Overseas Security Advisory Council (OSAC), a joint venture between the government and the private sector, was founded in 1986 to help Americans overseas deal with terrorism. The OSAC's goals include providing regular exchanges of information between security officials in both public and private sectors. There is also the Threat Analysis Division of the U.S. Department of State, which consists of specialists covering specific geographic regions to assess the terrorism potential in that area. For instance, the senior analyst for the Middle East region reports that the two main current concerns there are the situation in Israel and the occupied territories and the Persian Gulf situation. References: Robert E. Lamb, *OSAC: A View to Global Security;* Ralph F. Laurello, Jr., *Security Management* 32, 9 (September 1988), pp. 103–16.

Item: *The Federal Advisory Council (FAC)*

The Federal Advisory Council (FAC), which was created by the Federal Reserve Act, confers with the Federal Reserve Board (FRB) on general business conditions. Specifically, it makes recommendations concerning discount rates, open-market operations, note issues, and other activities of the FRB. In order to determine the effectiveness of the council, minutes of joint meetings between the FRB and the FAC were analyzed to determine how soon the FAC recognized changing economic conditions. The study showed that the FAC recognized peaks and troughs, on average, three months after they occurred and had a recognition lag for upturns and downturns of 5.4 months. Review of recommendations by the Federal Open Market Committee shows they identified changes earlier than the FAC, 75 percent of the time. It is argued that the FAC does not serve a useful purpose and should be eliminated. Reference: Edward B. Selby, Jr., "The Recognition Lag of the Federal Advisory Council," *Journal of Finance* 34, 1 (March 1979), pp. 237–40.

Item: *Pension Plan Funding*

During its recent annual meeting, the Pension World Editorial Advisory Board addressed the direction that government policy should take in the next five years with respect to regulating the pension industry. To remedy the lack of direct pension industry representation in the executive branch, establishing an office dedicated to pension policy was suggested by the board. Hershey Foods Corporation's Merrill C. Horine suggested that to address the long-term nature of the pension area, an agency should be created. Steven E. Schanes of Schanes Associates said the administration needs a focal point involving policy. Board members suggested that the proposed agency's head not be a tax expert or an attorney. Prudential Asset Management Company's Eugene B. Burroughs suggested that the individual have a "broader perspective." David J. Pittman of NCNB Texas cited the main problem as the lack of a long-term pension policy in the United States. Reference: John D. Marsh, "Editorial Advisory Board Members Address Future of Government Policy," *Pension World* 24, 10 (October 1988), pp. 38, 40.

Item: *Advice on Ethics*

Duane Kullberg, managing partner of Arthur Andersen & Company, was a participant in a recent roundtable discussion on business ethics. He states that there is a growing concern that business teachers do not feel prepared to address ethics. In response to this problem, Arthur Andersen is developing and underwriting an educational program called the Partnership for Applied Curriculum on Ethics (PACE). In 1987, to air a variety of opinions and practical suggestions, the company brought together a group of teachers, writers, and business executives who shared a common concern about the condition of the nation's ethics. This meeting was followed by the establishment of an Advisory Council on Ethics to develop a realistic approach to teaching business ethics. The resulting PACE program will integrate ethics into existing business courses and incorporate case studies into coursework. Instructor reference materials dealing with principles of ethical reasoning and the skills required to cope with ethical issues in business will be made available. Reference: Duane Kullberg, "An Ethics Roundtable: Business Ethics: Provides Lessons from "Real Life," *Management Review* 77, 8 (August 1988), pp. 54–55.

Item: *Independent Manufacturers' Representatives Advisory Board*

Hoffman Air Filtration Systems, a division of Clarkson Industries, introduced a "manufacturers' rep" advisory board in 1978. Eight members from the rep group serve three-year terms along with six permanent members from the Hoffman organization. The prime function is to provide advice that would benefit marketing policies and programs. Expenses are paid for all members who meet for three days annually in plenary session which is highly structured and planned. Results include a new inventory stocking program, introduction of new sales tools, development of a "dust control" movie to explain unique features of dust control equipment, organization of a trade show customer contact program, an audiovisual program for an equipment assembly, and a new delivery program.

Item: *STAG*

The Science and Technology Advisory Group (STAG) was created in January 1980, according to Minister K. T. Li, Minister Without Portfolio, the Executive Yuan, Republic of China (Taiwan), speaking at the first meeting of the Board of Advisors on Science and Technology. For many years, research and development had been carried out in Taiwan in such fields as agriculture and telecommunications. In January 1978 a conference was held to assess the status of science and technology and recommend improvements. The following May the government invited a team headed by Dr. Patrick E. Haggerty and Dr. Willis A. Adcock of Texas Instruments, Inc., to recommend and discuss directions for industrial and technological development in the Republic of China. The government representatives generally adopted Texas Instruments' "Objectives, Strategy and Tactics" (OST) approach to research and development, and STAG was approved by the cabinet on May 17, 1980. Pat Haggerty chaired the initial group of six distinguished advisors from the United States. The guidelines were:

1. Management of science and technology to achieve social and economic goals; policies, issues, strategies, and priorities.

2. Effective use of Taiwan's science and technology educational programs to meet industrial and national requirements; vocational training; undergraduate and graduate degree programs; and continuing education. Consider modifications of admission requirements.

3. Development of attitudes that will promote the social acceptance of science and technology.

4. Promotion of government-industry-university interactions for the application of technology.

5. Inducement of more active research, development, and education (RD&E) investment in the private sector.

6. Monitoring of government's RD&E projects.

7. Assessment of alternatives for development and/or acquisition of technologies required to fill critical gaps.

8. Role of basic science, applied science and engineering in Taiwan's technological, industrial, and economic developments.

9. Promotion of multidisciplinary and interdisciplinary research and development activities.

10. Assessment of selected projects by individual board members.

11. Other topics of interest to the board.

STAG has been meeting once in Taiwan and once in the United States every year since. The current roster includes eight from the United States and one from France. Seven topic areas are discussed: general policy, health and environment, electronics information, chemical science and technology, telecommunications, technical manpower and education, energy and agriculture.

The use of advisors is as old as biblical times. The variety of use varies with the needs of the times. For those who would advise, there is a well-known caution: Do not offer advice that has not been seasoned by your own performance. Further, the advocacy is only counsel. The person in responsible charge makes the decision. The admonition reminds me of Henry VIII's famous line to his legal advisors as he dismissed them, "Let's forget about alimony, I have a better solution."

NOTES

1. The Federal Advisory Committee Act P.L. 92–463, October 6, 1972, defined advisory committees as "any committee, board, commission, council, conference, panel, task force or other similar group which is established by statute or reorganization plan or established and utilized by one or more agencies in the interest of obtaining advice or recommendations for the President or one or more agencies or officers of the Federal Government."

2. R. Jeffrey Smith, "Carter Reducing Plan Adds Pounds," *Science* 198 (December 2, 1977), p. 900.

3. *Councils, Committees and Boards:* A handbook of advisory, consultative, executive and similar bodies in British public life. Edition 5, CBD Research Ltd., copyright 1982 (391 pages), Beckenham, Kent, England.

4. An interesting sequel to this advisory role example is the luring away in 1986 of Louis Fernandez, sixty-four, to become head of Calgene, a New Jersey Company, just four months after he retired as chairman of Monsanto. The original advisory enterprise continues in duo form.

2

DRIVING FORCES

Two strong forces are creating a new wave of corporate interest in advisory boards. The more acute force is the D&O liability insurance crisis discussed later in this chapter. Complexity of doing business, a chronic trend, is increasingly significant and is forcing companies to seek outside counsel. While reignited interest in corporate advice squads is driven by these current pressures, many of the boardroom issues are old. Before examining the recent liability insurance issue, the impact and nature of the basic issues need to be reviewed in their current context.

During the 1900s, environmental challenges increased substantially. Technological turbulence, saturation of first-generation industries, emergence of new industries, multinational markets, government markets, leisure markets and technology-created industries challenged traditional ways of doing business. Late in the twentieth century, sociopolitical impacts, developing world markets, loss of control over the environment and socialist markets became issues of primary concern.[1] These trends are further explored in Chapter 7. These environmental and contextual changes and the resulting turbulence increased the need for corporations to be more aware of external forces. The governance role embraced linkages with and sensitivity to these outside forces. Outsider advice has, indeed, become more relevant and necessary. This need for external perspective impacted boardrooms by changing criteria for directorship.

The Korn/Ferry International Thirteenth Annual Board of Directors Study (February 1986) revealed some disturbing facts in the 592 responses it received from United States companies in a wide array of business and industry sectors. One out of five qualified candidates turned down an invitation to serve as director. Reasons were (1) time commitment requirements were too great, (2) inadequate director and officer liability insurance, and (3) exposure to public censure. Despite this general reaction to invitations to serve on a board, the search for a greater proportion of independent directors continues. Outside directors elected to corporate boards in the last six months of 1985 rose to a record 63 percent, up from 57 percent in the comparable span of 1984, according to *Director Trends,* a study conducted by the Heidrick Partners (Chicago). There was also renewed interest in outside advisory boards and advisory councils to provide independent input relatively free from the liabilities accompanying statutory board membership.

BUSINESS COMPLEXITY

The worry list of issues challenging multinational companies is scary: acute industrial crisis prevention and management, environmental assurance, takeover defense, merger damage control, industry and corporate restructuring, devastating global competition, deregulation, surprise technological shifts, social reform, political upsets, terrorism, and many others. Business complexity has reached a new level of challenge. Nobel Laureate Herbert A. Simon's concept of bounded rationality helps explain the rising need for qualified advice at the governance level.

Individuals as well as organizations often cannot comprehend problems that exceed a certain level of complexity. When this level is passed, directors and managers can no longer understand what is going on in the environment nor develop rational response strategies. Evidence suggests that today's international business complexity, in some cases, may have passed the bounds of boardroom rationality.

There is also evidence that certain organizations have grown too complex to be governed and managed rationally. This shifts the focus from governing a corporation within a complex environment to governance of the complexity. Some cage-rattling consequences are already evident: decentralization or fragmentation of decision power, network-type company formation of the "hollow corporation" variety, de-glomeration, previously unthinkable spinoffs, leveraged buyouts, downsizing, strategic concentration, and re-vectoring.

All this is a boon to the advice field. During last year, I have responded to inquiries on the role of advisory boards from corporations in Finland, Sweden, Holland, France, Switzerland, the United Kingdom, Venezuela, Hong Kong, and, of course, the United States. Advisory boards have long been established on the international scene.

Much in vogue in the 1960s and 1970s, they followed a welter of international subsidiary company formations. Advisors can be a valuable resource for top-line thinking about external and internal forces at work that neither insider group-think nor prayer-wheel spinning can cope with.

Scholars in the field of decision and management sciences continue to struggle with the treatment of complexity. In 1982 the National Science Foundation (NSF) established the Decision and Management Sciences Program (DMS) and provided funds for basic research. An NSF workshop held in Dallas in April 1984 identified four of the most promising research areas, many of them inviting crossdisciplinary efforts. In addition to the treatment of complexity, measurement-based models for operational processes, choice theory and decision support were judged to be the most fertile areas where increased knowledge would be likely to have a valuable long-run impact on management practice.

Three types of complexity were identified: prescriptive, descriptive, and communicative. The type most related to the role and function of advisory boards and councils is the treatment of prescriptive complexity. The goal of the treatment is to help the CEO and other decision makers (that is, the statutory board of directors and top management). Better decisions are needed to cope with complexity in the corporate decision setting, which is the turbulent, uncertain world context in which corporations must exist today.

There are at least two useful directions for coping with such external and internal complexity. One is for outside experts to observe and study interactions in complex settings both within and without the firm. Experienced advisors can observe relationships, for example, between the top management, middle management, employees, suppliers, customers, and governmental interests, shareholders, and competitors. Suggestions for structural and policy changes, interventions, comparative analysis, new programs, and perspectives can be offered by a diverse group of qualified advisors.

A second complementary activity that an effective advisory group can offer is occasions for reviews, workshops with key principals of the firm where specific significant issues and problems are tackled in depth. Many problems on a corporation's agenda are reasonably likely to be soluble at present, but, for whatever reasons, have received insufficient attention.[2]

In addition to the treatment of complexity, outside advisory groups have been formed in the past to offer specific know-how about technology, market or political trends, and environmental and consumer affairs. In 1968 Conoco (then Continental Oil Company) created an international advisory council to the board to advise the directors and senior management on international matters. The council was created because the company was making its first exploration, refining, and marketing moves in Europe. The United Kingdom, Switzerland, Germany, Italy, and Sweden were represented on this council, which was active until 1975, when there was a change in the corporate chairmanship. By that time, the company felt reasonably experienced in operating in Europe on its own without the external advisory council.

Large international business firms obviously need regional, social, economic, and political advice. The viewpoint of distinguished foreign nationals can offer a guest company valuable insight and access to networks in a world region far from corporate headquarters.

D&O LIABILITY INSURANCE

In 1986, the National Association of Corporate Directors' blue-ribbon panel of corporate personnel and insurance and legal experts surveyed the impact of soaring cost and drastically curtailed availability of director and officer (D&O) liability insurance coverage. Impacts readily observable were director defection from some boardroom rosters and the increased cost of doing business. For example, in September 1985 six outside directors of the Continental Steel Corporation quit en masse when the company dropped its D&O insurance. On February 4, 1986, Armada Corporation had eight of its ten directors resign because the company refused to pay the sharply higher D&O insurance costs, thereby leaving Armada without a chairman or chief executive officer.

The survey results were widely distributed as a "white paper" setting forth the issues and the attitudes of a sizeable group of knowledgeable business and professional people on the potential impact of the insurance situation. This survey was made available on a nonpartisan basis to any public, legislative, government, media, and professional interested parties. Below are some highlights from the 363 responses (a 13 percent return on the questionnaire). The respondents averaged 308 hours a year on board duties. The survey of directors indicated:

85 percent believe compared to five years ago, that being named in a lawsuit related to service on a board of directors was currently more probable

46 percent served on boards of corporations where directors or officers have been sued in actions covered by D&O policies

19 percent had been named as a defendant in actions covered by D&O policies

93 percent recommended federal or state legislation establishing a cap on the liability of independent outside directors

95 percent recommend legislation at the state level penalizing those who bring frivolous suits against officers and directors

55 percent see benefit in federal codification of the business judgment rule

61 percent do not believe certification of directors would minimize the number of suits brought against directors

48 percent were acquainted with persons who had refused a directorship offer because of lack of D&O insurance

24 percent indicated willingness to serve as a director of a business corporation that did not carry D&O insurance

Sadly, this disruptive D&O development comes at a time of growing need for improving corporate conduct through more accountable directorship and strengthening management effectiveness. Willing and qualified statutory directors are harder to come by in these litigious days. Advisory directors can be one of many different species, as described in Chapter 6. They have unique roles and need special arrangements to make them effective. They are not a surrogate for statutory directors, but they can provide needed outside, independent perspective unencumbered by the same degree of individual liability exposure, public scrutiny and need to disclose financial affairs that are part of being a director. Otherwise they may act as a governance resource.

What is relatively new is the realization that outside advisors may be retained without being exposed in the same degree to increasing liability exposures of statutory directors. The concept of the behaviorist's "nonteam" notion is relevant here. A clutch of peer-respected outsiders can come together on a continuing assignment basis, each bringing a greater commitment to the interest and expertise they represent than to one another or their common task. Independent professional advice is their input regardless of fiduciary or vested interests within the corporation or the top management's tendency to "mow its own grass." A chief executive who creates new fields of endeavor in his development of the corporation but stays too long has to tend the repetitive "mowing" rather than planting new seed plots for growth or modernizing the corporation.

D&O insurance originated in the 1930s, following the crash of 1929, the New Deal, and new yardsticks for the courts, based on the Securities Acts of 1933–34. Federated Stores and GAF Corporation, at that time, recognized the limitations in indemnifying their directors and officers for personal liabilities incurred in relation to their corporate activities. The key legal concerns were potentials for derivative litigation by shareholders and violations of the Securities Acts.

Both companies purchased policies from Lloyds to supplement the ability to indemnify directors and officers. In the 1960s, emerging liability problems caused a sudden rise in demand for D&O insurance from U.S. and British underwriters. The increasing crescendo of legal action causing floods of litigation began to threaten to drown vulnerable industries. Three Mile Island, Watergate, Bhopal, Johns Manville, and Continental Illinois were episodes along the way. According to Albert L. Salvatico, managing director of the professional liability department of Marsh & McLennan, Inc., the demand in 1986 was such that virtually 100 percent of the Fortune 500 companies purchased D&O coverage (*Risk Management,* January 1986, pp. 16–19).

Until late 1984, excess D&O insurance could be purchased for as little as $133 per million per year on the basis that no claim had ever exceeded $25 million. In the meantime, changes in the legal community were taking place. Attorneys were wringing $15 million claims out of a $20 million D&O policy. This caused the insurance market to contract and according to Salvatico, pricing of D&O policies reached levels of forty-five times the expiring price, if coverage was available at all. A survey of purchasing conducted (by Alliance) during the second quarter of 1985 reported premium increases from 50 to 500 percent with a true availability problem existing in certain industries.

The increased cost and limited coverage available have caused customers to look for alternatives to insurance. For example, in January 1986, twenty-three of the largest banks were studying options such as pooling arrangements and formation of their own insurance company—referred to as a "captive" insurance company. Some industrial companies are "going captive" or even changing corporate strategy to get out of certain business sectors considered especially risky and "uninsurable."

One of the ways out of the director liability trap may be the Delaware legislature's answer. On June 18, 1986, Delaware Governor Michael N. Castle approved legislation permitting Delaware corporations to limit or eliminate the personal liability of directors for monetary damages. The new Delaware law enables Delaware corporations, in their original certificates of incorporation or by amendment, to immunize directors from liabilities for breach of their fiduciary duty. The legislation specifically prohibits any limitation of director liability for breaches of the duty of loyalty, for bad faith or intentional misconduct, for illegal acts, or for improper personal benefits. This law took effect July 1, 1986, and spawned a rush by many Delaware corporations to amend their charters. The legislation also improved Delaware law relating to the advancement of litigation expenses to directors.

Governor Castle and the Corporation Law Section of the Delaware

State Bar Association considered the permissive, limited immunity provision of this new law to be the most balanced response of several alternative approaches studied to deal with the problem of director liability. Just as trust beneficiaries may agree to limit the liability of their trustees, the 1986 Delaware Director Immunity Law permits shareholders to agree to shield their directors from liability where no misconduct, intentional wrongdoing, or illegality is involved. Even with a limitation on director liability, furthermore, shareholders will retain the ability to seek injunctive or other equitable relief from the courts regarding a transaction alleged to be the product of a duty of care violation. With these changes in its General Corporation law, Delaware hopes to maintain the ability of its corporations to attract and retain highly qualified individuals to serve on their boards of directors.

Another alternate response to the increasing uncertainty surrounding personal liability exposure of corporate directors is the subject of this book. The engagement of advisory boards, groups, or councils of outsiders who are experts or generalists with wisdom and judgment may be of governance value to the company and also avoid the liability exposure problem. Contracting for such advice is not a new phenomenon, but the extent and formalization of such adjunct organizational entities is relatively novel and yet to be generally adopted.

The liability issue is not clear and has not been tested yet in the courts. Conventional wisdom is that such an advisory role having no conflict with the statutory board's role and not involved in decision making or in any manner substituting for the board of directors will not be exposed, at least to the same extent, to the liabilities of the role of a statutory director. A caveat to keep in mind is that if compensation for advisory services is received, some liability is implied in relation to the value of services rendered. One protective provision in an advisory contract is to limit the liability exposure to the compensation paid for such services.

One caveat, further discussed in Chapter 9, needs mentioning here. The limited availability and high cost of D&O liability insurance is generating interest in the formation of advisory groups. This raises other concerns associated with organization and operation of such advisory boards or councils. Bryan F. Smith, former general director of Texas Instruments, Inc., a fellow of the National Association of Corporate Directors and of the Academy for the Advancement of Corporate Governance, points out, "My basic worry is that board of director input to the organization; i.e., definition of such groups is minimal at best, and that consequently de facto delegations of subject matter later occur which create organizational confusion and perhaps even default by the board of its required duties under established standards of care."

Mr. Smith has given permission to quote his elaboration of this important concern:

Advisory boards or councils are having a new wave of popularity stimulated in part by a misguided feeling that in some way service thereon will avoid the legal exposure incident to service on boards of directors. In the more traditional sense where such groups are not intended to be de facto boards of directors but rather to provide broad insight and information, they can indeed perform very useful functions. Since membership by design is expected to include distinguished persons who are usually not only competent but outspoken and with strong convictions, great care must be taken from the outset to define its duties and responsibilities so that they will not (a) conflict with those of the board of directors or (b) become an alternate board or super board, or a body dealing with substantive board matters with respect to which the directors have clear legal duties and obligations. Consequently, the board of directors should carefully prescribe and review the charter of the advisory group and should formally approve its members. There is great risk that advisory groups—even with the best intentions and careful definition—can become glorified "chowder and marching societies" whose activities degenerate into expensive gratifications for the participants. Their status can be misinterpreted by the management who feel compelled to attend to their care and feeding to unproductive excess, particularly when the advisory group has an international orientation. Additionally, scheduled periodic and structured meetings between the advisory group and the board of directors will usually serve as an effective monitor and control.

Care should be taken that the support costs for such advisory activities, including fees paid to members, are appropriately in line with costs of supporting the board of directors.

In carrying out its own duties, the Board must decide what subject matter it reserves to itself and what, in turn, is appropriate for consideration by other formally organized groups—be they management committees, ad hoc board committees or advisory bodies. Failure to define these respective roles can lead to confusion and potential abuse.

Fred A. Tillman, professor of legal studies in the Department of Risk Management and Insurance at Georgia State University, Atlanta, Georgia, offers this legal advice. To avoid being treated either as a board of directors or as its alter ego, an advisory group must be separate from the board and must function only on an advisory basis. According to Professor Tillman, steps to ensure this include:

The advisory group should be formed as an advisory council, not as an advisory "board";

Membership of the council and the (statutory) board should not overlap except where necessary (e.g., the chief executive officer);

Clear, complete records of council meetings should be kept;

The (statutory) board should explicitly accept or reject council recommendations made to it, if any, and the board's minutes should be certain to document its acceptance, rejection, or decision to take no action;

It is unlikely that all the council's suggestions will be brought before the (statutory) board, but even suggestions that are not submitted should be covered by file memoranda. These records document the council's independent thinking and affirm its separation from the board.[3]

My experience with advisory boards has been much more informal in the structure, process, and linkage with the advisee organization with a minimum of paper trail involved. The legal points suggested have been carefully set forth in the advisor's contract with each individual advisor. His or her obligations and liabilities in the relationship are carefully spelled out to ensure distinction between the advisory role and any statutory board role.

NOTES

1. See H. Igor Ansoff, "Conceptual Underpinnings of Systematic Strategic Management," *European Journal of Operational Research* 19 (1985), pp. 2–19, for an interesting discussion on strategic or adaptation activity of the firm in the changing environment.

2. For further discussion on the treatment of complexity, see John D.C. Little, "Research Opportunities in the Decision and Management Sciences," *Management Science,* 32, 1 (January 1986), pp. 11–13.

3. Fred A. Tillman, "Commentary on Legal Liability: Organizing the Advisory Council," *Family Business Review* 1, 3 (Fall 1988), pp. 287–88.

3

COUNSELING VERSUS CONSULTING VERSUS MENTORING

> To have no assistance from other minds in resolving doubts, in appeasing scruples, in balancing deliberations, is a very wretched destitution.
>
> —Samuel Johnson (1709–84)

A precursor to the next chapter's examination of the role of advisory boards is a better understanding of the process of consultation and advising in general. In particular, there are subtle distinctions between counseling, consulting, and mentoring. We do not have in the fields of management or governance a neat typology of the advisory process. Professor Edgar H. Shein of the Massachusetts Institute of Technology offers some help with two process models.[1]

The most prevalent model in organizational consultation is the *purchase model*. This means the purchase of expert information or an expert service with or without joint diagnosis by the client and consultant.

The *doctor-patient model* involves an outside team of consultants or an individual expert looking over the situation to define the problem and recommend a corrective program. The process may or may not be a joint one between client and consultant. According to Schein, "Process consultation is a set of activities on the part of the consultant which helps the client to perceive, understand and act upon process events which occur in the client's environment." Process consultation is not normally the focus of outside advisory boards. They are generally focused on the external environment. Advisory board activity is, however, of the purchase model type and normally of a counseling rather than a consulting nature.

A consultant works as a staff resource with a client who purchases the advisory service for one or more of half a dozen reasons: (1) on jobs the client might do for himself but needs temporary help, (2) providing services or skills not available on the client staff such as special knowledge of perspective or to stimulate new ideas, (3) innovate or intervene using outside help, (4) provide an uncommitted point of view acting as "strawman," (5) be an expedient, or (6) act as a surrogate of management.

The popular stereotypes for consultants are either positive as experts, gurus, or innovators, or negative as hired guns, unemployed executives, or witch doctors. Of most definitions of consulting that can be found, there are certain key distinguishing criteria, including (1) independent service orientation, (2) staff relationship to the client, (3) expertise involving professional mind-set, education, and training, (4) experience and insight, (5) analytical and diagnostic ability, (6) problem identification and solving skills, and (7) integrity, reliability, and discretion.

A consultant's advice implies knowledge and experience, often professional or technical, on the part of those advising. The advice may apply to any of the affairs of life. The range of advice goes from the "Dutch-uncle" variety of frank, even severe criticism offered in a professional manner to the consciousness-raising variety proffered for the purpose of expanding client perspective or thinking process.

Counseling is different, although it is also advice with a price tag. Counseling often stresses the "fruit of wisdom or deliberation," according to dictionary definition. It presupposes weightier occasions than advice or more authority or a closer relationship in the person(s) who counsels as in Shakespeare's: "I do in friendship *counsel* you. To leave this place." An attorney is often called a counselor, suggesting instruction or advice of a lofty, legal, or ideal character as in the expression "the Christian *counsel* of perfection."

The key point regarding an advisory board is the involvement of the board members in conferring, discussing, deliberating frankly, sometimes unofficially, with the client. The Scotch proverb, "He that winna be counselled canna be helped" frames the raison-d'être for most advisory councils.

The wise advisor may be called a mentor. The common role model is that of a paternalistic father figure. The term comes from a friend of Odysseus entrusted with the education of Odysseus's son, Telemachus. A mentor is a trusted counselor, guide, tutor, coach, and teacher. Mentoring is an individualized process and may be a consequence of a senior or junior's initiatives, or it may be a matter of organizational policy or culture. Jewel Companies, for example, have a policy in which vice presidents are assigned as mentors and as "first assistants" to their apprentices. Many other organizations, such as Bell Laboratories, have formal mentoring programs internal to their organizations.

Mentoring requires individuals who can tolerate emotional interchanges. They must be able to accept conflict as a dispute over substance, not as a personal matter. Mentors accumulate power, respect, and future access to information from those individuals they help to develop. Mentoring is a satisfying, creative, rejuvenating experience.

Worldwide, advice is offered for a fee to companies needing outside expert orientation, counsel, problem solving, introductions, industrial-business-societal scans, or just plain handholding. A significant part of these professional solo or team advisory services is at the board level, subsidiary and main board, or at the top of the management hierarchy.

In a more innovative direction, an interesting development is underway in the educational field that is related to advice for boards. It is worth including here as a possible new approach to improving board effectiveness. The board-mentor service was conceived in 1974 by the Association of Governing Boards (AGB) to provide assistance to colleges and universities troubled with their trustee effectiveness and to provide member boards with on-campus workshops to assess their organization and performance. This concept could well have application in the business world as an addition to the environmental scan function of advisory boards.

In September 1976, the first group of experienced and knowledgeable trustees and administrators, representing a broad range of higher education institutions across the United States, were invited to serve as board-mentors. They were then given an intensive orientation session conducted by the AGB with the assistance of the Institute for Educational Management of Harvard University and the Cheswick Center of Boston.

Field tests with these thirty-two board-mentors began in January 1977, and a second orientation session was launched for a new batch of volunteers. The cost of employing a board-mentor is nominal to the educational institution, and the service is available only to AGB member boards. The thrust of the advice is on trusteeship in the evolving societal context. In addition to offering filmstrips on topics ranging from the board's role in institutional strategic planning to fund raising, the basic role of the board-mentor is to serve as a catalyst to engage boards in discussions of matters of special concern. In this regard, the technique and contribution of the board-mentor is to the proper role of the trustees, the most useful concepts, and the methodology of the stewardship process. Through this process, there is an awakening of the trustees to the realities of functioning in the future world of education.

The AGB describes its program as follows:

One of the important responsibilities of a college or university governing board is to assess its performance periodically. The AGB Board-Mentor Program is designed to assist trustees as they review their commitment to and understanding of their roles and responsibilities. This process is facilitated by a qualified peer trustee from another, but similar, type of institution—the Board-Mentor.

Because the Board-Mentor Program is tailored to address the specific needs of individual boards, the potential benefits are as varied as the participating institutions. Some of the more common outcomes include:

· Greater understanding of the governing board's roles and responsibilities.
· Renewed sense of institutional mission and purposes.
· Better understanding of the institution's strengths and needs.
· Closer working relationship between the board and the chief executive.
· Consensus on priorities for strengthening board organization and bylaws.
· Improved communication with the board's various constituencies.
· Greater camaraderie among board members.
· Renewed understanding of goals and priorities to enhance board effectiveness.

The agenda for each workshop is determined collectively by the chief executive, the board chairperson, and the Mentor, based on their understanding of the major issues facing the board and the responses to AGB's "Self-Study Criteria."

A typical Board-Mentor workshop lasts from one to two days and is held in a retreat setting, preferably off-campus with comfortable lodging and meeting facilities. It is highly recommended that the trustees commit themselves to at least eight hours of meeting time, and that the session extend overnight. All board members are encouraged to attend and participate. One of the program's strongest assets is that it affords trustees an opportunity to meet informally with one another in a relaxed environment. To encourage candor and camaraderie, it is recommended that the chief executive officer be the only administrator present.

The Board-Mentor helps to plan the workshop agenda, serves as facilitator in leading discussions, and provides an objective perspective on the board's and chief executive's concerns. Every Mentor has extensive personal experience as a college or university trustee, and has been fully prepared by AGB to lead such workshops.

Because the Mentor plays such a critical role in the success of the program, careful attention is given to selecting the most appropriate Mentor for the participating board, keeping in mind his or her experience and background.

Typically, three or four Mentors are recommended, and the descriptions of their professional and volunteer experience are sent to the president and the board chairperson.

The participating institution—not AGB—makes the final selection after discussions with AGB staff, review of the Mentors' backgrounds, and perhaps consultation with boards that have previously participated. (AGB staff coordinates all communication with prospective Mentors throughout the selection process.)

The Board-Mentor concept features more functional advice than environmental scan-type advice, and it is focused on college or university governing boards. Both types of advice are needed when a company seeks to operate in a new business environment or geographical locale. What is going on there that is different from other operations and how best to function are equally valuable advisory inputs. Perhaps some business corporations could use a board-mentor for their subsidiary boards—perhaps even for their main boards. The essence of either counseling, consulting, or mentoring is emotional detachment and professionalism. A Quaker advises us:

The true secret of giving advice, is after you have honestly given it, to be perfectly indifferent whether it is taken or not, and never persist in trying to set people right.[2]

NOTES

1. Edgar H. Schein, *Process Consultation: Its Role in Organization Development* (Reading, Mass.: Addison-Wesley Publishing Company, 1969).

2. Logan Pearsall Smith, *Philadelphia Quaker: The Letters of Hannah Witall Smith* (New York: Harcourt Brace Jovanovich, Inc., 1950).

4

ROLE OF AN ADVISORY BOARD OR COUNCIL

Unlike a statutory board, an advisory group can avoid some unwanted powers and responsibilities. The advisory board can function without a legal right to depose management and without legal responsibility to external publics. There are various reasons for using advisory boards:

1. A gap-filling function when the owners or owner-representatives lack time or expertise to cope with the difficulties of governing or managing an organization in a dynamic environment;

2. A resource to the top management and the statutory board. The advisors supplement the expertise of the internal staff. They avoid the consequences of group-think, concinnity, and lack of objectivity when the advocates of a decision are involved in its justification or are beneficiaries of the action;

3. Providing special peer-acceptable insight in the gray area of entrepreneurship, innovation, and professional business administration;

4. As an adjunct to the corporation's intelligence-gathering system for purposes of activity or societal scans on an international or specific functional or strategic area of interest (technology, economics, marketing);

5. To identify and evaluate alternative courses of action not foreseen by the management or the main board;

6. To assist the CEO in resolving or reconciling serious internal differences of opinion by an objective outside judgment;[1] and

7. To provide introductions to potential customers, suppliers, or clients; develop business, government, and trade relations; keep abreast of political,

social, and technical developments in industry, government, or universities.

It is important, in adopting any of these seven (or other) reasons for having an advisory group, to steer completely clear of any ambiguity or uncertainty regarding accountability in corporate decision making. Advisors should not, de facto, make decisions or unduly influence the accountable decision-making body—the board of directors—or the chief executive and his immediate staff who are by charter, policy, legislation, or regulation the decision makers. An advisory group functions as a resource and must avoid de facto dominating the decision process or permitting the board or executive management to abdicate or abandon their roles and accountabilities.

Given the positive reasons for creating advisory groups, it is important to distinguish further between their policy role and the legal role of the statutory board. My long-time colleague on advisory councils, J. Keith Louden, president of The Corporate Director, Inc., points out that there are important differences between serving in an advisory role and in a legally accountable role, but the risk of litigation may not be one. The unavailability or high cost of adequate liability insurance may make it difficult, too expensive, or impossible for companies to obtain D&O liability coverage, and some companies are considering placing their boards of directors on an advisory status, rather than having them legally constituted and accountable. Louden says, "This, in my mind, is not only a major step backward but a totally unsatisfactory solution to the problem. First of all, it is not clear that even though a director is serving in an advisory capacity that, should the company be involved in litigation the advisory director would not be held accountable if it developed during the trial that management followed the advice of the advisory director or directors."[2] Louden further points out that to have just an advisory board is to deprive management of the quality of judgment and advice that they have the right to expect from a board of directors.

Patrick J. Head, vice president and general counsel of FMC Corporation (Chicago), observes, "I am not aware of any regulations that deal specifically with the legal liability of advisory directors, except that it would undoubtedly be the same as any other consultant or advisor. It would, therefore, be different than the normal director who has the additional legal protections of business judgment in regard to his or her service. An advisory director, like any other consultant, or lawyer if you will, would be held to the same standards of liability for professional advice."

FUNCTIONAL AND PROCESS ROLES

Statutory boards of directors can be conceptually characterized by three governance *functional* roles and by five governance *process* roles. Advisory boards or councils have different parameters. They normally overlap statutory board roles in only three of the process roles and in none of the functional roles. This abstract comparison is important for these multiple role designations, and role distinctions are key to understanding an effective advisory board. It is useful to compare the roles of statutory boards of directors with those of an advisory board.

United States courts generally agree on three fiduciary and statutory roles of a board of directors. These roles concern the functions of legitimization, auditing, and supervisory oversight or direction. By virtue of its incorporation, a company must legally have a board of directors, and thus its existence, in part, legitimatizes the corporation. State statutes require boards to audit the affairs of the corporation to see that it is properly managed on behalf of its owners and to serve the charter granted by the state for incorporation responsibly.

Advisory boards have none of these functional responsibilities; they are policy creatures of the statutory board or of the top management. They perform as adjunct resource groups and are formed by the corporation, not the state, for a variety of purposes described in Chapter 6.

Statutory boards of directors have multiple *process* roles, some of which are kinetic or active; others are latent or relatively quiescent. There are at least five process roles to consider: (1) the statutory/fiduciary role, (2) evaluative role, (3) participative role, (4) resource role, and (5) catalyst or change agent role. Assumption of all or some of these roles varies in relevance and intensity depending upon the nature of the company's industry and business size, the life-cycle stage of the enterprise, its ownership patterns, and other considerations. No two boards are alike. The roles assumed will change with competitive, environmental, social, economic, legal, and political conditions.

The first role of *statutory and fiduciary* responsibilities is defined by law and custom. The board must assume responsible charge of this function and the requisite processes to keep current. The advisory board does not engage in carrying out these responsibilities.

The second role of *evaluation* is also critical. Boards must lead and act in a judicious and objectively prudent fashion to evaluate compliance with the law; ensurance of management performance, succession, and development; conformance to plan, objectives, and board standards and criteria for corporate performance (on behalf of the stakeholders); and the company's relationships with the society that sanctions the existence of the corporation. The advisory board can contribute input to various evaluative exercises, keeping clear of the decision-making process.

The *participative* role is controversial. It deals with the involvement of directors with the executive and operational levels on selected matters such as financial auditing, strategic considerations, technology trends, organization and compensation, and environmental assurance. The extent of director participation depends on the talent and interest of board members and the attitude of the CEO in either dealing with the board at arm's length or encouraging selective participation. The issue here is one of clear accountability, responsibility, and authority. If requested, an advisory board can act carefully in selected participative exercises as long as its role is clearly side-saddle, staff-oriented, and not confusing to those in responsible charge as to where the authority, responsibility, and accountability lie.

The *resource* role of directors concerns the nature and composition of the board. Specific experience and expertise are increasingly called for as business becomes more complex. Willingness of the CEO to draw on director expertise is the key. The board can take leadership by insisting that qualified board members or outside experts be used as a resource.

The *change agent* role of the board has been more or less relegated to action in crisis (for example, removal of the CEO, response to a takeover threat, or governmental intervention). Tomorrow's board should take leadership in acting and planning before a crisis or outside intervention. This will require a proactive attitude, more time commitment, and a close working relationship—teaming—with management. Consultants and boards or councils of advisors are obvious resources when an outside perspective is required.

Of those cited above, the most common process roles of advisory boards are the evaluative, resource, and change agent roles. In this regard, advisory board input may overlap or supplement, but not intervene with, the statutory board activity from either of these three perspectives.

Evaluation of external threats and opportunities; evaluation of competition, political, social, environmental, and economic trends, public opinion; assessment of state of the art or innovative technology, can make up a complex sensing and evaluative process. Where the advisors have special expertise, networks, experience, or instincts about these forces and phenomena, their advice and counsel can augment a corporation's awareness. Advisory board activity does not compete with the regular board's evaluation of executives or directors.

One company, Monsanto, recently created an inside advisory board

Table 4-1
Conventional Statutory Boards versus Quasi-Boards or Advisory Boards

Function	Conventional	Quasi or Advisory
Accountable to numerous interests for corporate conduct	Yes	No
Required to make certain public disclosures	Yes	No
Review and approve major corporate objectives, policies, and budgets as initiated by CEO	Yes	Yes--plus taking some initiatives
Monitor the company's financial structure, performance and management	Yes	Yes
Evaluate performance of CEO and key executives	Yes	Yes
Ensure company compliance with all applicable laws	Yes	No
Have or need directors' liability insurance	Yes	No
Appointment and tenure	Elected by stockholders for stated term.	Appointed by owner who determines tenure

made up entirely of senior executives of the company. They advise the board and provide specific linkage to board committees. The arrangement legitimatizes nonvoting presence of insiders at board meetings. This device reverses, in a nonvoting sense, the ratio of inside to outside members in this boardroom. The arrangement has been in operation at Monsanto for several years. It has provided a more solid relationship between key members of management and the outside board, according to advisory director Robert L. Berra, senior vice president for administration. The rationale for creating this arrangement is related to Monsanto's historical evolution of its statutory board role. The present composition and terms of reference are given Chapter 6.

How small companies can enlist expert advice, at low cost, through a few independent overseers has been referred to as a quasi-board of directors or an advisory board (see Table 4-1) by Harold W. Fox. The following is excerpted from his article.[3] Quasi-boards perform many of the functions that conventional boards do (or should do) in publicly held corporations, but without the latter's legal power and account-ability. The preceding table compares some of the functions of the two boards.

A quasi-board/advisory board critiques management's actions, raises new questions, and offers suggestions to strengthen the company. The board's effectiveness depends on the proprietor's voluntary decision to respect its advice. And because the board has no legal power, the owner does not feel threatened when it exposes problems, worries, and ideas.

An advisory board functions best if it is small. Ordinarily four or five members—the owner (chairman) plus some outsiders with over-lapping expertise—suffice. Members should have empathy for small business problems, care about the company's success, and work effec-tively with other board members. Members of advisory boards usually receive far less pay than directors of large corporations. Typical fees range from $500 to $1,000 per session.

An advisory board must avoid meddling in procedural details. For-bearance helps allay the apprehensions of department heads. As in any new relationship, the owner-manager, executives, and members of a fledgling board may be skeptical. Early successes and reassur-ances help dispel these misgivings. Ideally, the company's owner and executives handle the exigencies of the moment and look to the ad-visory board for guidance on basic, long-term challenges.

A typical action is a recommendation for a logical organization de-sign including, where needed, position descriptions for the top man-agers and organization charts. At several companies, these requests have forced management to strengthen internal control, fill func-tional gaps, and eliminate overlaps. As byproducts, internal squab-bling dies down, and the need for policies in some operating areas (such as inventory control or insurance programs) becomes evident.

The quasi-board does not usurp the role of consultants. It does not conduct detailed studies, install systems, formulate procedures, or im-plement special projects. It is concerned with important policies, ques-tions of strategy, and decisions that promote a company's lasting prosperity. Successful quasi-boards also contribute to the growth of not only the company but also the owner-manager, executives, and their own members.

ADVISORY TASKS

From a task standpoint, advisory boards are often engaged to per-form any number of the following charges. All of them can fall in the purview of the statutory board, but when they are performed by an advisory board, the advisors take no part in the decision process.

1. To comment on the reasonableness and propriety of a proposed corporate decision without necessarily endorsing it as the only, the best, or the wisest decision that could be made.

2. To identify and evaluate alternative courses of action not foreseen by the management or the main board.

3. To confirm or verify important factual data underlying a particular proposition, project, or policy request.

4. To relieve some of the pressure on inside management and the decision-making process in times of explosive growth or business pressure. Advice by an advisory board on key decision elements can facilitate management decisions if the advisors are expert and trustworthy.

5. To provide independent assistance in the formulation of long-term objectives, goals, and strategy and advice on how to operate in an uncertain or foreign environment.

6. To provide objective and disinterested evaluation of corporate or management performance and competitive or government activity.

7. To supplement management with needed expertise and experience not available internally.

8. To assist the company in resolving or reconciling serious internal differences of opinion by offering an objective outside judgment or recommendation. The advisors are not involved in the decision process itself.

9. To provide a level of confidence to top management when there is some lack of confidence but no desire or ability to bring in new, better qualified management at the time (a short-term interim solution at best).

10. To advise the company where there is a high risk of material litigation or other potentially serious adverse consequences to the community, environment, or corporate reputation.

11. To watch for conflict-of-interest (real or perceived) overtones of a proposed activity or transaction. This could involve an acquisition, merger, joint venture, spin-off, stock issue, or entry into a new business.

12. To provide introductions to potential customers, suppliers, or clients; help develop business and enhance trade relations; assist in recruiting key personnel; assist in obtaining industrial property rights, permits, and licenses; and offer knowledge to keep abreast of social, legal, and technical developments in industry, government, or universities.

13. To provide a mechanism for monitoring the external environment for multinational corporations.

14. To act as sort of "agent provocateur." The advisory group decides nothing or virtually nothing; it only makes proposals. If the proposals are too far out, if they are too far ahead of the top managers or board members and where they may be persuaded to move—then the advisors may be wasting time. If such proposals are too modest—if they simply summarize what others are already doing—they are not worth making, nor are they

worth the cost of the advisors. So the role is to examine what is needed and make doable proposals for the enterprise to consider.

One further suggestion worthy of consideration has been made by John E. Martin, an independent consultant. This concept is that certain specialized functions requiring board attention can be handled by a single director with the support of advisory counselors. The concept is referred to as a committee or council of peers. The peer director thus defined provides services for the others on the board, either as an individual and liaison between the advisory counselor and the board or as a chairman of a board committee. In order not to compromise his independence, the peer director should not also be an officer of the company. The concept proposes

instituting a board structure that would provide specialized communications and counsel to the directors. A diverse group of independent advisors and corporate monitors, or examiners, would constitute a council selected to service the numerous needs of the directors. . . . The services they would provide would be in the nature of advice and counsel, analysis and special studies, auditing and monitoring sensitive operations, answering inquiries and advocating the views of special constituencies.[4]

Although this approach has obvious problems of potential conflict with management, information overload, and duplication of staff, it is an idea to be aware of even though use of the full-blown concept is yet to be seen extensively. The concept has many of the ingredients of the less complicated and traditional advisory board that have proven of value to many corporations.

In September 1979 Hercules, Inc., formed an advisory council of senior outside experts drawn from business with international experience and expertise in science, technology, and government. Alexander F. Giacco, chairman, president, and chief executive officer, created the panel to improve the review process and primarily to advise him and top management on complicated decisions that often involved sophisticated technology. The panel met regularly on a quarterly basis with occasional individual exchanges between meetings.

The initial mandate was to evaluate the company's plans and assess potential new markets for the company's products. Subsequent agenda topics included review of prospective acquisitions, strategic changes in corporate directions, materials sourcing, and competitive activity. The advisory council was a transition step to provide Hercules with independent, outside perspectives. "After a while you get steeped in tradition," commented Al Giacco in a *Business Week* interview on November 12, 1979. "It is often difficult for an in-house expert to tell his boss he's off his rocker."

After five years of advice and counsel, the Hercules main board ratio of outsiders to insiders swung in favor of the former. This was the first time in Hercules's corporate history that such a transformation had taken place. The advisory council was gracefully phased out at the end of 1984 after five years of advice and counsel to the CEO.

COMPANY-SPECIFIC ROLES

The role of an advisory board is company-specific. Its value cycles with the needs and resources of the corporation. It is not surprising that public statements of the role of advisory groups are tailor-made, often very broadly stated either in the annual report or the bylaws, in policy statements, or to the media. It is interesting to note that the life cycle of the Hercules Advisory Council was five years (1979–84). The following samples of other advisory groups are taken from publicly available sources.

Texas Instruments Annual Report

Board Advisory Council. The board advisory council advises the board of directors on a wide range of economic, political and social issues. Members are available on a group or individual basis, and spend between seven and 30 days a year performing such duties. The 1987 members were:

William M. Batten, Chairman, Board Advisory Council; retired Chairman and Chief Executive Officer, New York Stock Exchange

Cecil H. Green, one of the founders of Texas Instruments

Tadao Kato, former Japanese Ambassador to the United Kingdom

Paul W. McCracken, Professor, The University of Michigan

Lord Peyton of Yeovil, former member of Parliament, United Kingdom

Mike Shepherd, Jr., Chairman Texas Instruments

Joachim Zahn, retired Chairman of the Management Board, Daimler-Benz AG

Bank of America Bylaws

Section 1. Advisory Directors. The Board of Directors may appoint such number of advisory directors as shall be determined by the Board from time to time to be appropriate. Such advisory directors shall serve at the pleasure of the Board of Directors and shall have the function and duty to attend the meetings of the Board and to advise the Board, the committees and the officers of this Association. The Board of Directors may from time to time request any or all of the advisory directors to attend meetings of designated committees of this Association. Advisory directors shall receive the same fees and expenses as may from time to time be paid to the members of the Board of Directors. No advisory director who receives a salary as an officer or employee of this Association shall receive compensation for attending any meeting of the Board of Directors or of any committee of this Association.

Section 2. Management Advisory Council. The Board of Directors shall appoint a Management Advisory Council composed of such number of members as the Board may from time to time deem appropriate. Such members shall be officers or retired officers of the Association, and such other persons as the Board of Directors may from time to time designate and appoint. The Chairman of the Management Advisory Council shall be appointed by the Board of Directors. All members of the Managing Committee shall be Ex-Officio members of the Management Advisory Council. The Managers Advisory Council and the Junior Advisory Council shall each appoint one of said councils' members to represent said councils at each meeting of the Management Advisory Council. The representatives of said councils shall be Ex-Officio members of the Management Advisory Council when present at meetings of the Council.

The Management Advisory Council shall meet at such times and places as the Managing Committee may determine and shall give advice and counsel to the Committee and to the officers of the Association, as from time to time may be requested.

Anta Corporation Bylaws

Section 11. Advisory Directors. The Board of Directors may appoint individuals who may but need not be directors, officers, or employees of the corporation to serve as members of an Advisory Board of Directors of the corporation and may fix fees or compensation for attendance at meetings of any such Advisory Boards. The members of any such Advisory Board may adopt and from time to time may amend rules and regulations for the conduct of their meetings and shall keep minutes which shall be submitted to the Board of Directors of the corporation. The term of office of any member of the Advisory Board of Directors shall be at the pleasure of the Board of Directors and shall expire the day of the annual meeting of the stockholders of the corporation. The function of any such Advisory Board of Directors shall be to advise with respect to the affairs of the corporation.

Genuine Parts Company. Notice of Annual Meeting and Bylaws

Election of Advisory Directors. The By Laws of the Company provide that Advisory Directors are entitled to attend all meetings of the Board of Directors, but do not have the power to vote and are not to be counted for the purpose of ascertaining the presence of a quorum. Advisory Directors are available for consultation with and advice to the Board of Directors but are not members of the Board of Directors for any purpose.

3.3 Advisory Directors. (a) Effective at the annual meeting of the shareholders to be held in 1970 and at each annual meeting thereafter, all directors who shall have attained the age of seventy (70) years on or before the first day of January preceding the annual meeting shall be retired as directors of the corporation; provided, however, that such mandatory retirement shall not be applicable to any director holding office on April 1, 1969 who had on or before such date attained seventy (70) years of age.

Upon the nomination of the Chief Executive Officer any director of the corporation as he is retired under the provisions of this section, may be elected an Advisory Director of the corporation by the shareholders, to serve until the next annual meeting of the shareholders. Thereafter, upon the nomination of the Chief Executive Officer such retired directors may be re-elected by the shareholders from year to year at the annual meetings as Advisory Directors in the same manner as directors are elected.

(b) Any officer of the corporation who is a director of the corporation and who shall retire or be retired by the corporation shall be eligible to be nominated and elected as an Advisory Director in the same manner as provided in Section 3.3 (a) above, even though he has not attained the age of seventy (70) years on the date of such retirement.

(c) The Advisory Directors shall be entitled to attend all meetings of the Board of Directors and may participate in any discussion thereat but shall not have the power to vote and shall not be counted for the purpose of ascertaining the presence of a quorum. Such Advisory Directors shall be available for consultation with and advice to the Board of Directors for any purpose. The same fee paid to directors for attendance at meetings of the Board shall be paid to the Advisory Directors who attend Board meetings.

Northwest Natural Gas Co. Bylaws

Article III, Section 2. Advisory Directors. Any person who shall have served as a director of the company may be elected by the board as an advisory director of the company for one or more terms of one year or less. An advisory director may attend meetings of the board but shall not have the right to vote at such meetings.

Section 4. Compensation. Advisory directors shall receive such reasonable compensation for their services as may be fixed by resolution of the board of directors and shall be reimbursed for expenses properly incurred in connection with the performance of their duties as advisory directors.

Unidentified Industrial Company Prospectus

Excerpt from Prospectus for an Advisory Board. With the growth and diversity of the business, major decisions are made relative to marketing, manufacturing, production, finances, personnel, and corporate structure. Our management is marketing-oriented and requires expertise and counseling in other areas to establish perpetuity of the corporation and provide counseling to management.

As can be seen from these examples, the purpose, focus, boundary, criteria for membership, linkages, and relationships of advisory boards or councils are in no way uniform. Nor should they be. These aspects depend on the role of the advisors and their capacity to contribute. Creating an "advisory" role for ceremonial or political reasons may be justifiable. However, if true independent advice and counsel is the objective, such "advice with a price tag" should be a distinct, peer-respected addition to management and governance of a corporation.

Need for tailored contract advice varies with the industry or business maturity, the ownership and strategic position of a company, its history of using outside directors or advisors, and the capabilities and preferences of the chief executive officer and/or chairman of the board. Some specimen contracts between advisors and advisee companies are included in Chapter 10 as guidelines for agreement contracts.

INTERNATIONAL ADVISORY COUNCILS (IAC)

Prescribing the role of an advisory board is usually (and carefully) ambiguous and general. This allows fit and reception of advisory input with the corporate or boardroom culture. Many advisory boards of large corporations contacted in my 1986 survey of international advisory council practices have only a very general invitation letter agreement. This is due to change to more formal contractual form with the increasing litigation and liability exposure occurring around the globe. Some interesting developments are underway in advising international corporations.

A 1983 survey by *International Management* identified an elite fraternity of about 250 of the world's top multinational corporation executives who advise each other on policy and strategic issues via participation on numerous advisory councils. These are global, regional, or national advisory bodies functioning as closely knit peer groups. Individuals are drawn from industry, finance, government, research and development institutes, and consulting organizations. The councils ranged in size from six members on Sperry's advisory council, to twenty-four on Morgan Guaranty's.[5]

International advisory councils are not new. The 1973 oil crisis substantially increased the movement toward corporations seeking outside advisors. This notion had been introduced in the 1950s by a few American multinational companies actively extending their interests overseas.

The 1983 survey was interesting in the increasing interlocking nature of these international advisory councils. Forty-six persons served on two or more advisory councils. Eight belong to three councils, and six serve on four, two on five, and one individual sits on seven councils. In 1983 the busiest advisory councillor was Guido Carli, former governor of the Bank of Italy. He served as an advisor to Merck & Co., Inc., IBM Corp., First Boston, Inc., Chemical New York Corp., and Rockwell International Corp., all U.S.–headquartered firms. In addition, he served on advisory councils of Robeco NV of the Netherlands and the Canadian Imperial Bank of Commerce.

Dieter Spethmann, chairman of Thyssen AG of West Germany served on five advisory councils: Merck, Ford Motor Co., and the Conference Board, Inc., of the United States; Unilever of Britain and the Netherlands; and the Swiss Bank Corp.

The other five-star advisor at the time of the survey was Otto Wolff von Amerongen, chairman of Otto Wolff AG of West Germany: he served on the advisory council of AMF Inc., IBM, United Technologies Corp (UTC), Rockwell and the Conference Board, all of the United States.

Four-star advisors were:

Arthur Furer, chairman of Nestlé SA of Switzerland, who was advisor to Valmont Industries, Inc., Rockwell, Morgan Guaranty Trust Co., of New York, and the Conference Board, Inc., all of the United States.

Pehr G. Gyllenhammar, chairman and CEO of AB Volvo of Sweden, served on the advisory councils of Chase Manhattan Corp., Tenneco Europe Inc., and CPC International Inc., all of the United States, plus Lafarge Coppée of France.

Ichiro Hattori, president of Daini Seikosha Co. Ltd. and Suwa Seikosha Co. Ltd. of Japan, sat on the advisory councils of AMF and Security Pacific National Bank of Los Angeles, both of the United States; Touche, Remnant & Co. of Britain; and Lafarge Coppée of France.

Walther Kniep, former president of CPC Europe Ltd., served on advisory councils of Chemical Corp., Tenneco, CPC and Volvo of Sweden.

Roger L. R. Martin, former chairman of Saint-Gobain-Pont-à-Mousson of France, served on advisory councils of AMF, Sperry Corp., General Motors Corp., and AT&T International Inc.

William Cochrane Turner, former U.S. ambassador to the O.E.C.D. and chairman of Argyle-Atlantic Corp. of Phoenix, Arizona, was also chairman of AT&T's Asia Pacific and European Advisory Councils and a member of American Can Co. and Caterpillar Tractor Co. councils.

Other heavy hitters on the international advisory council circuit to the extent of serving on three councils:

Giovanni Agnelli, chairman of Fiat SpA of Italy, an advisor to Chase Manhattan, UTC, and the Conference Board.

Umberto Agnelli, vice chairman of Fiat, serving as councillor to AT&T,

Allianz Versicherungs AG of West Germany, and Thyssen-Bornemisza NV of the Netherlands.

Carlo De Benedetti, president of Olivetti SpA, served on advisory councils of AMF, Morgan Guaranty, and AMAX Inc.

Sir Maurice Hodgson, chairman and CEO of British Home Stores was on the advisory council of Chase Manhattan, AMAX, and Air Products and Chemicals, Inc.

H.F. van den Hoven, chairman of Unilever NV of the Netherlands, an advisory councillor to AT&T, Rockwell, and the Conference Board.

Jean-Paul Christophe Parayre, chairman of Peugot SA of France, served as advisor to Merck, Chase Manhattan, and Burroughs Corp. on their respective advisory councils.

Ambroise Roux, former chairman of Compagne Générale d'Électricité of France, an advisory council member for Ford, Swiss Bank and Touche, Remnant of Britain.

H. Johannes Witteveen of the Netherlands, former chairman of the International Monetary Fund, Washington, D.C., was on the advisory councils of Morgan Guaranty, General Motors, and Thyssen-Bornemisza of the Netherlands.

It is easy to see how international human networking occurs as relationships develop through peer respect, personal trust, and familiarity. This leads to multiple nominations and membership at the top level of the multinational corporate "elite corps of jet-set power brokers," as Jules Arbose refers to them in the *International Management* 1983 survey.[6]

While concerns may be voiced from some quarters at the interlocking and self-perpetuating oligarchies of the advisory councils serving large corporations in the developed countries, particularly Western Europe and the United States, the benefits to the corporations can be significant. These networks of advisors are able to spot international trends, hazards, and opportunities that can be vital to strategic directions, even to survival of far-flung business activities. They offer effective backup sources of guidance in taking tough decisions abroad or in a sector of business activity unfamiliar to top management.

It is important to understand how these international advisory boards actually function and how their role differs from that of the statutory board of directors and of top management of the corporations being served by an advisory council. The councils are advisory, act as symposia, and are not decision-making groups. They meet relatively infrequently, although members understand that they may be called on occasionally for ad hoc advice. Some companies keep the dates and venues of council meetings secret for security, policy, or competitive reasons. Other companies take advantage of the "star power" of the membership and use meeting occasions as major public or customer relations events.

Common problems, both to advisory councils and statutory boards, include dealing with strong egos, political and ideological orientations, celebrity versus working members, tenure versus rotating or term membership, establishment-biased views, passe advice, conflicts of interest, unintentional commercial security leaks, the life cycle of an advisory council, and advisory versions of the duty of care and duty of loyalty parameters set forth for statutory directors' conduct. All these characteristics of advisory councils can be managed properly, albeit sensitively. Chapter 9 discusses in more detail the "care and feeding" of these high-geared, high-priced groups and influential individuals. My experience over thirty years of advisory council service for corporations of various sizes and types leads me to offer some not-so-obvious points.

Advisory councils are relatively easy to create if you are willing to pay the price for such advice and worry with the idiosyncrasies of the members. However, advisory councils' role and purpose are often transitional, serving as a timely, specialized resource or an organizational option. An example of the organizational option role would be where an advisory council provides a responsible set of part-time advisors in a world region. This might be where operations are diverse or are not of sufficient size to warrant institutionalizing an incorporated-type board of distinguished and experienced directors or establishing a top management staff resident in the territory. Another example is where the council serves as a resource until the composition of the main board can be altered to provide outside directors with the needed experience and perspective.

One caveat: avoid implying tenure for those invited to serve on an advisory group, especially in a foreign country where business cultures and practices may not be the same as in the United States. One multinational U.S.–headquartered company where I assisted the chairman establish a distinguished international advisory council of prominent European corporate chairmen and CEOs had a delicate and difficult time on this score. The matter concerned not renewing the contractual agreement for serving on an international advisory council when the advisor, a chairman of a major European bank, retired from his active role as bank chairman. The local national culture and business practice did not abruptly retire a distinguished executive from such an advisory role because he retired from his primary executive position. The chairman of the American company engaging the advisors held firm on his policy of only having advisors in active business roles. The retired banker was replaced with an equally distinguished European, still actively in responsible charge of a major European enterprise.

A delicate balance is necessary between bringing outside advisors up to speed with the dynamic nature of the company's business, and timing the rotation of the membership appropriately in order to keep the most suitable and relevant advisors is a company- and situation-specific problem. Administering this has to be done from the top of the corporation being served; otherwise, the advisors will get the signal that their service and advice is secondary to the use of their name and position on the annual report of the corporation.

A friend of mine, chairman of a United States company in Europe, has some advice with which I heartily concur. He advises (1) don't take nominations for an advisory council from subsidiary company executives, since you will have a business problem when it is necessary to sever their advisory council membership; (2) council members should be chosen based on personal achievement and position in industry-outside activities, industry fit, geographic fit, and other than industry experience in public sector, academia, economics; (3) have only one or two specific issues on the meeting agenda, provide reading materials on the subjects in advance, and arrange to facilitate group discussions confined to these few issues; (4) include spouses at least once a year at meeting occasions to provide important social cement.

It is useful to examine an example of a prestigious and active European advisory council. This illustrates a real, current situation making the most out of this increasingly useful organizational device.[7] Tenneco Europe administers its European Advisory Council program from the corporate office in London, England. The Advisory Council, initially formed in 1980, is a group of European business executives appointed on a yearly basis with a rotation membership policy in force. The council meets quarterly to discuss topics of interest to Tenneco's management and to provide advice concerning relevant economic, political, and social trends in Europe. It is not a decision-making body, and does not have the legal responsibility of a board of directors.

When the company's Advisory Council was set up, James Ketelsen, Tenneco's chairman and chief executive officer, commented, "Tenneco has substantial and growing business interests in Europe and we feel that it is important for us to have the benefit of direct advice and counsel from people who intimately understand what is happening there today and what the operating environment there is likely to be in the future."

The Advisory Council helps Tenneco's management in three principal ways. First, the council can identify and analyze long-range potentials and threats in the European operating environment, acting in this capacity as an early warning system. Second, the council can act as a group of consultants for Tenneco's management by evaluating strategic issues affecting the company. Third, and important, association with the council members serves to enhance Tenneco's credibility in European business circles.

The twelve members of the Advisory Council, as of April 1986, were:

Senator Howard H. Baker
Senior Partner
Vinson & Elkins, Washington, D.C.

Rainer E. Gut
Chairman of the Board
Credit Suisse, Zurich, Switzerland

John P. Diesel
President, Tenneco Inc.
Houston, Texas

Pehr G. Gyllenhammar
Chairman & Chief Executive Officer
AB Volvo, Gothenburg, Sweden

James L. Ketelsen
Chairman of the Board & CEO
Tenneco Inc., Houston, Texas

David W. Livingstone
Deputy Chairman & Managing Director
Albright & Wilson Ltd., London, England

Oskar A. Munch
President & CEO
Elektro Union A/S, Oslo, Norway

Jaime Urquijo Chacon
Director, Banco Urquijo;
Chairman & Senior Executive
Energía e Industrias Argonesas SA
Madrid, Spain

Dr. Jur Klaus Liesen
Chairman of the Executive Board
Ruhrgas AG, Essen, West Germany

Raymond H. Marks
Chairman
Tenneco Europe Inc., London, England

Jacques Solvay
Chairman
Solvay & Cie SA, Brussels, Belgium

Bernard M. A. Vernier-Palliez

President of the Supervisory Council
Poclain SA, Le Plessis-Belleville, France

The program for the Advisory Council is run by a small economics
and business analysis corporate staff in London, which handles the
administration for the quarterly meetings and performs background
research for the discussion topics. There are generally two or three
planned discussion topics for each meeting. Some deal specifically with
the business strategies of Tenneco's operating units, for example, the
changing European market, investor relations, labor relations trends,
countertrade, the French economy, and prospects for gas markets in
Europe. Once a year, the council reviews the Tenneco financial results, with particular emphasis on the European operations.

Once each year, the council members meet Tenneco's board of directors in Houston. The remaining three meetings are held in Europe.
On occasions, outside council members have hosted meetings at their
own companies' headquarters. In September 1981, for example, the
council was invited to the headquarters of Volvo in Gothenburg, Sweden, providing Tenneco members a chance to compare the operations
of a European corporate office to their own.

Informal contacts between the council members are enhanced at a
dinner before each meeting where the council members are joined by
a guest speaker. Speakers have included Helmut Schmidt, former
chancellor of West Germany; Sir Ian McGregor, currently chairman
of Britain's Coal Board; and Edward Heath, former prime minister of
Britain and a prime mover for Britain's entry into the European Economic Community. Contact with Advisory Council members has been
restricted to members of Tenneco's senior management. Council opinion has been of value in some specific strategic moves. For example,
Advisory Council experience helped Tenneco's energy divisions establish innovative programs to market natural gas in the United States,
and Tenneco's entry into the venture capital industry and a multidi-
visional trade mission to Hungary were discussed with the Advisory
Council. Actions taken have been consistent with council opinion on
the subjects. According to Raymond H. Marks, former chairman of
Tenneco Europe, the Council provides an objective prism through which
Tenneco's management can look at strategic issues affecting the company's businesses in an environment of cultural, political, and economic diversity.

Another example of a current successful advisory group is that of
Merck's European Advisory Council. John Lloyd Huck, president and
later chairman of Merck & Co., Inc., attended most of the meetings of
this council and found them of great interest, but most specifically of
value to Merck's European executives. Huck observes, "One of the

greatest values is the contacts you make with some key people in Europe and the ability we had to call on them for assistance, in addition to the regular meetings." He described the role of the council (as it was constituted in 1983) as follows:

MERCK & CO., INC.
European Advisory Council

I. *Function*. Established in 1971 and composed of leading business executives, financiers and statesmen from various countries, the Merck European Advisory Council meets with Company executives to provide perspective on the political and economic outlook abroad and on the Company's broad strategic plans for growth in Europe.

II. *Members*. The current members of the European Advisory Council are:

Dr. Ernst van der Beugel, Professor of International Relations, Leyden University, Netherlands

Dr. Guido Carli, former Governor, Bank of Italy, Italy

John J. Horan, Council Chairman, Chairman and Chief Executive Officer, Merck & Co., Inc.

Dr. Hans Igler, Partner, Schoeller & Co., Austria

Dr. Henry Kissinger, former Secretary of State, United States

Baron Lambert, Chairman, Compagnie Bruxelles Lambert, Belgium

Jean-Paul Parayre, President, Peugeot S.A., France

Lord Roll, Chairman, S.G. Warburg & Co., Ltd., United Kingdom

Dr. Dieter Spethmann, Chairman, Thyssen, A.G., West Germany

Prospective members are invited to serve for an initial term of three years, with such membership subject to extension for additional periods by mutual agreement of the Company and the member.

Company participants, in addition to Mr. Horan (then chairman, Merck & Co.), were:

John L. Huck, President, Merck & Co., Inc.

Abraham E. Cohen, Senior Vice President, Merck & Co., Inc., and President, Merck Sharp & Dohme International Division

Bernard J. Crowley, Senior Vice President, Merck Sharp & Dohme International Division

William B. Van Buren, Vice President and Secretary, Merck & Co., Inc.

III. *Meeting Dates*. The Council meets twice a year, in the spring and fall, at various locations throughout Europe. Every second or third year, one of the Council meetings is scheduled in the United States.

IV. *Meeting Format*. To assure adequate coverage of meeting subjects and permit a full exchange of views, two-day meetings are scheduled, commencing in the early afternoon on the first day and concluding at around

4:00 P.M. on the second day. A Council dinner is held on the evening of the first day.

A formal agenda is prepared and circulated in advance of each meeting, with specific discussion topics suggested for each member.

V. *Fees and Expenses*. Fees for service as a member of the Merck European Advisory Council are reviewed and adjusted periodically.

Council members are also reimbursed for all reasonable travel and other expenses incurred by them in the course of their service as members.

Other examples of successful, long-standing advisory councils are those of AMF, Inc. AMF has had the AMF European Advisory Council for a number of years and subsequently formed the AMF Asia/Pacific Advisory Council. The role description and functions of these two councils are similar with their focus on different geographical regions.

Merlin E. Nelson, former vice chairman of AMF, actively directed these councils, and comments,

There was no contractual agreement other than an exchange of correspondence in which the individual was appointed as a council member for a term of years at a specified annual fee. In this letter they were informed that there would be an annual meeting and given some description of the role they would play and the purpose of the meeting was included.

The following in an outline of the European Advisory Council's role with the membership of the two AMF councils, as of 1984:

1. *Objectives of the Council*
   a. The primary mission of the Council was to provide advice to the CEO and other senior officers regarding general subjects which were relevant to the conduct of the company's business in the designated international territory. This included information concerning economic, fiscal, financial and political trends in the company's territory. Topics reviewed included labor relations, interest rates, taxation and government regulation of business in general.
   b. Council members also provided advice relating to specific industries in which the company was engaged or interested in entering.
   c. When the company was considering a major investment in a country within the international territory, council members were consulted on an individual basis.
   d. Council members were available to provide assistance to the company in connection with specific matters such as public relations, labor relations disputes, pending legislation or regulations which would directly affect the businesses of the company, etc.
2. *Composition of the Council*
   a. The European Advisory Council was composed of five members.
   b. One member each was selected from Germany, France, the United Kingdom, Italy and Austria since these were the major countries of

investment for the company in Europe. Generally, they were senior chief executives or retired CEOs from the industrial and financial sectors.

   c. Members were appointed for a term of three years. No person could be appointed after reaching the age of seventy.

3. *Conduct of Council Meetings*

   a. One meeting was held each year of one-day duration. Meeting locations tended to alternate between one in Europe and one at company headquarters in the USA.

   b. The meetings were two-way exchanges; that is, at the beginning of each meeting the company reviewed its operations in order to familiarize and update the members of the council regarding the company's current status overall and in Europe in particular. At the first meeting, it was necessary to spend more time in providing this familiarization regarding the company's business, its organization and systems of operation in the United States.

      Following the indoctrination regarding the company, there was a discussion concerning the current state and forecast of the European economy and also regarding the political outlook.

   c. Well in advance of each meeting, council members were sent an agenda; a set of forecasts regarding their countries; and a short list of questions regarding current events in each of their countries and in Europe generally which were of particular interest to the company. Council members were asked to come prepared to comment on the forecasts and questions and to add any remarks they felt would be of interest to the company executives and the other council members.

   d. Company executives in attendance included the chairman, president, and vice chairman, plus one or more group executives when the meeting was in Europe. When at the U.S. headquarters, other senior staff officers were invited. On several occasions, the U.S. meeting was scheduled on the afternoon of the day of the company's Board of Directors' meeting so that they could attend the council meeting.

   e. Usually a dinner was held the night before to which spouses were invited.

4. *Compensation*

An annual fee of $6,000 plus expenses was paid.

5. *Other Matters of Importance*

   a. Council members were put on the company's mailing list for all publicly distributed documents such as interim and annual reports, press releases, etc.

   b. Council members were encouraged to visit the company's plants and offices, which might be of interest to them, when it was convenient on their travels in connection with other professional activities.

Asia Pacific Advisory Council Members

Australia, Sir David Zeidler, C.B.E.

Hong Kong, The Honorable Michael G.R. Sandberg, C.B.E., Chairman, The Hongkong & Shanghai Banking Corp.

Japan, Mr. Ichiro Hattori President and CEO, Seiko Instruments & Electronics Ltd.

Singapore, Mr. Richard Lim Kee Ming M.Sc. Managing Director, Lim Tech Lee (Pte) Ltd.

European Advisory Council Members

Austria, Philipp von Schoeller, Jr. Bankhaus Schoeller & Co.

France, Roger Martin

Germany, Otto Wolff von Amerongen, Chairman, Otto Wolff Aktiengesellschaft

Italy, Carlo De Benedetti, Chairman & CEO, Ing. C. Olivetti & C., SpA

United Kingdom, Sir Trevor Holdsworth, Chairman, Guest, Keen & Nettlefolds plc

With the increasing environmental turbulence, business complexity, and the litigious trends in the United States, the importance of outside advisors, their company-specific role, and modus operandi cannot be ignored.

NOTES

1. Edward deBono, originator of the term "lateral thinking," has also introduced the concept of "triangular thinking" in which a third party can assist in conflict resolution by helping design a "road" out of the conflict by looking at the situation from a third-party angle. This third party is neither a judge nor negotiator but a creative designer. For more, see Edward deBono, Conflicts: A Better Way to Resolve Them (Middlesex, England: Penguin Books Ltd., 1985).

2. J. Keith Louden, "The Liability of Advisory Boards," Directors & Boards 10, 3 (Spring 1986), pp. 19–20.

3. Harold W. Fox, "Quasi-boards: Useful Small Business Confidants," Harvard Business Review (January-February 1982), pp. 158–65.

4. John E. Martin, "The Board Advisory Council and Peer Directors," Directors and Boards 1 (Fall 1976), p. 46.

5. Jules Arbose, "The Men Behind the Multinationals," International Management (November 1983), pp. 21–26.

6. Ibid., p. 21.

7. "Tenneco in Europe: The Essential Overseas Market," Tenneco Magazine 18, 4 (Winter 1984), pp. 5–13. Quarterly publication by Tenneco, Inc., Houston, Texas.

5

ACTIVITY AND
SOCIETAL SCAN

A corporation normally has its own network of plants, laboratories, offices, agents, and representatives that furnish a continuing flow of information necessary to plan and operate the business. But when it comes to sensing developments in remote locations or in broad economic, cultural, or social trends, it is important to tap outside experts to avoid the group-think pathologies that tend to develop internally.

BUSINESS RISK ASSESSMENT

Political scientists have long had techniques for charting international indicators of the degree of friendship or enmity that currently exists among nations. New methods are being continually developed in this field of nonlinear political risks to business. The techniques are of increasing value in estimating the relative likelihood of future changes.

Social and behavioral scientists have also advanced their observational techniques and instruments to deal with such emerging issues as (1) the general decoupling process when societies retreat from the complexities of life and attempt to restore a more human scale, (2) terrorism, and (3) the recognition of social traps or the tendency of organizations and societies to start in a direction that ultimately proves unacceptable but cannot then be reversed without causing even greater problems (such as exploitation of limited resources, reliance on technology, or disposal of wastes).

Technology and economic forecasting methodologies have also advanced substantially with a host of techniques, including systems modeling, alternative futures, scenario development, and refinements to most of the conventional basic forecasting techniques. This array includes qualitative (such as Delphi, panel consensus, visionary forecasting, historic analogy), time series analyses (trend projection, exponential smoothing, moving average), and causal methods (life-cycle analysis, leading indicators, input-output, diffusion index).

Risk management concerns attempts to reduce locational risks to a level of firm-specific risk that is consistent with the company's risk-return trade-off. This requires knowledge about the futurity of cash returns from the locations involved, which gives rise to a need for insights about what countries will be taking what action at what time.

American executives, more than their foreign counterparts, are likely to see external political interaction as some kind of social aberration that interferes with the pursuit of corporate objectives and private foreign policy. But as a result of worldwide operations, top managers must have or develop statesman-like skills: a knowledge of nation-building and the commonalities of its purposes and problems; a sensitivity for national and international economic, social, and political trends as related to differing paths to development; and an appreciation of broad historical realities that give some order to what seems like global confusion. In this regard, independent advisory boards can be a valuable resource to the chairman or CEO of a corporation. There are many well-known and conventional approaches to provide continuous scanning of the external environment, including use of foreign advisory councils, hiring of former foreign service officers, use of federal agencies' advice, use of consultants specializing in world area know-how, establishment of private intelligence systems, and creation of international studies and research units within the corporate structure.

In addition, there are data bases available for more quantitative approaches. These include use of computerized and other resource services providing country-specific programs. Some examples:

PRISM (primary risk investment matrix, a country rating service, reduces some 200 variables for each country to two digits: an index of economic desirability and an index of risk payback (measures of political and economic stability).

United Technologies Corporation has its own computer-based program for measuring foreign risks in the many countries in which it does business. Data are fed in from questionnaires filled out by the company's overseas staff, outside business, government, and academic sources. This provides ratings of sixty-five countries on ninety-six different factors ranging from labor unrest to economic health.

BERI (business environmental risk index) is another computerized country-ranking system. Countries are ranked on a scale of 1 to 100, depending on increased riskiness. The system uses the Delphi Technique with a panel of 100 individuals and is based on fifteen factors. This index grew out of the original work by Frederick T. Haner of the University of Southern California in 1966 combining economic and political factors in an overall rating of investment potential.

Business International Country Rating has a country index advisory service for multinational corporations covering most countries of interest to the international business community. This is an annual rating of the intensity of weakness and strengths in the fifty-seven countries of greatest interest to corporate investors. Using regional experts, thirty-four factors are grouped under four basic categories: (1) political-legal-social, (2) commercial, (3) monetary, and (4) energy vulnerability.

WPRF (World Political Risk Forecasts) is a service of Frost & Sullivan's business research group. It gives odds on potential business losses due to political developments.

Forecasting International, Arlington, Virginia, provides country forecasts based on a combination of statistics and intelligent judgment. Vital signs or stability indicators of various nations are numerically rated by experts. Factors such as welfare figures, procedures to deal with injustice, treatment of dissidents, political stability, military security, and self-image are integrated and compared with trends that may affect the country.

Data Resources Incorporated (DRI) offers an econometric data-based model approach to about nine industrialized countries.

The Wharton School of Business of the University of Pennsylvania has a computerized "Project Link," which was funded by the National Science Foundation. Economic models for about twenty-five countries (mostly industrialized OECD members) provide economic forecasts and examine transmissions (exports and other flows) between countries of economic fluctuations and disturbances. This service is not available commercially.

Wharton's World Model Project, an outgrowth of Project Link, is available commercially and has a wider country coverage. Present major focus is on OECD countries and South Africa.

Probe International and other firms provide tailored custom information on political changes and trends based on broad forces at work and the implications to specific companies.

Conference Board has sponsored a long-term effort involving a dozen multinational corporations jointly engaged in an international political and social analysis program with 193 corporations. This is an in-depth key country study.

Control Risks, Ltd., is a British security consulting firm specializing in countering threats to personnel. This company is a subsidiary of the Hogg Robinson Group, one of the larger, quoted Lloyds Insurance Brokers. The firm uses various survey methods to evaluate inherent security risks as a basis for recommending strategies to cope with such risks.

WEIS (World Event/Interaction Survey) at the University of Southern California in Los Angeles is a project originated by Charles A. McClelland. It is operated by the Consolidated Analysis Centers, Inc. (CACI) and uses a system for coding and analyzing data on nonroutine, newsworthy events occurring between governments. Since 1966 more than 50,000 international events reported in the *New York Times* have been coded and developed as international indicators. Sixty-three different types of action and more than 150 nations and international organizations are involved. These categories include military incidents, coercions, pressures, communications, support agreements, reconciliations, and military disengagements.

Policon (Political Consultations, Inc.), Ann Arbor, Michigan, provides systematic estimates of the political capabilities and stabilities of countries to supplement economic indicators of economic risks.

To sum up, there is a host of formal damage-control approaches and surprise avoidance techniques to help the multinational corporation cope with discontinuous and divergent changes in the political-risk game. The nonlinearity of political environmental and other risks makes such Achilles-heel type analyses both an art form and quantitative discipline. No technique will replace actual field observation, the checking out of readily available intelligence sources, strategic thinking, and experienced intuitive judgment from advisors in the territory. The computerized techniques can be useful supplementary tools but not ends in themselves or replacement for sophisticated advisory boards or councils made up of independent and knowledgeable persons.

INDEPENDENT CORPORATE ADVISORY BOARDS

The illusion of invulnerability held by many internal decision groups (and hence high-risk propensity), the rationalization of warnings that may force reassessment of current policies, the belief in the inherent morality of the decision group, the pressures on members of management to conform to accepted company or group policies, the suppression of personal doubts, and the cognitive biases or faulty conceptualization are all symptoms of company group-think pathologies.[1] An advisory group consisting of independent, well-situated, experienced, and expert persons can avoid these characteristics of group-think, which may breed in some corporate organizations. A glance at the present advisors on the Tenneco, Merck, and AMF European advisory councils (Chapter 4) illustrates the independent talent providing outside perspective to these multinational corporations. The advisory board can be viewed as an adjunct to the corporation's intelligence-gathering system. In this context, two useful conceptual approaches have been employed in describing their setup of information systems for social reporting.[2]

The first approach may be characterized as an activity scan (see Figures 5-1 and 5-2). The activity scan can be positioned in at least two different sectors. The most obvious is when the advisory board is made up of industrial, specialized disciplinary, or nation-oriented experts. This is represented in Figure 5-1 as an industry-focused advisory board. Justification for situating an advisory board in an industry domain may be dictated in a new venture or at the start-up or crisis stage. Or it may be targeted at a selective industrial market where the determining factors for viability of the enterprise are in the hands of competition, a set of particular customers, a restricted source for raw materials, or in a regulated or service-regulated industry.

In 1985, AT&T launched a couple of semi-independent business units in high-risk, high-return markets. The medical information systems and nondestructive testing products division were spun off from AT&T's New Ventures organization as separate strategic business units. Medical Information System (Morristown, New Jersey) integrates computer, communications, and software custom systems for large hospitals and medical professionals. It will jointly develop software with Health Information Systems (New York, New York). Nondestructive Testing Systems has introduced a portable nondestructive tester.

The New Ventures organization has a statutory board of directors to which the two new semi-independent businesses report through their respective managers. The units are free to pursue their own decisions, strategies, and marketing. They may enter agreements with outside firms or use existing AT&T resources. A Venture advisory board of industry experts decides which proposals may proceed.

The statutory board of any corporation, whether start-up or well established, may need input from a special group of advisors who are unaffiliated, disinterested, and independent and who are credible and outstanding in the industry involved. The broader social concerns may be shielded from the enterprise at any particular stage of its development. Knowledge of long-term trends may be of secondary or tertiary consequence at a particular stage of development. When these concerns become important, a different focus for outside advisors may be in order.

The model in Figure 5-2, with the business (rather than industry) focus, calls for an advisory board made up of persons with broad business and business-related backgrounds, but not necessarily from the particular industry or business in which the corporation has its primary interests. Financial, economic, political, scientific, or technological advisors are obvious advisory director candidates where such a broader cognitive sweep of the business community and its trends is germane and determining to the company's operations and future plans. Examples of companies using business-focus-activity-scan advisory

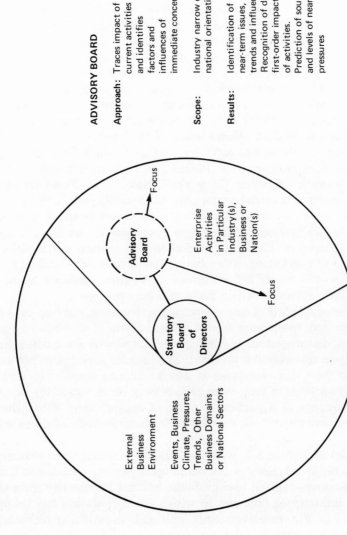

INDUSTRY FOCUS

External
Business
Environment

Events, Business
Climate, Pressures,
Trends, Other
Business Domains
or National Sectors

Statutory
Board
of
Directors

Advisory
Board

Focus

Focus

Enterprise
Activities
in Particular
Industry(s),
Business or
Nation(s)

ADVISORY BOARD

Approach: Traces impact of
current activities
and identifies
factors and
influences of
immediate concern

Scope: Industry narrow or
national orientation

Results: Identification of
near-term issues,
trends and influences.
Recognition of direct
first-order impact
of activities.
Prediction of sources
and levels of near-term
pressures

Figure 5-1
Activity Scan of an Advisory Board (Industry Focus)

BUSINESS FOCUS

ADVISORY BOARD

Approach: Same as Figure 5-1 against broader business range of activity

Scope: Business community oriented

Results: Figure 5-1 plus interrelationship with worldwide business interests. Identifies some second-order impacts and cross-impacts with industry and business more broadly

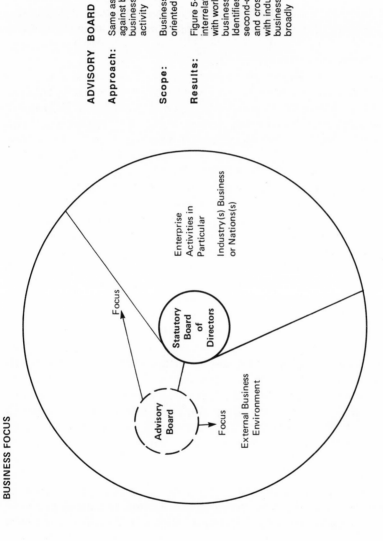

Focus

Enterprise Activities in Particular

Industry(s) Business or Nations(s)

Statutory Board of Directors

Advisory Board

Focus

External Business Environment

Figure 5-2
Activity Scan of an Advisory Board (Business Focus)

boards are conglomerates, multinational companies, multiproduct and service firms, holding companies, and investment management of financial services organizations. Large, fairly complex organizations in services and manufacture can often use an advisory board composed so that its perspective is that of the broad international community.

W. Michael Blumenthal, chairman and chief executive officer of the Burroughs Corporation, made a particular point of the company's international advisory board on the occasion of Burroughs' 1985 annual general meeting of stockholders at the Detroit Institute of Arts. During the century of growth being celebrated on that occasion, the emphasis on Burroughs' overseas presence was punctuated by the presence of distinguished business and financial leaders from the major countries in which Burroughs does business. These leaders serve on the International Advisory Board, providing their economic, political and societal perspective to those in responsible charge of Burroughs' overseas business. The personal distinction of the advisors also helps reinforce the world's understanding of Burroughs as a strong and growing force.

Figure 5-3 is a model of the advisory board concept at a higher level of information sensing and cognitive scope. The societal focus of such a board dictates an entirely different board mix, locale, and composition. Its purpose is more long range, futuristic, global, and social change–oriented. The issues studied are more sweeping and concerned with the purposeful and normative nature of the enterprise. The overview meta-scan type of advisory board serves the corporation at the highest level of this relevance tree. Such advisory boards are being employed by many large multinational companies, such as financial institutions and international manufacturing corporations.

The strengths of each of these three separate approaches—the industrial, business, or societal focus—give rise to their respective limitations. An advisory board formed for either of the first two activity-scan situations offers the advantages and familiarity with the company's current activities, problems, and opportunities. It also provides knowledge of previous crises, conflicts, disputes, pressure points, and vulnerabilities of the firm. The shortcomings stem from these same sources. Familiarity with the activities lends itself to some of the pathological conditions referred to previously. Other related shortcomings may be a priori notions, predispositions, or prejudice regarding sources of pressure and conflict or the merit of certain claims. In addition, there may be a tendency to overcommit to certain goals.

The overview or meta-scan approach, shown in Figure 5-3, balances the weaknesses of the more provincial scans by analyzing broad societal trends that are often relatively detached from the firm's current activities. By refraining from assumptions about the significance of

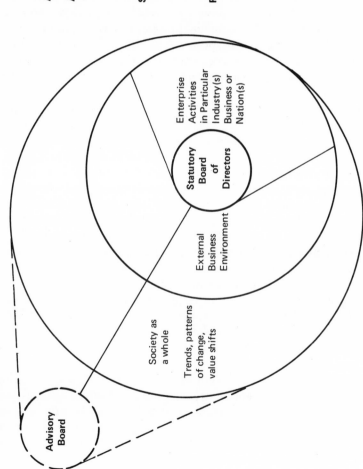

ADVISORY BOARD

Approach: Identifies broad social trends, movements, issues, conflicts, interactions, potential surprises, discontinuities, force fields, patterns of change, value shifts, traditions, beliefs, ideologies

Scope: Global and meta-system view of economic, military, social, cultural, political, ethical, moral, legal, religious, scientific, technological and environmental factors and change. Understanding society and human affairs as a whole.

Results: • Forecasts of alternative futures, trends and impact of forces at work

• Projection of long-term continuity and discontinuity between activities and trends

• Visualizes end state of society of the future, including new roles, issues, dilemmas and opportunities for the corporation

SOCIETAL FOCUS

Advisory Board

Society as a whole

Trends, patterns of change, value shifts

External Business Environment

Statutory Board of Directors

Enterprise Activities in Particular Industry(s) Business or Nation(s)

Figure 5-3
Meta-Scan of an Advisory Board

these invasive and illusive trends or forces and by offering alternative futures, the advisory board can force a continual redefinition of the parent organization's activities. Such reexamination is becoming more necessary as the world increases in interaction and interdependency.

This broad societal approach has some obvious shortcomings, including its unlimited scope of inquiry, its often abstract level with inconclusive indicators, and the difficulty in relating results of the advisory group's perceptions and suggestions to the real activities of the company that it is supposed to serve. It can also be expensive and inconclusive. Only certain firms can afford to explore this approach. It is being used with increasing effectiveness by large, multinational corporations.

The complementarity of these three approaches suggests the development of an advisory board that combines the focuses in an integrated approach. This can be done by careful design of the composition of the advisory board to achieve a proper balance of advisors who can contribute the different perspectives. A planned turnover through specified terms of service can keep such an advisory board tuned into and intelligently related to the current activities and the future course of an enterprise.

One model of a sophisticated, international, business, scientific combination of statutory board and advisory boards is that of a relatively new public company, Nova Pharmaceutical Corporation (Baltimore), a molecular biotechnology research and development enterprise. Sales are less than $1 million but growing rapidly. The fifteen-person board consists of experienced talent drawn from international business, the pharmaceutical industry, and government. John Lloyd Huck, former chairman of Merck, Inc., is currently CEO and chairman. Among the directors are Gerald Ford, Donald Kendall, Charles Edwards, and Edward L. Hennessy. The five-person Scientific Advisory Board is equally high-powered: Dr. Soloman Snyder, Johns Hopkins neuroscientist; Dr. Soloman Snyder, Johns Hopkins neuroscientist; Dr. Julius Axelrod, Nobel laureate in medicine; Dr. Floyd Bloom, neuroscientist and endocrinologist, Scripps Clinic and Research Foundation; Dr. Paul Greengard, molecular and cellular neuroscientist, Rockefeller University; and Dr. Bertram Pitt, cardiologist, University of Michigan School of Medicine.

The American yearning for credentials and the temptation to place star-quality scientists, economists, educators, business leaders, and celebrities on an advisory board of start-up companies raises a note of caution in this discussion of the scan and scope of such boards. There is no question that star quality on an advisory board sells stock. The going price for Nobel laureates, astronauts, past presidents and diplomats, distinguished educators, scientists, technologists and financial gurus can run anywhere from $25,000 to $150,000 (and up) in annual fees for advisory services.

Underwriters of a public offering of stock in a start-up, high-tech company often seek Nobel Prize winners or persons of equivalent distinction on the scientific advisory board. Kevin Kimberlin, vice president of D.H. Blair & Company, expressed it this way to the press: "The idea is, if a guy can win a Nobel Prize, he's obviously got something important to say about breakthroughs in his field." Thomas Unterberg, chairman of the underwriting firm of L. F. Rothschild, Unterberg and Towbin adds: "It's easy to class up an unclassy deal if you put a few Nobel Laureates on your scientific advisory board." The fault in this approach is that just because a scientist is on an advisory board doesn't mean that the company can lay claim to his research. The counter is that distinguished scientists have reputations as wise persons. People pay heavily for wise people's counsel.

The new ventures field is strewn with troubled start-up companies, particularly in biotechnology and electronics, which have access to advisors with distinguished university credentials and professional recognition. Decorating the board with stars has a place in governance of corporations, but ultimately it is the management, the product, process, or service that makes the company, not the advice and counsel of those not in responsible charge.

NOTES

1. Carolyne Smart and Ilan Vertinsky, "Designs for Crisis Decision Units," *Administrative Science Quarterly* 22 (December 1977), pp. 640–47.

2. James E. Post and Marc J. Epstein, "Information System for Social Reporting," *Academy of Management Review* 2 (January 1977), pp. 81–87.

6

SPECIES OF ADVISORY BOARDS

My current service on several international corporate and educational advisory boards and past service on ten editorial, professional society, financial service, and industrial company advisory boards or councils leads me to appreciate the expert and referent power of such resource groups. Review and guidance of corporate activities is as ancient a function as the organization of human groups. Anthropologists point out the similarities between our modern corporations and the original tribal organizations. Many of the same basic tribal principles are retained in the contemporary corporate form. Both tribes and corporations function with review and guidance from one or more councils of elders. Both tribes and corporations avail themselves of advice and direction from "men and women of knowledge." According to consulting psychologist, Keith D. Wilcock, the terms, "headshrinker, high-powered attorney, financial wizard, fetisher, brujo, bara'u, sorcerer, consultant, shaman, doctor, medicine man, prophet, and priest" as well as "sorceress, witch, priestess, and prophetess all refer to archetypal roles common to tribes, modern and primitive, past and present, throughout the world."[1]

I have been exposed to a number of different role model species.

INTERNATIONAL ADVISORY COUNCILS

Foreign nationals provide local political, social, economic, industry, and business "gray power" viewpoints and network contacts. Lyndon B. Johnson once hankered: "I wish there were some giant-economy size aspirin that would work on international headaches. But there isn't. The only cure is patience with reason mixed in." If a corporation has the time and the patience, an international advisory board can provide some of this necessary reasoning. With the growth in influence and the challenges facing multinational companies in recent years, the use of international advisory boards has come into vogue with a welter of U.S. and foreign-headquartered firms. Some well-known American firms that have established such boards are listed in Chapter 1.

The viewpoint of the foreign nationals—usually distinguished citizens active in their own noncompeting companies—can offer a guest company some valuable insight and knowhow of the international scene in a foreign region. The value to a guest company of having expert advice from prominent residents of the host country is the obvious advantage. No legal or statutory entanglements are involved, and the meeting schedule requirement is usually limited to three or four times a year for formal meetings. In addition, contacts with advisory board members in overseas locations are frequently made on an individual basis to help with spot assignments, effective introductions, or an exchange of views with visiting executives or by trips for the advisory director arranged by the home office.

One general observation may prove valid over the next few years. Frank X. White, former vice president of Business International Corporation and an experienced internationalist of long standing in the business world, pointed out that "in the industrialized countries, the trend seems to be among U.S. companies to move away from the traditional 'dummy' inside boards to boards with numerous local, outside directors. This would seem to militate against advisory boards at the national level, but they seem to be multiplying at the regional and world level."

William C. Turner, former U.S. ambassador to the Organization for Economic Cooperation and Development (OECD) in Paris, is chairman of Argyle Atlantic Corporation which advises multinational corporations of economic and political affairs. Turner serves as a member of the board of directors and on the international advisory councils of several major companies. He and Norman E. Auerbach, former chairman of Coopers & Lybrand, consider international advisory councils (IAC) as "one of the most sophisticated and widely used approaches to overseas assessment of business conditions." A survey made in 1977 by Turner and updated in 1982 identified more than forty IACs organized on a global, regional, or national basis by American or foreign multinationals.[2] The sponsoring companies found that the IAC proved to be an effective "damage control" mechanism for monitoring the external environment for multinational corporations. Turner and Auerbach cite examples of assistance IACs have given to multi-nationals.

In Europe, one group helped an industrial products company to overcome the impediments of government bureaucracy and red tape when closing down an operation that was losing money. In Asia, a council provided valuable insight and assistance to a company entering a country to establish a joint venture. In Scandinavia, a council arranged key introductions that resulted in a major computer contract. In Japan, a member led an American firm through the complicated administration (non-tariff) barriers that had restricted imports of their products. A Brazilian IAC was instrumental in removing some long-standing regulations and price controls that were deterring profits and growth.

My 1986 survey of advisory boards of companies headquartered outside the United States and Europe revealed only limited use of this advisory resource other than subsidiaries of European and American-based companies operating in the regions. For example, a long-time friend, Abraham Friedman, chairman of the state Bank of Israel, advises that his bank is the only corporation in Israel with a formal advisory board. W. Sycip, chairman of the SGV Group, Manila, a professional accounting services group, advises that he is unaware of any Filipino company that has an advisory board. Dr. S. P. Adarkar, a colleague of mine at Monsanto for many years when he was managing director of Monsanto Chemicals of India Private Ltd. (Bombay), checked out the current existence of advisory boards or councils in India. He was unable to find a single company with an advisory board. He advises, "This concept is totally unknown and therefore not practiced. I, today, met with Mr. Kesule Mahindra who presides over the Mahindra empire in India, and he agrees with this observation."

As one would expect, use of independent advisory councils in politically and economically controlled parts of the world is somewhat counter to the culture and way of conducting their affairs. To get a perspective on this, I visited with a former Russian-speaking Belgian colleague, Dr. Nicholas Chorine, who, after twenty years working for U.S. firms, established his consulting firm specializing in European and Soviet affairs. Chorine points out that the business sector in the Soviet Union includes industry, science, technology, and trade, as distinct from the political and military areas. He observes,

To my knowledge, the Soviets do not employ non-Soviet organizations or individuals on a normal business basis to advise them on non-Soviet business. In-house; i.e., within the Soviet Union system (party and government), there are various organizations (ministries, state committees, institutes, academic bodies) that advise leadership on non-Soviet business and affairs. Three worth mentioning besides the normally specialized ministries are: The Institute of World Economics and International Relations. (It comes under the authority of the USSR Academy of Science and [I] understand is influent[ial] at the highest levels); The State Committee for Science and Technology; and the Institute of United States of America and Canada.

Of course all three are bona fide institutionalized and fully-owned Soviet organizations. Besides them and other various in-house bodies that counsel the Soviet Union on non-Soviet affairs, the Soviets participate in mixed international organizations (UN, Atomic Agency, UNESCO, etc.) from which they draw some amount of advisory inputs. A special worth mentioning is IIASA in Vienna [see Chapter 1 discussion of IIASA]. Hardly necessary to also mention Soviet intelligence collection structures in which participate some non-Soviet individuals or organizations. In the extreme, and I leave you the choice, they could be also quoted as advisory bodies to the Soviets on non-Soviet affairs.

I have heard in Moscow that at times the Soviets have received advice on non-Soviet business matters from certain non-Soviet individuals, described as "consultants," but to my knowledge this was always discreet and never became institutionalized.

No doubt there would be benefit to the Soviets themselves and to a better world-understanding if some pattern and flow of West-toward-East business counsel could be established in an honest and responsible fashion. It does not appear to exist today.

ASSET IMPACT ADVISORS

The epitome of elitism, this species has a preference for big-name, celebrity advisors. Presumably possessing Olympian qualities, these stars offer the perception that the corporation benefits (on its balance sheet) by their advice, personality, and luster. This is also called the Rubbia Effect after Italian-born, Harvard's Nobel laureate physicist, Carlo Rubbia. Professor Rubbia is now at the European Organization for Nuclear Research (CERN) in Geneva. The National Institute for Nuclear Physics secured Parlimentary approval in 1985 for a four-year budget allegedly due to the Nobel prize won by their Professor Rubbia. The ego factor cannot be underestimated for a chairman or CEO who can "command" a board of well-known heavy hitters.

There is a contrary point of view to the significance of using the "star" system for an advisory council. It's called the Sukhomilov Effect. This refers to the fetching theory that in war, victory goes to those armies whose leaders' uniforms are the least impressive. This alludes to the excessive emphasis on form versus substance in a value scale, whether it be military, social, political, economic, or advisory governance conflict. General V. A. Sukhomilov, war minister of Russia in 1914 and Fascist Italy's Benito Mussolini, Il Duce, each postured in glittering swank on the eve of tragicomic disasters. Winston

Churchill in his starkly simple suit, Dwight Eisenhower in his modest jacket, Mao Zedong in peasant tunic, were plain winners in comparison to their respective fancy losers. General George S. Patton, a successful commander, went counter to this effect, but allegedly that merely demonstrates the variable of pure idiosyncracy influencing the Sukhomilov Effect.

PLACEBO PERCH

An organizational artifact is often employed as a transitional model to deal gracefully and empathetically with director redundancy after a merger or bylaw age-determined retirement of distinguished directors, that is, "statutory senility." As an advisory "attic" for nonvoting emeriti or excess directors, the appointment to an advisory board can be a decompression stage as a final parking place before all ties with the company are severed. This "percussive sublimation" maneuver can preserve identity and dignity and corporate memory, honor worthy governance alumni or senior managers, and enable continued perquisites and board fee payments without encumbering the management or governance process.

For example, the National Life Insurance Company of Vermont has both a Director's Advisory Council and a Director's Emeriti group. The 1984 council consisted of five members; three were former National Life officer-directors ranging in company service from seventeen to thirty-four years. Two others were former outside directors having twenty and twenty-five years of service, respectively, on the statutory board before becoming advisory council members. The two directors emeriti were the retired chairman of Dresser Industries, Inc., a director of National Life for eleven years, and the former vice chairman of the board and a former director of National Life for two years.

COUNTRY CLUB ADVISORS

Bryan F. Smith, former general director of Texas Instruments, Inc., refers to this species of advisory boards as a "marching and chowder society." The main purpose is ceremonial and social exchange among well-known and well-regarded persons who allow their identity to be connected with an organization that expects little and asks little in return. Country club–type advisors tend to be ornamental rather than functional. The advisor's name and reputation are used by the advisee company for public relations or ego gratification of the chairman or CEO. The advisor's personal network outside the company served are expected to be accessible in return for the privilege of advisory service.

PROBATIONARY FARM CLUB

An advisory board or council affords the advisors and the company served respectively to assess the value and relationship between the firm and an individual without formal participation and obligations on the statutory board. Three multinational companies that I have been associated with have used a trial period of two to five years for a mutual size-up of the arrangement before an invitation was issued to stand for election to the corporate board. This contract governance advice approach allows a "tryout" period before being called (or not called) to "play in the major league" of statutory directors. The potential liability exposure on the statutory board makes such an opportunity a matter to be carefully considered by a candidate director.

In the case of closely held corporations, an outside advisory board can be a significant factor in insuring effective leadership continuity. One recent case comes to mind in this respect. A closely held company with revenues of $150 million in a diverse set of businesses had a problem of agreeing on which members of the founder's family should assume the position of chief executive. An experienced consultant was engaged to work with the group and was invited to become the chairman and chief executive officer after a one-year probation period. Upon assuming responsibilities, he immediately created an advisory council of three outside experienced businessmen to help steer the company and provide objective advice on the ultimate choice of a CEO successor.

INTERNAL ADVISORY AND MULTIPLE MANAGEMENT BOARDS

One interesting species is the internal advisory director group recently created by Monsanto. While the purpose is not indicated as a probationary role for top executives to become visible to the board or to be prospective director candidates, it does have this feature. The main purpose is to redress the balance of insider knowledge to the predominantly outside director board without changing the official composition of the board.

In 1981 Monsanto Company named six of its senior executives as advisory directors, then a newly designated position believed the first of its kind in any large U.S. corporation. John W. Hanley, then chairman and chief executive officer of Monsanto, said the six executives will "bring to the deliberations of the Board, judgment, experience and expertise which will serve the Board well." Advisory directors were Executive Vice Presidents Earle H. Harbison, Jr., and Nicholas L. Reding; Robert L. Berra, senior vice president, Administration; Dr.

Howard A. Schneiderman, senior vice president, Research and Development; and Francis A. Stroble, vice president and chief financial officer. Mr. Hanley pointed out that the Monsanto Board's composition had changed markedly over the past decade from a predominantly "inside" or employee board to one that now consists of ten outside and only six inside directors. Hanley said,

The Board of Directors periodically reviews its charter to be certain that its objectives, structure, and operations reflect its contemporary responsibilities. Out of such a review grew the recognition that while it is important to maintain the independence of the Board—assured by the mathematical domination of the outside members—it is important for the Board to have access to the best of management's knowledge and expertise. It is for that reason that the advisory memberships were created.

It is expected that these senior officers will not only play a role in the deliberations of the Board as a whole, but where appropriate will participate in the activities of our Board Committees.

The Monsanto creation of inside advisory directors as participants in the main board deliberations is a variation of a much older organizational device. The construct is focused on providing internal management and input to the statutory board of directors. An earlier version, geared at providing internal advisory input to top management was the participative-management concept introduced in 1932 at McCormick & Company, Baltimore. The innovation was introduced by a former friend of mine and fellow director. Charles P. McCormick, now deceased, was nephew of the founder of the country's leading spice manufacturer. Charlie, as president, was forever extolling the value of advice derived from his "multiple management boards" to anyone who would listen. In fact, in the first five years of its existence, more than 2,000 board suggestions were adopted to help turn the company around in the depths of the Great Depression.

In 1986 the company had eighteen operating units and fifteen multiple management boards comprised mainly of younger middle-management employees. The board is comprised of from six to twenty members with widely differing disciplines and expertise, and they serve for a six-month term. They have the authority to investigate every aspect of McCormick operations with the exception of compensation and benefits. Hillman V. Wilson, current president, is a great supporter of this advisory process of internal boards: "They present an ongoing momentum for change . . . they give members a feeling of belonging, an opportunity to participate, make a contribution, and are recognized for it . . . and the boards serve as a valuable process for developing future management."

FUNCTIONAL ADVISORS

Financial services industry firms and consumer-oriented corporations often engage advisors who can attract or place business. The advisory board becomes a marketing arm. Technology and development-oriented firms engage scientific experts from universities, institutes, and consulting organizations to supplement internal capabilities. For example, Incentive AB, the Swedish holding company involved in building and construction materials, instruments, earth-moving and mechanical handling equipment, and motor vehicle distribution, has a Scientific Advisory Council made up of fifteen faculty members on the general committee, plus forty-two members scattered among seven development committees (biochemistry and medical technology, energy and heating technology, marketing and technology, polymer technology, and others) plus an executive committee. Members of these committees come from Swedish universities, institutes, and industrial firms.

Other professional specialists, including economists, educators, political analysts and human resource experts, are frequently asked to be on advisory boards. They can imply a comfort level to the firm by their professional association on its advisory group. In addition, they can bring new network contacts that can lead to additional business, sources of capital and other resources.

INDUSTRY EXPERTISE

Corporations entering a new business sector or having a diverse scope of businesses can tap specific industry-wise counselors via advisory assignments.

INDUSTRY AND COMMERCE LINKAGE MODEL
(UNDER CODETERMINATION LAWS)

Codetermination laws in certain European countries require that boards of directors include representatives of labor unions, employees, and/or certain other stakeholders. The practice is to have a double-decker or two-tier system of legally constituted boards. One is the executive board made up of executive directors actually involved in running the company; the other is the supervisory board with workers represented. Supervisory board members may also be distinguished national figures whose names and presence add outside status. The concept of codetermination was introduced in Germany in the Ruhr steel industry in 1952, setting forth composition of the advisory board as an equal number of representatives of shareholders, trade unions, and employees. (Law on codetermination; that is, *Mit-bestimmungsgesetz.*)

This corporate governance architecture is supplemented by advisory boards and advisory councils, notably in the financial services and a few industrial sectors. One of the more notable examples of these supplementary advisory resource groups is the extent to which Deutsche Bank A.G. engages councils of advisors for the Supervisory Board *(Aufsichsrat)* and the Board of Managing Directors *(Vorstand)*. Dr. Rev. Pol. H. C. Hermann J. Abs, distinguished emeritus chairman of Deutsche Bank and internationally respected financial leader, first introduced the concept of councils of advisors to the bank many years ago to strengthen the linkage and understanding of the bank with commerce and industry. The councils supplemented the two-tier governance structure. In personal correspondence with Abs, with whom I had business contact years ago, he kindly gave me permission to explain his linkage concept for Deutsche Bank. His letter reads, in part:

I appreciate your views concerning the reasons for creating and availing oneself of advisors and counc[i]llors, and do agree, since some of those mentioned by you as well as other considerations led to Deutsche Bank's councils of advisors.

As you may know, Deutsche Bank AG has one council of advisors for the bank as a whole (Advisory Board) of presently 17 members, and, besides, 14 regional committees of advisors (Regional Advisory Councils), comprising more than 500 personalities of industry and commerce. These councils are established on the basis of the Articles of Association of Deutsche Bank AG, which reads in its non-binding English translation in paragraph eight as follows:

"For the purpose of closer contact and business consultation with trade and industry, the Board of Managing Directors may form an Advisory Board for the entire bank and Regional Advisory Councils, lay down rules of procedure for their business and fix the remuneration of their members. The Supervisory Board shall be informed of any changes in the membership of the Advisory Board and the Regional Advisory Councils at the Supervisory Board meeting immediately following such changes."

These councils have, accordingly, their own rules of procedure setting out their objects, the election, term of office, maximum number and retirement of their members, as well as particulars, including secrecy concerning their meetings.

Although the laws of the Federal Republic of Germany permit the establishment of such advisory councils for stock corporations (section 160), para. 3, no. 8, German Stock Corporation Act mentions the same. I would like to stress, however, that they may in no way interfere with the legal rights and powers of the Supervisory Board, the Board of Managing Directors, and the shareholders. That is why among stock corporations in the Federal Republic of Germany only several banks, insurance companies, and major enterprises have formed such advisory councils in order to avail the management of expert opinion, contacts to business partners, and a forum of discussion of problems or developments of mutual interest.

Enterprises which are not incorporated under the German Stock Corporation Act and which—under the co-determination laws—are not obliged to establish a supervisory board, use to the extent permitted by the appropriate laws advisory councils more frequently and often attribute to the same some supervisory and/or managerial functions, controlling powers to provide for a smooth succession, means to channel the decision-making of partners or arbitration competences.

It goes without saying that the liability risk increases with the power conferred to such an advisory council.

Despite a considerable number and tradition of such advisory councils in Germany, there have been only a few court cases and very few publications. I can only add that with respect to stock corporations in Germany, a certain increase of advisory councils was noticeable already in 1931 when an amendment of the then applicable laws on stock corporations formed advisory councils in order to retain the expert advice of their former supervisory board members.

The Dresdner Bank has a similar group of advisory boards and advisory councils. The 1985 annual report identifies 36 members of the Advisory Management Council and eight Regional Advisory Councils having fifty to sixty members each. The certified translation from the German language of the Articles of Association of the Dresdner Bank describes the provisions for these advisory groups as follows:

The Advisory Management Council, Advisory Councils (Verwaltungsrat, Beirate).

Section 15:

1. The Corporation has an Advisory Management Council.
2. The Advisory Management Council consists of personalities from domestic and foreign business. It has the task of advising the Board of Managing Directors in economic matters in the performance of the Board of Managing Directors' duties. The statutory rights and duties of the Supervisory Board remain unaffected.
3. The members of the Advisory Management Council are appointed by the Chairman of the Supervisory Board upon proposal by the Board of Managing Directors. The Chairman of the Supervisory Board is, in this capacity, also a member of the Advisory Management Council. The term of office of the Advisory Management Council is the same as that of the Supervisory Board.
4. The Advisory Management Council shall be chaired by the Chairman of the Supervisory Board. The Advisory Management Council may elect one or more Deputy Chairmen.

WALKING STICK MODEL

Chairmen or CEOs occasionally need trusted, experienced outsiders to talk to *in camera*. Problems that are best explored with other than regular board members or subordinate management can be aired and tested with these trusted, paid outsiders. (The name of the model refers of course, to a handicapped person benefiting from a cane.)

EARLY WARNING RESOURCE

Weak signals of threats and opportunities are hard to separate from the noise in a complex world. Experienced counselors can focus on such incipient matters as long-term social, economic, technological, ecological, or political trends. Anticipating the impact of surprise events can be a valuable service.

The Center for the Study of Social Policy at SRI, Inc., Menlo Park, California, set out to try to identify the problems that may become critical in the years ahead. Eight different problem search strategies or techniques were developed for bagging their elusive quarry. The work was conducted under a grant from the U.S. National Science Foundation and was specifically aimed at providing guidance for the president's science advisor. The results are relevant to our discussion of advisory boards, which are usually created for the parallel purpose of forecasting trends in the future as well as advising on current activities.

Of the eight different techniques used, some will be of interest to management long-range planners and advisory directors:

Problem lists: review of existing known problems

Problem level analysis: compare alternative interpretations of problems at different societal levels

Opinion surveys: a conventional technique

Trend discontinuities: looking for trend breaks or gaps

Missed opportunities: latent or stymied technological or social innovations for exploitation

Cross-paradigm analysis: modeling and comparing societal conceptualization

Alternative futures: an obvious task for advisors

Science fiction: a controversial source of subjective anticipation, far-out and risky but playful

The study identified more than a thousand problems found in the literature. After consideration, only twenty ended up on the final list of forty-one potential crises or future long-term problem areas that were judged to be representative of the more critical problems that society may face in the years ahead. Surprisingly, many of these national-

and international-scale problems are not widely recognized as such at the present time.[3]

There are other roles that an advisory group can fulfill. For example, the transition model or task-oriented group of advisors is in common use. Assembled and engaged for a limited time and specific mission, such an advisory set phases out of existence when its interim role is no longer needed.

The next chapter expands on the opportunity for advisory boards to provide some sophisticated thinking about sensing surprise events from environmental weak signals.

NOTES

1. Keith D. Wilcock, *The Corporate Tribe* (New York: Warner Books, Inc., 1984), pp. 45–56.

2. Norman E. Auerbach and William C. Turner, "Risks and Opportunities of Foreign Investment," *Chief Executive* 21 (1982), pp. 37–40.

3. Peter Schwartz, Peter J. Teige, and Willis W. Harmann, "In Search of Tomorrow's Crisis," *Futurist* 11 (October 1977), pp. 264–78.

7

WEAK-SIGNAL GOVERNANCE/EARLY WARNING ADVISORY SYSTEMS

Walt Whitman once observed, "From any fruition of success, no matter what, shall come forth something to make a greater struggle necessary." For a number of reasons, many related to the impacts and devastation of World War II, American industry reached a pinnacle of success that lasted through the first two or three postwar decades. But, as everyone now recognizes, out of that success were born the seeds of a struggle that have literally become a life and death battle for survival for great chunks of our domestic industry. Because of this upheaval and the resulting turbulence, corporate management and boards of directors, in turn, face a greater struggle than they ever have before encountered. As a result, it becomes more difficult to conduct and govern our various organizations as in the past.

Harland Cleveland, dean of the University of Minnesota's Hubert H. Humphrey Institute of Public Affairs, notes that the informatization of society has changed the context of our human activities in which information is now our crucial resource.[1] Previously, the inherent characteristics of the world's physical resources (natural and manmade) made possible the development of five bases for hierarchy and discrimination. Cleveland suggests that these five hierarchies are crumbling today, based on the forces at work in our turbulent world. These five hierarchies are: hierarchy of power based on control (of new weapons, of energy sources, of trade routes, of markets and especially of knowledge); hierarchy of influence based on secrecy; hierarchies of class based on ownership; hierarchies of privilege based on early access to valuable resources; and hierarchies of politics based on geography.

CHANGING TURBULENCE

This turbulence is changing the role and modus operandi of the director and top management. How these changes can be used to advantage is the challenge. Advisory directors or councils can help, and we can benefit from the research thinking in academia on how to interpret both strong and weak signals emanating from the external environment.

It's proper to begin with a simple truism. We strive to govern and manage our corporations in a way that anticipates significant issues and allows corporations to address them creatively. Heretofore, those issues were comparatively easy to identify and respond to because they gave out strong signals. Such strong-signal issues still abound. Examples of current interest to boards are: the growing unacceptability of interlocking directorships; the increasing call for independent outside directors; the need for actual and perceived absence of conflicts of interest; the adverse public reaction to golden parachutes, multimillion dollar executives' salaries and greenmail; environmental and consumer activists' foci; legislation on foreign corrupt practices; attention to South African investment policy; women and minorities on the board; affirmative action in the corporation; and "sunshine in the boardroom."

There is an unusually strong signal in the novel type of liability that surfaced in Britain's new Insolvency Act when it was first introduced as a bill early in 1985. The act, which went into force in spring 1986, exposes U.K. directors to potential personal liability for company debts. The final act was a watered-down version of the original, but the thinking behind it is a signal to corporations.

The final version of the bill included the following provisions. Directors of U.K. companies that go into liquidation now have two main things to fear. One is being found guilty of a new civil sin called "wrongful trading." This means letting the company keep going when a person "knew or ought to have concluded" that it would go bust. The person found guilty may have to fork up personally for the company's debts. In addition, he or she may also be disqualified from being a director for up to fifteen years, and is automatically disqualified for three years from all directorships if the company goes into compulsory liquidation. These penalties will be hotly contested and may be relaxed in practical administration of this act. But the signal to boardrooms is there, and it is a strong signal. The Institute of Directors (London) hurriedly provided directors comprehensive protection for wrongful trading liability. Within a month of the scheme being launched, more than £5 million worth of cover had been placed with fifty company directors. By March 1986 more than £10 million worth of cover had been placed and over one hundred applications signed. The pace of signups continued in 1986 at an increasing rate.

Today, however, something new has been introduced—strategic issues that give off *weak signals,* imprecise early indications about impending events that may impact the corporation. To cite a few examples: epidemiological trends due to chronic exposure to toxic substances in the workplace or home (the acid rain phenomenon, asbestos, urethane exposure, and so on), political upheavals in the Middle East; resurgence of Mainland China as a market and as a competitor; continual discussion about federal chartering of corporations; the cry for constituency directors (labor, public, and environmentalists), that is, the stakeholder notion; the pressure for formal codes of corporate ethics; the comparable worth of individuals concept; extended liability for antisocial actions (for example, redundancy, pollution, safety) with community severance obligations; and social control of corporate behavior. These represent a host of issues that are in the turbulent future ahead but about which we get only relatively *weak signals* concerning their possible impact and existence.

A medical analogy is useful here. A premonitory symptom of disease is termed a *prodrome,* form the Greek word for "running before." This refers to the warning that certain symptoms indicate regarding anticipation of an event without conscious reason. If a company operates in a prodromal, or vigilant, state, it may catch sight of something that needs to be addressed quickly before it gets out of control. Current knowhow in crisis management has pointed out the significance of the prodromal stage in the Three Mile Island crisis, Union Carbide's Indian disaster, Tylenol poisonings and the Procter & Gamble/Rely tampon controversy.[2]

The essence is that the board of directors and chief executive officer can and should be the guiding influence of the corporation in anticipating these impacts. The corporation must see that appropriate responses are undertaken to deal with the potential impacts. No longer can the board of directors be the "wave pushed ahead by the ship" as Tolstoy opined many years ago. An advisory board can warn the CEO and the board of directors of turbulence ahead.

A SYSTEMS PERSPECTIVE

The interactions of the corporation historically have been through two coupled but distinctive activities. The first is the transactional activity of exchanging goods and services for dollars. This interaction was dominant in the first half of the twentieth century and was the main activity of a competitive operating business.

Second is the adaptive strategic planning activity. This activity seeks to cope with the changing markets that the firm serves, the changing technology that it offers, the different products and services it sells, and the way it sells and distributes them. This activity was visible and indeed dominant during the last half of the nineteenth century. It subsided during the first half of the twentieth century when the transactional exchange approach held sway. It has reappeared in a somewhat different form with a sensitivity to social, political, and environmental issues and values.

The two activities, though existing simultaneously in a corporation, have different goals. Strategic activities set the stage for future growth and profitability potential, whereas operating (transaction exchange) activities seek to convert the potential of yesterday's strategic activities into next year's profits.

Not surprisingly, the governance approaches for each also differ. Therefore, the model under which a CEO and board functions needs to be in tune with both the transaction and adaptation activities if the firm is to survive in the changing turbulence ahead.

Such a management-cum-governance model is, above all, a systems one. The systems model reverses the Humpty-Dumpty scenario: it puts all the pieces together into a meaningful whole, into an orderly arrangement of interdependent activities and related procedures that facilitates the performance of a major activity of an organization. A key element in this orderly arrangement is the equilibrium (or rather lack of equilibrium) in the system. Within the context of corporate governance, equilibrium means keeping a balance among the many components of the governance system. It is a consequence of growth and environmental context. If the dimensions of the corporation remain the same, forces that act on the system may change and disturb the equilibrium equation.

Galileo first expressed this idea in his general *principle of similitude*. He said that if we tried building ships, palaces, or temples of enormous size, the yardbeams and bolts would cease to hold together. The thing falls to pieces of its own weight unless the relative proportions are changed. And such changes will, at length, cause it to become clumsy, monstrous, or inefficient unless a new material is found that is harder and stronger than that used before.

This principle of similitude holds not just for changes in size but as well for any environmental change (political, market, and so on) that puts stress on the equilibrium of the corporation. To restore the equilibrium, we have to alter the structural "materials" of which our corporations are made through changes in our general management systems. Thus, over the past thirty years we have witnessed such management inventions as long-range planning, management by objective, strategic planning, and issue management as corporations sought to adapt to prevailing conditions.

Initially these new management systems were not industry-specific. They had to be adapted, for example, to the banking, semiconductor, chemical, and transportation industries to retain their underlying logic. Consequently, they became *environmental-turbulence-specific*. That is, each successful system was responsive to the particular turbulence level characteristic of the industry to which it was applied.

Because different corporations evolved along different turbulence paths, some needed the latest model management systems. Others were able to exist with predecessor systems. A repertoire of usable systems accumulated. Through trial and error, the system needed by a particular firm was chosen by diagnosing the future turbulence of the firm's environment and selecting a system most appropriate for coping with that environment.

I believe, that with the support of expert advisors, chief executives and boards of directors can apply this concept to deal with future turbulence . . . particularly the turbulence that contains issues about which we are receiving only *weak signals* at the present time. We first consider the internal and external environments of corporations and how they have evolved and are likely to evolve. The following adapts the logic and hitchhikes on the thinking of H. Igor Ansoff and his construct of systematic strategic management.[3] My interpretation is modified for the top management and governance level of corporations, in particular, an application of the concept for contract governance advisors; that is, advisory boards or councils reporting either to the statutory board or the CEO.

DIAGNOSING ENVIRONMENTAL TURBULENCE

The internal environment of corporations, according to Ansoff, has had at least three evolutionary periods. First was the turn-of-the-century production efficiency period calling for an honest day's work for a fair day's pay. Management was by authority. The environment was relatively stable and change was slow. The future was somewhat perceivable.

Second, from about the 1930s to 1950, evolution focused on marketing effectiveness, enrichment of the work environment, local participation and management by consensus. Third, in the period 1970 to 1990, we perceive a redesign of the workplace through CAD/CAM operations, participation in strategic decision making, management by power delegation or retention, the recognition of networking as a process for management, innovation as a process to be managed, and the study of alternative futures. All were products of an evolution in management and board thinking.

If we trace the external corporate environment during this period, at the turn of the century, it was essentially laissez-faire. From 1930 to 1950 there was some loss of social immunity: consumerism rose; there was pressure for social responsibility; and the public reacted adversely to environmental pollution and perceived or actual abuse of power by management and directors.

In the period 1970 to 1990, we are seeing the development of a new raison-d'être for the firm, according to Ansoff. There is greater application of "socialism" or "neocapitalism." Innovation, entrepreneurship, venture capital, small business importance, and deregulation are characteristic of this surging external sociopolitical environment. The international advisory council concept is an increasingly used mechanism for monitoring the external environment for multinational corporations.

The increasing turbulence levels through this century brought a counterpart evolution in the role of the board. About 1900, the environment was stable. The role of the board was repetitive—essentially that of responding to its fiduciary and statutory requirements. In 1930, the environment was reactive and the board became more involved in evaluating management and corporation performance. In 1950 turbulence changed the environment, and the board became more participative. In this period a few American firms began to employ advisory councils for their overseas activities. Directors also took active parts in audit committees, nominating committees, strategic planning, and other areas. In 1970 growing environmental concern caused more exploration of the external conditions on the part of corporations. There were discontinuities, predictable threats, and opportunities. The board role added to its portfolio of functions the role of a resource to the corporation, providing directors with expertise in special needs that management could call on. Advisory boards and councils, while relatively few, nevertheless were becoming of more apparent value to certain multinational companies.

In the 1980s (perhaps to the year 2000) we see our "familiarity of events" becoming more and more discontinuous. Novelty and rapidity of change have become shorter than the firm's response. The future is only partly predictable because signals are *weak*, and we are increasingly subjected to unpredictable surprises. Ansoff summarizes these historical evolutions in management and governance systems by suggesting that (1) in the second half of the twentieth century, the environmental challenges have been progressively more numerous and novel and not resolvable by the solutions that worked in the past; and (2) the multiplicity of challenges and international expansion of the marketplace increases the complexity of governing and managing our corporations. Novelty, complexity, speed, and likelihood of strategic surprise increase the probability of catching the board of directors unaware.

This translates the evolution to a turbulence scale that goes from an arbitrary level of one (low turbulence and stability, in 1900) to a level of five (strong turbulence, toward the end of this century). In other words, we will be faced with a need for a creative, adaptive response on the part of the firm and the board of directors.

In this area of strong turbulence *weak signals* need to be recognized and a creative response developed in advance and in anticipation of impacts on our corporations. Not surprisingly, most boards of directors or top managements may not have the time, capacity, or competency to recognize such weak signals. They can experiment with the idea by creating advisory boards or councils with experts especially qualified to perform this scanning and sensing function.

TURBULENCE PHASE CHANGES

According to Ansoff, a successful response must understand and cope with changes in the *familiarity of events,* the *rapidity of change,* and the *visibility of the future.* During the past hundred years, the *familiarity of events* has evolved from the familiar, to extrapolation of past experience, to discontinuous but related to the experience, to discontinuous and novel. The *rapidity of change* has ranged from slower than company response, to equal to the response, to shorter than the response of the firm. The *visibility of the future* has evolved from (1) recurring familiar visibility to (2) visibility forecastable by extrapolation to (3) predictable threats and opportunities, some of which were familiar and discontinuous to (4) partially predicted *weak signals* of issues to (5) unpredictable surprises to (6) a novel level of discontinuity.

All these forces at work were, of course, affected by competitive, technological, economic, and political changes. They moved at different rates in different parts of the world; for example, the postindustrial turbulence originated in the United States in the mid-1950s and then moved to Europe and the Far East. Within Europe, Germany's "economic growth miracle" remained distinctively nonturbulent until the late 1970s. Only in the mid-1980s have we begun to see strong signs of postindustrial turbulence in Japan.

The challenge is to diagnose the turbulent environment expected in the next five or ten years and to adapt the proper governance and management model systems. Ansoff's study of over a thousand managers around the world found surprising agreement among half of those in developed countries that their expected turbulence for the late 1980s will be on the "discontinuous level" with frequent interruptions taking place.[4] This means that changes will be faster than the firm's response and that events that will take place will be only partly predictable before they impact the firm.

MAPPING GOVERNANCE MODELS

If we accept the progressive evolution of more complex and dynamic governance systems, we need to map their corresponding levels of turbulence. Ansoff suggests a categorization that can be adapted to the role of an advisory board.

Stage I: Governance by after-the-fact control, the audit mentality. The underlying reality is a perceived climate of incremental, relatively slow change in an environment of limited turbulence.

Stage II: Governance by extrapolation. Change, while still incremental, becomes much more rapid.

Stage III: Governance by anticipation. This adaptation becomes necessary when changes become novel and discontinuous.

Stage IV: Governance through flexible real time response. This is the model that is emerging in progressive boardrooms to ensure that the management has planning, processes, and systems in effect to deal with significant challenges which develop too rapidly to be anticipated.

Stage I and Stage II systems have, until recently, been useful for most companies. But, now, when we try to peer into the turbulent future, we are concerned not only with predictable threats and opportunities but also with partially predictable or *weak signal* threats and unpredictable surprises. Top management and boards of directors need to become more sensitive to these external signals. The mechanism of an advisory council is one means to achieve this surveillance. What this means is that more and more companies will have to adopt Stage III or Stage IV systems if they are to thrive or, in some cases, survive.

STRATEGIC ISSUE MANAGEMENT

If the future is becoming too turbulent to predict from an extrapolation of the past, the challenge is to identify those issues that are likely to become critical to developing a corporate business strategy. How does a company filter out the "static" to tune in on weak signals? The conventional route to developing and managing a strategic portfolio is to (1) analyze company strengths and weaknesses; (2) determine the appropriate strategic posture; and (3) select the optimal approach to managing the portfolio.

These three broad steps will continue to obtain. To be competitive, a company must maintain a constant surveillance over the environmental, technological, economic, social, and political trends; estimate the impact and urgency of trends of key strategic issues; prioritize highly urgent and impactful issues that require immediate attention and action; and arrange for monitoring by management (and/or board committees or advisors) through surveillance systems. The impact and urgency of strong-signal issues must be taken into account along with issues from which only *weak signals* emerge.

Since weak signals mature over time and may become strong-signal issues, companies need a system that permits responses to graduate in concert with the progressive strengthening of the signals.

Ansoff divides signal strength into five stages.[5] Using these five progressively stronger signal-strength levels, we can interpret that an advisory board might recommend the following graduated response:

Stage	Strength of Signal	Graduated Advisory Response
I	Sense of threat or opportunity	Initiate environmental surveillance
II	Source of threat/ opportunities is known	Identify their relative strengths/ weaknesses
III	Shape of threat/ opportunities is concrete	Reduce external strategic vulnerability
IV	Response strategies are understood	Increase internal strategic flexibility
V	Outcome of responses is forecastable	Establish capability plans and response action plans

STRATEGIC SURPRISE GOVERNANCE

In spite of best efforts, some strategic issues slip by the surveyors and become strategic surprises. This means either that the issue arrived suddenly and was unanticipated and/or that it poses novel problems in which the corporation and the board have little prior experience. The development of international hostile corporate takeover phenomenon caught many corporations unprepared legally and financially to thwart unwanted predators. Failure to respond may imply a major financial reversal or loss of a major opportunity. The response characteristically is urgent and cannot be handled promptly or adequately by normal systems or procedures. Certainly in the United States and increasingly in Europe trends toward deregulation of transportation, banking, insurance, and other industries have caught many corporations ill prepared for the competition and changes in conduct of business.

Thus, if an advisory board expects that the environmental turbulence will be around the level of "strategic surprise turbulence," it needs to explore yet another system—a *strategic surprise system*. Here are some characteristics of such a strategic surprise system using the Ansoff model as a framework.

An emergency communication network needs to go into effect. This means eliminating the barriers from hierarchy, substituting a network process to deal with the transfer of information and communication. The network crosses organizational boundaries, filters the information, and rapidly communicates to whatever (or whoever) are the affected parts of the organization. Many of the large multinational industrial corporations have these networks identified in their disaster plans to help cope with acute industrial accident emergencies.

During the emergency, the responsibilities of the board and top management are *repartitioned*. The advisory board can assume defined roles such as: Advising a statutory board committee or management group devoted to control and maintenance of organization morale. Another advisory orientation could offer its input to assure continuance of business as usual with a minimum of disruption. In the third dimension outside advice could be to those who take charge of the response to the surprise.

A model example of this (albeit without a formal advisory board) was the action taken by the Union Carbide management and statutory board following the Bhopal disaster. Task forces at the board and management level were specially assigned along these lines. Some outside consultants were engaged to give an independent perspective.

Strategic task force networks are created along the lines of a *civil defense* vigilante model. Leaders and task forces cross normal organizational lines and execute strategic actions, serving not just as planning units. The communication pattern is star-shaped, directly between task force and central top management and/or board. Knowledgeable and especially qualified advisory directors can offer outside perspective.

The board formulates an overall strategy with the management given an advisory board input, assigns implementation responsibility and coordinates the implementation through delegated authority and power. Decentralized task forces implement their component of the new "surprise strategy."

Both task force and communication networks are *predesigned and participants trained* before a strategic surprise takes place. These networks can be developed along such lines as marketplace surprises, technological surprises, political or economic surprises, and others. Outside advisory council members have access to additional networks of their own which can be of value in coping with strategic surprise.

These networks are *exercised under noncrisis conditions* by addressing real strategic issues as if they were surprises (the "what if" game). Outside advisors can be particularly objective in such exercises.

The concept of alternative futures is useful here. Using scenarios of alternative futures, we can speculate about future governance requirements in different environments in which the corporation may find itself. Given such situational analyses, a realistic assessment of the uniqueness, if any, and an understanding of the governance process currently appropriate for the enterprise completes a setting for those in the boardroom or those advising the board or top management.

The usual approach is analytical, logical, rational, sequential, and qualitative. However, creation of alternative future scenarios departs from this algorithm into a perceptive, intuitive, simultaneous, qualitative mapping of the future. This exercise requires unique advisory director skills and an appropriate amount of thinking and debating time. Alas, too few board meetings permit or encourage time to be taken from the ceremonial, the statutory, and the fiduciary chores for such deliberation. Advisory boards can spend full time on a single issue.

Scenario building is a relatively recent adaptive tool for management and boards of directors. It can be simple and direct or complicated, indirect, and complex. Essentially it is a methodological attempt to view and combine various strong and weak signalled trends in a systematic way. Scenario writing has been termed science fiction, paranoidal, or unrealistic by critics. But it can indicate plausible or credible futures that a board of directors or advisors can contemplate and prepare themselves to fill their role as plotters of the strategic direction for the enterprise.

Here are specific suggestions (following Ansoff's model) for a top management or board of directors or board of advisors dealing with strategic surprise. First, examine strategic business units and their environments to establish a relative level of future turbulence. Second, rank the strategic business units by profit contribution versus the turbulence level. Third, "guesstimate" future levels of novelty, rapidity, and visibility of change within the chosen business area. Fourth, using the level of novelty, identify the strategic and tactical repositioning needed, that is, the control, long-range planning, strategic planning, and strategic issue management needed for the strategic business unit to survive and prosper. Fifth, pick the appropriate issue management governance and/or surprise governance system and implement it. A council of outside advisors can be focused on any of the five steps to provide an objective input.

CHANGING TURBULENCE AND CONGRUENT BOARD FIT

This discussion presents a two-step method by which a company can select its future system of governance and management. This method involves *first,* diagnosing the future turbulence of the firm's environment along the categories suggested previously, and *second,* matching the turbulence level with the appropriate system for governing and managing. The role of the statutory board is to see that executive management adopts the appropriate system to match the environment of progressively increasing turbulence. A well-qualified board of outside advisors can offer an objective perspective on this. While a large percentage of companies in the developed world will in the future need a system belonging to the "anticipation family," many other firms will need systems from the other response families.

Academics have questioned the basic usefulness of such concepts as the previously discussed anticipatory systems. Practitioners complain about the complexity and self-bureaucratizing tendencies, suppression of entrepreneurial creativity, and, in particular, system failure to improve corporate performance. The disappointments may come first from the mismatch between the system and the external reality of the firm. This can be corrected by matching the management and governance model with external realities. Second, any failure by the board (or management) to control the inertial tendency of the existing system, as well as failure to use other systems, inhibits entrepreneurial decision making.

A return to the basics of yesterday can be dangerous unless tomorrow's challenges are certain to be an extension of yesterday's. The observable behavior of firms such as ITT, RCA, Mobil, Union Carbide, and Monsanto suggests that after years of progressive increases in complexity such firms are moving to reduce complexity in order to make their companies more manageable. At this point, the focus of the problem definitely shifts from management and governance within the existing complexity to management *of* the complexity. The suggestion, therefore, is to design systems which provide a range of warnings and anticipations. One way to do this is by developing "alternative futures" reflecting political, social, cultural, technological, and economic forces that may prevail in the future. In postulating them, provision is made to recognize the importance of environmental weak signals. A well-qualified advisory board of experts may help in this regard, given Jonathan Swift's eighteenth-century reminder, "How is it possible to expect that mankind will take advice when they will not so much as take warning?"

NOTES

1. Harland Cleveland, *The Knowledge Executive* (New York: E. P. Dutton, 1985), pp. 34–35.

2. Steven Fink, *Crisis Management: Planning for the Inevitable* (New York: AMACOM, 1986).

3. H. Igor Ansoff, "Conceptual Underpinnings of Systematic Strategic Management," *European Journal of Operational Research* 2, 19 (1985); and idem, *Implanting Strategic Management* (Englewood Cliffs, N.J.: Prentice-Hall, 1984).

4. Ansoff, "Conceptual Underpinnings," pp. 6–7.

5. Ibid., p. 12.

8

ADVISING NON-PROFIT-SEEKING VERSUS PROFIT-SEEKING ORGANIZATIONS

> Most people think nowadays the only hopeful way of serving your neighbor is to make a profit out of him; whereas in my opinion, the hopefulest way of serving him is to let him make a profit out of me.
>
> —John Ruskin (1819–1900)

The great majority of nonprofits have no stockholders. What the full responsibility of being a trustee of a nonprofit institution means is often ambiguous. This complicates the role of an advisory board unless the scope is specifically focused on one or more definable elements of the institution's affairs. The general fiduciary obligation of the trustees is clear. The problem, in the event of alleged dereliction of duty by trustees, is how to determine precisely who the injured party is. "One of the outstanding characteristics of a charity . . . is that there is no beneficiary in a comparable position (comparable to the beneficiaries of a private trust or the shareholders of a business corporation) who is sufficiently interested to call the charitable fiduciary to account."[1]

This does not mean that trustees of a nonprofit institution are free from liability for negligent conduct. Nonprofit corporations' directors frequently have a much larger constituency and may be sued by donors, beneficiaries, alumni, and states' attorneys general. In this regard, advisors from such constituencies can be of great help.

Another difference between profit-seeking and non-profit-seeking organizations, according to the late Charles C. Abbott, former Converse Professor of Banking and Finance at Harvard Business School, is with respect to the handling of surplus or unexpended funds, if any, from operations. "Nonprofits are prohibited from distributing monies left over after paying expenses, so-called earnings of the institution, to private persons."[2]

A 1982 study of 103 not-for-profit organizations revealed that there is a significant void between trustees' and directors' activity in their policy-making roles. Business executives who become trustees too often are unable or fail to apply their managerial expertise to their volunteer efforts on not-for-profit organization boards of trustees. The study reveals the following significant ways in which boards of trustees differ from boards of directors on profit-seeking corporations. Not-for-profit boards are usually greater in number of incumbents, have fewer insiders, use the title of executive director for the person in responsible charge, have trustees with limited managerial experience and support services, have fixed terms of service, and demand less time of service devoted by volunteer trustees. The study found that trustees tend to ignore the task of discussing policies and normally accept the de facto decisions of the executive director. The volunteer relationship is a major cause for such a mental set.[3]

Advisory boards, where used, therefore are not normally assigned an overall role but rather advise on specific functions, trends external to the institution, new technologies, or political and economic forces that may impact the organization.

SPECIAL PROBLEMS OF NONPROFITS

The characteristics of a nonprofit organization make the legal function of governing by its board of trustees or board of directors one of seeing that the property and funds of the institution are devoted to the purposes for which they were given, and incorporate the ethic of service. This assumes that the trustees are clear about the aims and goals of the organization and that there is a conscientious and continuing effort to achieve them. A tricky set of problems follow, some of which may benefit by special advisory input.

Pricing of services is one such operating problem. Below-cost pricing of certain hospital services (such as emergency room) or below-cost tuition payments at universities are not unusual under the rationale that losses may be offset by other auxiliary activities such as gift shops, lunch rooms, university presses, or the investment income from endowment funds or grants from special donors.

Another problem is providing for future generations' needs by amortization of capital, research and development for the future, and "market" assessment. Future needs for services may change with shifts in demography, medical advances, standards of living, political support, competition, and so on.

Nonprofits have no automatic relationship between an increased demand for services and an increase in funding by public sources, gifts, contributions, or legacies. Most nonprofits deal with politicians, donors (not owners), and often with supplicants.

The root problem with most nonprofits is how to improve organizational effectiveness. Profit-seeking institutions tend to postpone or neglect some longer-term impacts on society (such as environmental, social responsibility, consumer protection, human rights, equal opportunity, and others) in pursuit of economic goals. Nonprofits, on the other hand, pursue the service ethic while often suffering from short-term crises of survival, political discontinuity, and the continuing task of maintaining financial integrity and viability and retaining qualified leadership.

Distinction between these two sectors is blurring. Profit-seeking institutions, despite their ethic of competition, are becoming what nonprofits always were; that is, more socially responsive and service-oriented. Advisory boards, visiting committees, boards of associates, and university councils can help build bridges between these sectors by having, for example, business persons, lawyers, and financial and other experts advise nonprofits. The principal functions of such advisory groups is to be informed about the academic goals of the institution and to counsel the respective administrative units on implementation of their objectives. A secondary objective is to raise friends and funds for the institution. In performing their functions, visiting committees or advisory councils can play a vital role in the formulation of policy and maintenance of high standards, as well as participate in the continual adjustment in the institution's educational and research programs to new conditions and new opportunities.

Conversely, educators, health service principals, clergy, other professionals, political leaders, and public representatives with special perspectives can offer significant advice and counsel that some business enterprises may sorely need. They can often be prime candidates for advisory councils to corporations.

The objectives of this cross-population via the advisory board or visiting committee route are to minimize ambiguity, distrust, conflict, and misunderstanding, and to conserve resources and allow both sectors to perform better with enlightened self-interest. Robert L. Gale, president of the Association of Governing Boards in Washington, D.C., remarks, "I think one reason for the success story of many community colleges in their external relations lies in their institution of the lay advisory board . . . functions of advisory boards group into four broad areas: finance, public, curriculum advice, and special kinds of expertise."[4]

SPECIAL ROLE OF AN ADVISORY BOARD

Advisory boards can do three things. First, they can raise the level of increased consciousness and concern about the present condition and perception of profit-seeking and nonprofit organizations and the relationship and relevance of this position to external circumstances and constituencies. Second, they help the nonprofit create a target model for improving its effectiveness given its purpose, objectives, and goals, and third, they help devise a transition model with enabling mechanisms to allow trustees of the nonprofit move toward improved effectiveness.

If we apply the process parameters of advisory boards in general, as discussed in Chapter 4, to nonprofit organizations, the following rationale and construct can "dock in space" with the unique governance and management characteristics of a nonprofit institution. An advisory group can be especially helpful to the board of trustees or executive director where there is a need for outside, independent, evaluative judgment of a trend or potential impact of external happenings, for example, changes in economic conditions, changes in public attitude and support of nonprofit institutions such as proposed tax regulations or liability insurance coverage; political shifts affecting funding; competitor strategy; invasion of the service sectors by profit-seeking organizations; advances in technology; or professional society and support service bargaining strategies. A carefully selected group of expert advisors can focus on an assigned element of the institution's concern and devote sufficient volunteer time to make an assessment. Usually volunteer trustees have support services available to them from their primary place of employment and contribute such at no cost to the nonprofit organization.

The *resource process role* is an obvious role for advisors. If the advisory group is formed, it can be in a standby mode until the board of trustees or the executive director needs outside help in the form of credible, objective advice and counsel.

The *change agent role* of an advisory board can be of special value in crisis situations, a search for a new executive director, or the revision of trustee criteria for service where the advisors are not eligible. Where some major strategic question is involved, such as combination of several hospitals or educational institutions to deal with redundancy, underutilization of capacity, or divestment of fixed assets, an advisory input can be invaluable. The advisors can be free of internal and external political pressures, professional biases and out-moded traditional hangups, and the influence of dominating donors or other constituencies.

Professional societies, trade associations, professional institutes, educational institutions, governmental departments and commissions, and social activist and political and religious organizations frequently form ad hoc or standing advisory boards, boards of associates, or visiting committees to perform any of these process roles. An invitation to serve on these groups should be carefully considered. It is not uncommon to use the formation of such a group as a fund-raising device.

To express the nature of a volunteer advisory group for an educational institution, the following specimen charter illustrates a typical charter for a liberal arts college. Note the relationship with the college trustees and administration.

BOARD OF ASSOCIATES

In order to extend the influence, outreach, and work of the College, the Board of Trustees of _____ College hereby establishes the _____ College Board of Associates.

  I. Purpose.
    A. To assist the Trustees in attracting the human and financial resources necessary to the College's continuing growth and health.
    B. To assist the Trustees in the articulation, dissemination, and achievement of the College's goals and objectives.
    C. To assist the Trustees and President in special projects.
    D. To augment Trustee expertise in various areas of college concern.
    E. To counsel with the Trustees and President, as requested, regarding programs, services, and activities of the College.
    F. To serve _____ as an integral constituent group and, together with the trustees, the alumni society, the faculty, the students, and the administration, to provide for the continuation of the College's strength, vitality, and high quality of undergraduate instruction.
  II. Organization and Structure
    A. Members shall be elected for terms of three years and shall be eligible for re-election. Members may, from time to time, be elected for terms of less than three years. During the initial year, members shall be elected by the Board of Trustees and, thereafter, by the established membership of the Board of Associates.
    B. Officers
      1. A Chairman, a Vice Chairman, and a Secretary shall be the officers of the Board of Associates.
      2. The Chairman and Vice Chairman shall be invited to attend all regular and special meetings of the Board of Trustees.

C. Committees
   1. No formal standing committees shall be established.
   2. Ad hoc committees and working groups shall be formed from time to time, as the need arises.
   3. Individually, members of the Board of Associates shall be invited to serve, from time to time, as associate members of existing or special committees of the Board of Trustees.

III. Program
  A. Meetings
    The Board of Associates shall hold at least two meetings each year.
  B. Special Projects
    The Board of Associates, or selected persons from its membership, shall undertake, from time to time, special projects involving various segments of the life of the College. In addition to self-initiated work, projects may also be invited by the Board of Trustees or the administration.
  C. General Responsibilities
    Members of the Board of Associates shall be expected to:
    1. Participate in special Board projects and major college events.
    2. Serve as hosts for the College in individual geographic areas for the purpose of student recruitment and financial resource development.
    3. Officially represent the College, as requested, at local functions such as installations or inaugurations of church officials and college or university presidents.
    4. Be alert for opportunities to attract financial support from individuals, corporations, and foundations outside the College's close constituencies.
    5. Utilize personal influence, prestige, and energies to advance _____ College in association with the Board of Trustees and the President of the College and his colleagues.
    6. Act as ambassadors for _____, telling the College story and extending a positive image of the institution.
    7. Acquire and maintain a thorough knowledge of the College and its purpose and objective.

An understanding of the aims and goals of the inviting non-profit-seeking organization is necessary before accepting an invitation to volunteer one's advisory service. The situation in the nonprofit sector is often as described in the old German proverb: "Less advice and more hands" are what is really needed.

NOTES

1. Kenneth Karst, "The Efficiency of the Charitable Dollar: An Unfilled State Responsibility," *Harvard Law Review* 73, 3 (January 1960), p. 436.

2. Charles C. Abbott, *Governance—A Guide for Trustees and Directors* (Boston: The Cheswick Center, 1979), p. 12.

3. Israel Unterman and Richard Hart Davis, "The Strategy Gap in Not-for-profits," *Harvard Business Review* (May–June 1982), pp. 30–40.

4. Robert L. Gale, "Lay Advisory Boards as an External Public Relations Tool," *Peabody Journal of Education* (April 1976), pp. 162–65.

9

CARE AND FEEDING OF ADVISORY BOARDS

What takes place after dinner must never be taken as counsel.
—Philippe de Commynes, *Memoires* (1524), 2.2.

An engagement to be a member of an advisory board is like an engagement in love. It is a period of occupation without possession. You contract to advise even if nothing happens to your advice. If it weren't for our admiration of those who come to us for advice, we wouldn't join an advisory board. Besides, it's no fun being a distinguished advisor unless the people you know, know how distinguished you are!

From a company's standpoint, the last thing most companies need is more advisors who know what the company needs. But it is hard to see the picture when you're inside the frame. Hence, the basic rationale for a corporation to create an advisory board or council of outside experienced experts.

One important key is to consider the formation of such a group as a contracted resource for a specific purpose and over a fixed, if renewable, period of time for the contract advice. Advisors should not be tenured any more than top executives or statutory directors.[1]

NATURE OF ADVISORY BOARDS

My perspective is that an advisory board is like the health care profession. It is one of but a few activities that strives professionally to destroy the reason for its own existence. An advisory board is relatively easy to establish. The problems that arise are in keeping the role of the group effective, both from a quality of advice and cost-effectiveness standpoint for the corporation and a rewarding experience for the advisors.

Advisory boards often march to a different drummer from that of the organization served. In fact they should, to some degree. The mutual challenge to advisors and advisees is to learn the respective identity, characteristics, stage of maturity, and experience of the advisory group and those in responsible charge in the corporation. The "musical training" of the two drummer groups should complement and eventually entrain each other if the advisory board relationship is to be productive and provide a forum for debate on independent business philosophies and separate experiences.

Two other issues are important to the maintenance of a good working relationship between the advisory group and the institution. First, the boundary between advisors and management or board must be drawn somewhere. When circumstances change, you can always agree to draw another boundary. The lesson is to have a fixed, mutually understood boundary for the advice under contract. Otherwise, the ambiguity will lead to confusion, uncertainty, conflict, and diffusion of accountability.

Second, the advisors require careful "care and feeding" by the liaison person and/or the chairman or CEO in the company being served. My experience is that advisory boards tend to accomplish very little unless the principals in the corporation served pay personal attention to and interact directly with the advisors. Otherwise, I have found that advisors get together to renew acquaintances, exchange business gossip, and redirect their pent-up frustration, even hostilities and hurt feelings at being engaged but not listened to.

The desire of distinguished persons to join an advisory elite, if not the directorship elect, is a stirring force in the business world. The driving forces are the service ethic, ego gratification, and, more recently, liability exposure of being a statutory director of a corporation. To keep these forces working for the benefit of all concerned, there are certain guidelines that I have found to be helpful in warding off dissipative effectiveness or lagging interest in an advisory board setup.

POINTERS TO CONSIDER

There are at least eight points to think about.

1. Social Cement. An invitation to an advisory board of distinguished persons can be heady. Monitoring the interface between the task and the sentience (or emotional bond) that develops between members is most im-

portant. Social cement binding the group collegially is the psychic income of providing service that is rewarding to a busy distinguished advisor. Caveat: Watch out for status sneakers who have social climbing as their prime objective.

2. Term of Engagement. Avoid implication of tenure. Engagement contracts should provide for negotiated renewal and escape.

3. Compensation. Pay can be based on comparative consulting fees or value of the advisor's time in his or her regular vocation. One formula is to match the fee, perks, and emoluments afforded statutory board members.

   Remember that the real compensation to most experienced and successful candidate advisors is the psychic income of being useful, cohabiting with a distinguished peer group of advisors, and serving an interesting, perhaps exciting, company peopled by those who command respect and are seriously in need of counsel and advice.

4. Legal Protection. While avoiding fiduciary responsibilities of a statutory director, indemnification and liability insurance need to be provided to the advisor. The corporate veil limiting liability exposure of individuals normally protects a statutory director. Merely resigning from a regular board and becoming a surrogate director identified as an advisor is not likely to escape this statutory director liability unless the role is defined differently and the advisor is not involved in the decision-making process and has no voting power. An expert engaged for specific professional input is in a different exposure category.

5. Conflict of Interest and Confidentiality. Provisions should be as explicit as those for a statutory director.

6. Dedication of Service. Include some requirement of the advisor for diligent attention to his role with any limitations and exclusions. The reciprocal is the obligation of the corporation to receive advisory input responsibly.

7. Accountable Flesh. It is unlikely, but advisory directors may be exposed to charges of acts of negligence, including malpractice, or to giving nonprofessional knee-jerk advice, any of which may cause alleged damage. Criteria for advisor selection, indemnification, and insurance can address this issue.

8. A final caveat. Companies resorting to advisory boards as a partial replacement for defecting statutory board members should carefully spell out the role of advisors, particularly the relationship, if any, to the statutory board. This is important to eliminate ambiguity or confusion as to the resource role of the advisors, versus the fiduciary and statutory role of main board members.

The temporal nature of an advisory council as a transitional structure helps address one of the most critical parameters of this organizational device. This concerns the potential for dereliction of duty of the statutory board or confusion over the executive management role by their deference in decision making to an advisory group.

If the advisory group has a limited term of existence and/or its members are not tenured and may be replaced from time to time, then the advisory role can serve as a useful resource. It should not have a permanent, overbearing influence on those who are accountable for conduct of the corporation. Legal and functional accountability rests with the formal governance organ of the corporation, the board of directors, in its role as a statutory and fiduciary body.

The executive management placed in responsible charge by the board of directors must fully accept such delegation of authority and responsibility to manage the company properly and to make the necessary decisions. Use of an advisory group as a resource only in arriving at decisions can be helpful. But careful attention must be paid to avoid allowing the advisors to make actual decisions or dominate the decision process at the expense of executive management or the board of directors.

Several situations bordering on this hazard come to mind from my service on advisory councils. The first occurred when the Hercules advisory council was proposed in 1979. The initial reaction of the statutory board members to this proposal was understandable concern over encroachment on or usurpation of their role, introduction of ambiguity in the corporate decision process plus the basic question of why the company needed such an organizational appendage. These questions were amicably resolved by the chairman citing the international experience and technical knowledge of the proposed individual advisors. This council clearly supplemented without conflict, in an objective, independent way, the attributes of the statutory directors and executive management.

The group was identified as an advisory *council,* not an advisory board, to emphasize distinction and the nondecision resource role. Further, the advisory council met only with the chairman and executive management and never convened jointly with the board of directors. This arrangement served its purpose for five years before phasing out. No misuse of the council or misunderstanding occurred to complicate or confuse corporate decision making accountability, responsibility, or authority.

Another advisory council situation was handled differently by the chairman who created a group of three experienced advisors to provide an independent perspective on the company's affairs. This was a diversified, closely held, U.S. firm that was dominated by the founder's family. They were members of the board, experienced senior management, as well as controlling owners. In this case, the outside director role was essentially absent from the statutory board. Outside directors were not welcome at the time. The small advisory council of carefully selected and respected outsiders was the temporary solution. This gave the owner-director-manager group an independent perspective without power sharing. Accordingly, our advisory council met with the regular board at some—but not all—board meetings. We were careful to offer advice but not to get into the trap of attempting to force or make decisions. This worked out well due to the chairman's ability in monitoring the relationship and the contributions and personal conduct of the advisors.

A third example of an advisory council's possible flirtation with the role of the statutory board took place last year with a European company. The company formed an advisory council of three senior, internationally experienced, independent, technically knowledgeable individuals to provide a resource to the essentially insider board of directors.

At the start of the advisors' contract term of two years' service on the council, only meetings with the statutory board and top management took place. There was no distinction made in conduct of the regular board meeting or in recording of board actions in the minutes, which clearly differentiated the role of any advisors present from statutory board members.

The initial setting was understandable, as the group was small, friendly, and communal in nature and style. This startup use of the council was later changed so that there were separate sessions of the advisors with the chairman. The perception of the board meeting was changed to emphasize the observer-advisor nature of the advisory council members whenever they attended a regular board meeting.

One multibillion dollar, multinational corporation with a distinguished advisory board is currently struggling with the undue influence that the celebrity advisors individually exert on the chairman–chief executive officer of the company. This power is tolerated by the statutory board, some of the members being also swayed by the dominating nature of the advisory board members. The result is some uncertainty about who is calling the shots and where the accountability (and liability) lies. The advisors are so prominent in the international business sector in which the company competes that disregard for this advice or termination of the advisors' service is politically difficult. The basic flaw in this setup is the apparent abdication of the statutory board to assert its accountability and to govern the corporation in an initiative rather than a reactive manner, taking full responsibility for strategic decisions with or without the input of the advisors.

THE APPROPRIATE SETTING FOR CONTRACT ADVICE

Many conditions set the stage for engaging an advisory board. Obvious needs may be for wider experience in various industries, an international venue, or provision of a fresh, independent perspective and long-term view.

From both the advisor and advisee standpoint, the existence and membership of an advisory group does not need to be disclosed. The advisory meetings can be devoted to key specific issues and not consumed by routine executive, operating, legal, or administrative matters that must be handled by the statutory board or executive management.

The members of an advisory board should be chosen as well-rounded persons of equal status, peer reputation, or position as that of the CEO and/or chairman. Advisors should be equal to the principals of the advisee company and not beholden or subordinate to them. They should be persons who can be trusted and respected.

Advisors should not represent any constituent group such as suppliers, customers, clients, shareholders, lenders, or borrowers. Advisors have no legal responsibilities, no equity participation, and no legal status, and serve only at the discretion of the chief executive and/or chairman. This assures an open approach to sensitive matters without inhibitions due to internal politics or expected quid pro quo. Advisors, carefully chosen, are not encumbered by past history or personality problems that may tend to inhibit regular directors of the company. Ironically, because of its lack of official power and detachment from daily operations an advisory board can gain the CEO's confidence and thus become an important strategic influence.

The *Small Business Report* of January 1985 has suggested six ground rules to establish in order to have an appropriate setting for an advisory board to provide the chairman or CEO with effective peer support. While this is conventional wisdom, it is important to keep in mind.

No advisory board member shall misuse the position for personal profit. And advisors must disclose any personal interests that could jeopardize their objectivity or cause personal conflict. Each must abstain from board actions that could mean personal advantage.

No advisory board member shall serve concurrently on the board of a competing firm.

Board members must attend meetings regularly, and provide input by taking an active part in discussions, analyses, and proposals.

Members shall be kept informed of all actions requiring their input. Any information from questionable sources must be verified.

Board members shall inform the company of any business opportunities made available by their positions before pursuing the opportunities.

All information received by the board members must be held in strictest confidence.

For a not-for-profit institution's advisory board, there are some other guidelines to consider. The following is a specimen offered by the Indiana State Advisory Council on Vocational Education.[2]

The Indiana State Advisory Council on Vocational Education has several ideas for maintaining an active advisory board. (An underlying assumption is that an advisory board can be effective only if it receives adequate and accurate information on which to base recommendations.)

1. Good communications are essential—keep informed.
2. Periodic meals as part of meetings can be helpful, make meetings pleasant.
3. Student presentations to the board (students are the product).
4. Publicity and recognition for members—everyone likes to feel important.
5. Reimbursement of major items of expense incurred by members.
6. Close coordination between staff person and board chairperson.
7. Board members are aware of objectives, goals, and direction of educational program.
8. Recommendations of board are thoroughly evaluated and implemented if feasible.
9. Responsibility is shared by all members of the board—likewise recognition and credit is shared by all members.
10. Provide opportunity for members to improve their ability to be effective—the institution is an example.
11. Formal publicity about the board and its work should be released by administrative offices.
12. Board should not engage in political activity.
13. Members must understand the scope and nature of their responsibilities.
14. Constant evaluation must be made of the board's work.
15. The structure and organization of the board should be reviewed periodically to assure they are appropriate.

GENERAL NOTIONS ABOUT CONTRACT ADVISORS

Like most organizational innovations, creation of an advisory board, council, or committee has become more fashionable recently. Many multinational companies, of course, have employed this device for years, particularly with respect to getting political perspective from advisors in countries away from their headquarters. Next there was a trend toward creating advisory councils whose main focus was technology. Lately, advisory boards have been created for many purposes: environmental assurance, social responsibility, consumer affairs, and political surveillance.

Any advisory group is very company-specific. In my judgment, this is often a transition model, but it may be institutionalized if found valuable and a turnover of advisors is planned to keep the group on the leading edge. The conflicts, or perception of conflict, must be managed between the advisory group, the statutory board, and top management.

The number one concern is to tailor any such advisory adjunct organization to specific company needs and revise its membership and role as needs change. Some random observations (many are conventional wisdom) have proven useful in my experience on advisory boards over the last thirty-plus years.

There are no standard guidelines or international conventions concerning advisory boards, councils, or committees. The structure and positioning of advisory groups depend a great deal on the legal context of the country involved as well as the idiosyncratic needs of the enterprise served.

There are some obvious policy matters to be clarified. These could be generically referred to as (1) determining the purpose of the advisory board and stating this explicitly. This would be followed by (2) a statement of specific objectives; (3) the role and relationship of the advisory board to the organization; and (4) conditions of service of advisory council members, such as the amount of time, compensation, spheres of interest, conflicts, and other issues.

From my own experience on statutory and advisory boards for many years (of private and public nature, for-profit and not-for-profit institutions) probably the biggest hazard in approaching this subject is failure to obtain a personal commitment by the chairman, CEO, and/ or statutory board members and top management, depending on role and reporting relationships of the advisors; and the proper management of advisory groups after they are formed. There is a definite life-cycle problem here. A problem presents itself after the initial euphoria of formation and getting acquainted as to where and how the real advisory input can be linked to the corporate strategy. This depends on the personal chemistry of the individual council members with those in the corporation being served. Another issue, of course, is the one of liability and appropriate dealing with insurance and the indemnification of those engaged in giving advice. This varies by country and by the nature of the business, and can range widely. In the United States, it also deals with the concept of malpractice.

The administrative problems of an advisory group should not be minimized. While simple in concept, it takes time and expense to administer the relationships of distinguished members of an international advisory group properly so that their understandings, allegiance, commitments, and contributions are properly handled from personal, political, accountability, and strategic standpoints.

Public and internal relations aspects concerning the formation and activity of an advisory group must be considered. The expectations of either the statutory board, the management, the shareholders, the public customers, investment community, or others may be unduly raised as to what is taking place and why such "extra" advice is needed. The company may be perceived to be in trouble, or the perception may be that this is an enlightened move to tap talents not readily available with the statutory board. The public and internal relations aspect should be carefully thought through with the principals involved.

The conflict-of-interest matter is one which can be managed but also must be carefully considered. Most qualified persons who would be of value on an international advisory board will have relationships and identity with interests that may be (or may be perceived to be) in conflict with the corporation served. This matter requires legal review as well as consideration from a public relations standpoint, so that the advisors are considered to be "independent, unaffiliated, and disinterested"—to use the terms adopted by the Securities and Exchange Commission in their outline of attributes for a "model" statutory director of a U.S. corporation.

The role of an advisory group needs to be clear in its relation (or lack thereof) to the various statutory and fiduciary board roles to see that these are in harmony or perhaps in creative tension. An advisory group provides a resource free from hierarchical constraint and relatively free of legal and statutory obligations. It should be peer-respected and presumably is independent of internal and external politics.

My experience in creating and serving on advisory boards leads me to suggest some *process* steps once a decision has been made to create such an organizational device. These have been detailed in Chapter 4 but are summarized here, as they are vital to successful "care and feeding" of an advisory board.

1. *Purpose:* Develop a statement of purpose and objectives for the advisory resource group. This involves a simple statement of the concept behind the formation of the group.

2. *Role description* of the advisory group and duties of members. Clarify the reporting relationships with the chairman/CEO and with any other top management representatives, the statutory board (if there is expected to be any relationship).

3. *Issue identification* with policy resolution of any issues that may be raised by creating this device, such as external and internal perceptions of the reason for creation of such a group and/or relations with statutory directors.

4. *Criteria* for membership, that is, attributes desired in the prospective candidates under consideration.
5. *Conditions of service:* duration of advisory service, number of meetings, compensation, and so on.

Given an understanding of these five points, it is useful to develop a "woodbox" list. This is a list of prospective candidates who may fit the criteria. The list can be developed from personal networks, advice of colleagues, and other sources, but initially without any contact with prospects.

The second step is a rank-ordering of most desirable prospects and an exploration of their interest and availability. It is important to avoid any misunderstandings or misrepresentations. The focus is on the expectations of the company and the individuals contacted. The problem here is that the type of people normally sought may have conflicts, real or perceived, have limited availability, and may or may not have interest.

Step three is actual recruitment and commitment. This is usually done in a formal way by the chairman or CEO to whom the individuals or group will report. Developing a personal relationship is important, and the invitation should clarify what is expected of the candidate. Some letter, contract, or other arrangement needs to be formalized to deal with such matters as time requirements, compensation arrangements, liability indemnification, period of engagement, and so on. This would include a forward calendar of meetings, location, general agenda, and other arrangements.

One last note: I believe that the success of any group of advisors acting as a resource to a corporation depends on several things. The first (and foremost) is the personal interest and commitment of the top executive. Second, how meaningful are the meetings to the company? Third, the psychic advantage of advisors getting to know other members on the advisory council should not be underestimated. Such contacts may not flow from other industry or business exposure. When you get a group of experienced and talented individuals from different domains to serve together, they form new and valuable relationships not only with the corporation served, but with each other.

This all sums up to the importance of the "care and feeding" of such a group. It takes time and energy on the part of all involved. In concluding this chapter, I like Oscar Wilde's dehortation, "It is always a silly thing to give advice, but to give good advice is absolutely fatal."

NOTES

1. Portions of this material originally appeared in *The Journal of Business Strategy* 9, 4 (July/August 1988), Copyright 1988 by Warren, Gorham and Lamont, Inc.

2. Hugh Thompson, "Are Boards Other than Trustees Needed?" and James T. Laney, "Using Visiting Committees," *AGB Reports* (May–June 1984), pp. 27–32.

10

INSURANCE,
INDEMNIFICATION,
AND CONTRACTUAL
MATTERS

He who builds according to everyman's advice will have a crooked house.

—Danish Proverb

It used to be that the fees, the public distinction, the ego gratification, the exclusivity, elitism, and the privilege of providing a needed service made directorship a much desired goal. Now the legal responsibilities of a corporate director expose statutory board members to liabilities for which indemnification provisions and insurance protection may be inadequate to protect a corporate director at least in the United States. I fear that one of our country's greatest exports is the litigiousness that accompanies doing business in these complex days. The conventional wisdom is that being an advisory director avoids the liability exposure of a statutory director as long as there is no participation in the decision-making process.

There is no voting power attributed to the advisor (see specimen advisory contract language later in this chapter). This advisory role is yet to be tested in court. However, the legal status of advisory directors is receiving increasing attention from corporate counselors. On May 1, 1986, Northwestern University School of Law held their sixth annual Ray Garrett Institute program. At the workshop on Protecting Corporate Directors, moderator Thomas A. Cole of Sidley & Austin, a Chicago law firm, discussed directors' and officers' liability insurance and the range of responses available to corporations and their directors upon learning that coverage will be subject to unac-

ceptably high deductible amounts, or that premiums have been raised
to a level that seems difficult to justify. The responses ranged from
suing the insurers, intensive contract renegotiation, expanding indemnification agreements, captive insurance, and risk reduction, to
resignation of directors from the board when all else fails.

The strategy of creating an advisory board presents some special
considerations. Cole made these interesting observations:

When all of the facts suggest that this is the appropriate response, consideration should be given to the establishment of an advisory board so that the
corporation may continue to benefit from the advice of outsiders. The members of the advisory board, unlike directors, would take responsibility only
for those matters on which they have given advice. Two notes of caution.
While the standard of review for directors' actions in most jurisdictions is
"gross negligence", it may be that advisors will be held to a standard of mere
negligence. In other words, the protections of the business judgment rule which
are afforded to directors may not be available to advisors. It would be appropriate, therefore for an advisor to seek an indemnification agreement from
the corporation, to purchase professional errors-and-omissions insurance and
to consider incorporating as a "professional corporation." Moreover, advisors
could be regarded, in certain situations, to be *de facto* directors. For example,
a member of an advisory board would be well advised to avoid transactions
which, if undertaken by a director, would result in Section 16(b) liability.

In order to appreciate the insurance protection and indemnification
problems further from both the advisory director and the statutory
director perspectives, it is useful to consider the insurance industry
trends during the last two years. Consumers of directors' and officers'
(D&O) liability insurance report they are facing larger deductibles,
lower limits, more restrictive endorsements, shorter policy durations,
and higher premiums. Premium increases in 1985 and 1986 ranged
50 to 500 percent. In a few industries there was a true availability
problem, for example, financial institutions, electrical (nuclear) utilities, new high-tech enterprises, wildcat oil and gas companies, research and development enterprises, real estate developers, petro-
chemical companies, and the steel industry.

Underlying problems responsible for the D&O insurance capacity
shortage include: [1]

Significant reduction in reinsurance because of the general condition of domestic and foreign reinsurance markets, combined with the reinsurers' perceptions of price inadequacy, the American civil justice system, and the increase in potential liability for directors and officers;

Policyholders are now breaking traditional relationships with D&O insurers and are suing some of their own managers, attempting to collect on D&O

policies (i.e., Bank of America, $95 million; and Chase Manhattan, $175 million).

Federal insurance agencies, such as Federal Deposit Insurance Corporation (FDIC) and Federal Savings & Loan Insurance Corporation (FSLIC), have insured failed banks and savings and loans and are attempting to recoup some of their losses by suing former directors and officers;

Court decisions hold directors and officers to an increasingly strict standard of conduct by changing the scope of the business judgment rule from true mismanagement into a "business judgment errors and omissions policy";

Increase in hostile takeovers and other business practices likely to generate claims (greenmail, poison pills, golden parachutes);

A greater concern that directors and officers are not representing the interests of their shareholders may also result from recent corporate battles;

The general financial condition of primary insurers;

Growth in demand for directors and officers coverage; and

Underpricing in prior years.

In 1984, rates were 20 to 25 percent inadequate. Reports are that in 1984, D&O insurers were paying three to four times as much in claims as they received in premiums. Average policy limits increased by 45 percent between 1982 and 1984, with a dramatic increase for those purchasing limits over $50 million. The number of companies seeking D&O insurance increased by 8 percent during this period with growth in demand greatest among companies with assets under $25 million. The average defense cost for claims in 1984 was $461,000 up from $365,000 in 1982. Average total cost of a D&O claim (defense cost plus losses) adjusted for inflation was $1.62 million in 1984 compared to $1.34 million in 1982 (up 21 percent).

Since 1984, there has been a dramatic reduction in capacity—the financial ability of an insurance company to offer its product. Several major insurance companies have withdrawn from the market and those remaining have significantly curtailed their writings and reduced coverage limits. The few new entrants are offering relatively low coverage limits.

Although the London market popularized D&O coverage, it has not been a major writer recently because underwriters thought U.S. rates were too low. London brokers are reportedly offering primary coverage with limits up to $20 million. Capacity reduction reflects the current financial condition of U.S. insurance companies and reinsurers. Portions of the reinsurance market have all but dried up. To date, primary carriers have been able to obtain some reinsurance coverage. However, it is expected that they will face some difficulties when current policies expire.

SOLUTIONS

Insurers have responded to broader liability with endorsements excluding certain liability from coverage. There is no standardization, but the new exclusions include claims arising from pollution and environmental damage, claims brought by government agencies (the so-called "regulatory" exclusion) aimed at FDIC and FSLIC suits, and the Bank of America–type situations where the policyholder sues its own directors and officers or where one director sues another.

Customers have responded by looking for alternatives to insurance. Twenty-three of the largest banks are studying options such as pooling arrangements and formation of their own insurance company, called a "captive." Another regional bankers' association has formed its own insurance company, capitalized at $3 million to provide D&O coverage to its 2,200 members. One organization is forming a new insurer to provide liability coverage for large companies. It reportedly will offer $50 million deductible.

Many of the largest chemical producers along with other large corporations are taking steps to fill gaps in their liability coverage left by the insurance upheavals of the past year. A group of sixty-six major firms have invested a total of $395 million in a new insurance company that intends to provide chemical and pharmaceutical producers eventually up to $75 million in general liability coverage on claims that exceed $50 million. Companies deemed to have less risk exposure will get coverage for claims starting at $25 million. The new carrier also will eventually provide directors' and officers' liability coverage of up to $15 million on claims exceeding $20 million. The company, X. L. Insurance, based in Barbados, was organized by insurance broker Marsh & McLennan, Inc., and Morgan Guaranty Trust. Most sponsors invested $10 million each and will pay annual premiums ranging up to $5 million, depending on risk exposure. Among the sponsors, major chemical producers are Air Products & Chemicals, American Cyanamid, Borg-Warner, Chemed, Chesebrough-Pond's, Ciba-Geigy, Dow Chemical, DuPont, Eastman Kodak, Hercules, International Minerals & Chemical, PPG Industries, Rohm & Haas, and Union Carbide. According to a *C&EN* report of June 16, 1986, the new firm provides liability coverage for claims at lower levels than that provided by other pools that have sprung up in response to the shortage of such insurance from traditional carriers.

Patrick J. Head, vice president and general counsel of FMC Corporation, speaking at the Garrett Institute, Northwestern Law School, Chicago, Illinois, on April 30, 1986, on "director's personal liability incurred under statute and regulation," offered the following perspective.

Even though directors may be named persons liable, the degree of actual exposure will be dependent more on the director's actual activities than on the violation of the statute itself.

This does not mean that there will not be actions against directors, especially in instances in which there are major events, such as catastrophic environmental problems, major antitrust exposure where the board was obviously not exercising an overview responsibility or where the violation of statute specifically becomes attached to their duty of care and diligence.

It may well be that though this area has not opened up significant exposure at this time, it furnishes a growing area of interest for derivative suit attorneys, and even for plaintiff's attorneys, interested in exerting pressure on board members in addition to the direct suit against the corporation itself.

This brief review has pointed up a number of apparent standards or guides.

1. Most civil (or criminal) liability will turn on the individual director's actual involvement, or in some instances, knowledge;

2. Some statutes (notably banking) add to the director's normal corporate fiduciary duties;

3. Some statutes will actually specify director liability (as Clayton or the Foreign Corrupt Practices Act), though most are silent;

4. Liability of directors will most often turn on breaches of fiduciary standards, as against specific violation of statutes themselves; and

5. There is an increasing possibility of director's deeper involvement by serving on committees with specific oversight or review assignments, as for instance, audit or public policy.[2]

INDEMNIFICATION

To indemnify means to save harmless or to secure against loss or damage that may occur in the future, or to compensate for loss or damage already suffered. Indemnification of officers and directors falls into three situations: where indemnification is a matter of right; where indemnification is allowed; and where a corporation is prohibited to indemnify because of public policy or a situation such as bankruptcy.

In this regard, insurance may be useful (1) to reimburse the corporation when they do indemnify a statutory director or advisory director, (2) when the corporation is not allowed to indemnify, or (3) when the corporation chooses not to indemnify its directors, officers or advisors. D&O policies are usually written to cover any director or officer of the corporation and may be extended to cover advisory directors on a blanket basis, usually without being specific as to names or positions. Indemnification, unlike D&O insurance, puts the burden on the director, officer, or advisor to show that there was some benefit to the corporation or that some interest of the corporation was threatened. My advice to prospective advisory board members is to seek indemnification and adequate D&O-type insurance by the company contracting for the advice. Otherwise, the risk of being an advisor may not be worth the reward.

SPECIMEN ADVISORY BOARD CONTRACTS

In surveying advisory board and advisory council practice in the United States and Europe, I found that the great majority of contract advisors, by far, were engaged with a simple letter of invitation agreement. On the other hand, some companies were exacting in the terms of service contract.

The usual arrangement between members of advisory boards or councils and the sponsoring company is an informal letter of invitation from the CEO or the chairman. This personalized invitation describes the charter of the council and the role and responsibilities of council members. It offers an admonition about conflict of interest and indicates fees paid to members and the nature and plans for the forthcoming meetings at least one year in advance. The invitation is usually for a designated period of service on the council, say two or three years, at the end of which another term might be renewed by mutual agreement. The invitee who has been informally contacted and has agreed in principle to serve, is, in effect, asked for his or her formal acceptance under the terms and conditions described. The letter covers all the important considerations but does not appear to be overly legalistic.

This type of invitation is common when dealing with the power elite, that is, CEOs, chairmen, former senior government officials, and distinguished academics. In dealing with other types of more functionally oriented advisory groups, such as a scientific advisory council, the letter agreement may have a format more like a consulting contract.

The general counsel of one of the corporations where I served as an advisory council member for over five years gave me the following statement as part of the official invitation to serve on the advisory council:

Since the Advisory Council will have no designated responsibilities other than advisory or consulting, members will have no liability comparable to that of a statutory director or management employee. If an advisory member for some inconceivable reason is considered to possess statutory director liability, the company's charter indemnification provisions would cover the individual, although not the indemnification insurance. Therefore, the liability insurance coverage will be extended to members of the Advisory Council. Potential liability as a consultant or advisor might arise by reason of being given access to confidential inside information provided in connection with the advisory role. Obviously, confidential information should be handled in such a way as to comply with the various securities laws and common sense rules regarding improper disclosure. To the extent a member is provided access to confidential information, such as unpublished earnings projections, potential acquisitions and the like, improper use and/or disclosure could create liability. Taking personal advantage of insider information in a proposed merger would be an example. Practically, it would be unlikely that any liability would be incurred, but this comment is included to help prevent inadvertent disclosures of confidential information.

It is concluded that no practical obstacles exist to serving as an advisory director from a liability standpoint.

The following contract specimens are offered as alternative guideline language for the various provisions of an agreement that are important in setting up an advisory board or advisory council.

Specimen Contract A

This agreement is entered into on this (date) between (first party) and (second party).

WHEREAS, the Board of Directors has authorized the formation of an advisory council to provide board members an independent source of information and advice (the "Advisory Council"); and

WHEREAS, (first party) has, as further disclosed herein, agreed upon terms and conditions under which he will serve as a member of the Advisory Council;

NOW, THEREFORE, in consideration of the terms and conditions herein provided, the parties hereto agree as follows:

1. (Second party) hereby appoints and engages (first party) as a member of the Advisory Council, and he hereby accepts his said appointment upon the terms and conditions herein provided. (First party) in his capacity as an Advisory Council member, is and shall be an independent contractor and not an employee of (second party).

2. The term of this Agreement shall be for a period of two (2) years commencing (date) and expiring (date), provided that either party may terminate this Agreement by giving the other party at least 90 days advance written notice thereof, in which case 1/12th of the annual retainer fee shall be paid for each month served.

3. During the terms of this Agreement, (first party) shall, subject to the limitations set forth herein, provide advice to the members of the Board of Directors of (second party) whether collectively or individually, with respect to (1) ongoing business activities of (second party); (2) strategic planning of (second party) regarding existing businesses or asset redeployment into other businesses and (3) the economic, political and social environment in which (second party) will conduct its business activities, both in the long and short term. Also (first party) shall, to the extent that he has awareness of applicable information and is otherwise ethically and legally permitted to do so, provide any information regarding (second party) customers, competition and suppliers which the company may deem useful as an ex-

ample of proper business conduct, efficient management technique or any other information or data in regard to said entities which may be of use to the company.

4. As a member of the Advisory Council, (first party) agrees to attend meetings of the Advisory Council as scheduled by the Chairman of the Board. In no event, however, shall he be expected to attend more than four (4) Advisory Council meetings in any one (1) contract year of this Agreement. (First party) also agrees to be available for advice to any member of the Board of Directors of (second party) by telephone, mail or personal visit between any of the meetings of the Advisory Council which are scheduled by the Chairman of the Board of Directors.

5. In consideration of his performance of this Agreement, (second party) agrees to pay to (first party) an annual retainer fee equal to (dollars) which shall be payable quarterly in arrears. In addition to the fees above described, (second party) herein agrees to reimburse (first party) for any ordinary and necessary costs or expenses which are incurred by him in attending council meetings or in the fulfillment of other duties specifically provided for herein.

6. Notwithstanding anything to the contrary herein, any and all comments, recommendations, advice and counsel given pursuant to this Agreement shall only be construed as the opinions of (first party) and, in no event, shall such opinions be deemed an act or decision for or on behalf of (second party) in connection with any of its business activities, operations or functions. (First party) shall have no authority to act on behalf of (second party) in any manner including, without limitation, the ability to bind or obligate (second party) to any third party or otherwise direct or control (second party's) internal actions or processes.

7. As additional consideration to (first party) for his services hereunder, (second party) agrees to indemnify, defend and hold him and all members of the Advisory Council harmless from and against any claim, demand, action, proceeding or suit which arises from or is otherwise connected with their performance under this Agreement. (Second party's) obligation to defend and hold (first party) and other members of the Advisory Council harmless under this Agreement shall include the cost of a reasonable fee for legal representation of any Advisory Council member.

8. (Second party) agrees to maintain information concerning the Company and its business affairs in a prudent and businesslike manner. In regard to information which is designated as confidential by (second party), (first party) agrees to treat such information as confidential and not to divulge said information to any third party. Further, (first party) agrees not to use any information acquired from (second party) for his personal financial gain without the written consent of the Company.

9. The parties intend and agree that the payment of fees to (first party) hereunder (i) constitute ordinary income to him (ii) are deductible from the federal gross income of (second party) as an ordinary and necessary business expense under Section 162 of the Internal Revenue Code of 1954, as amended, and (iii) do not constitute wages for purposes of the Federal Income Contributions Act ("FICA") but constitute earnings from self-employment for purposes of FICA. The parties agree to file tax returns and pay taxes consistent with such intentions and resist any assertion to the contrary by any governmental agency.

10. This Agreement, or any portion, may not be assigned without the written consent of both parties.

IN WITNESS WHEREOF, the parties hereto have executed this Agreement on the day and date first above written.

Specimen Contract B

This letter confirms the agreement reached with you as a member of the Advisory Council of (company).

You will be expected to provide consultation and advice to us on such matters with respect to the business and affairs of (company) as may from time to time be referred to the Council for its opinion and recommendations. As a part of these services, you will be asked to review corporate plans, strategies and directions and make suggestions thereon, with special emphasis on areas of high technology. You will not be expected to participate in the day-to-day management or operations of (company).

Commencing as of (date), you will be available to (company) for consultation and advisory services at mutually convenient times and places with the understanding you will devote such time in the performance of services as is reasonably necessary to fulfill the objectives of the Council. It is initially contemplated that meetings of the Council will require three or four days a year.

For these services, you will receive an annual retainer of (dollars) payable quarterly in advance installments of (amount) on each January 1, April 1, July 1, and October 1 of each year. An additional (amount) will be paid for each scheduled meeting of the Council you attend. You will be reimbursed for all reasonable travel and living expenses paid or incurred hereunder. Fees payable hereunder may be deferred by signing an agreement of deferral which will be provided on request.

All services under this agreement are provided as an independent contractor and not as an agent or employee of (company). You will have no authority to bind or otherwise obligate (company) in any way with a third party.

You will devote your best efforts to carrying out the services required hereunder. However, your liability, if any, will be limited in any event to an amount no greater than the amount paid for the services rendered and we will indemnify and hold you harmless against any costs or liabilities to third parties of whatever nature which may arise out of any use of the results of your work on the Council. (Company) will also extend to you its regular directors' and officers' liability insurance coverage.

It is probable that you will receive from time to time confidential information. You agree to preserve the nature of such confidential information and not directly or indirectly use or disclose it to others except upon the prior written consent of (company). These obligations shall terminate ten years following the termination of this agreement or any extension thereof. Any information which becomes available to the public generally is excluded from this commitment.

The period of this agreement shall be three years from (date) unless terminated earlier by either party on thirty days' prior written notice.

If the foregoing is acceptable to you, please acknowledge your acceptance thereof by signing and returning the enclosed copy of this letter.

Specimen Contract C

Purpose: The primary purpose is to assist the management in determining what business the company should be in. In accomplishing this purpose the following aims are appropriate:

To provide selected experts' advice and counsel to the management for its strategic planning process, particularly in the development of thinking about objectives, aims, scope, timing, resources, and directions for development.

To improve understanding of the opportunities, issues, trade-offs, implications, and integrity of the decisions the company may address in the short term on critical strategic matters that concern the long-term future of the company.

To catalyze and inspire the management's thinking about corporate strategy from the perspective of supportive independent outside perspectives. Council members are chosen from those having particular insight to externalities, risks, opportunities, and imponderables that may impact the company's longer-term future options and objectives.

Duties: The council will have the following duties:

1. Meet with the management at least twice a year to advise and counsel on strategic issues, planning assumptions, and externalities.

2. Bring to the attention of the management, any significant nonproprietary information received from external sources that may affect the company and which the council member may have reason to believe is not known to the management.

3. When requested, comment appropriately to the full board on the strategic plans for corporate development.

Composition and Term of Service: The council will consist of no more than four outside experts, including the chairman of the council to be appointed by the CEO.

The CEO will appoint (or reappoint) the council members annually at the first full council meeting.

Relationships: The council will have the status of an advisory committee to the CEO.

The council will serve as a resource to the management with no power as a council to intervene in the management's submission of its strategic plans to the full board.

Compensation: Council members (including the chairman) will be compensated for services and expenses at approximately the same rate schedule as the standing committees of the board.

Specimen Contract D

The following two letter agreements represent another approach to setting forth the conditions of service on an advisory board of a multinational company:

Date

Dear Sir:

We refer to the investigation which has been entrusted to you in your quality as Member of the Advisory Board of our Company concerning the administrative and managerial activities of the company and its subsidiaries.

It is understood that all data and information which will come to your attention in the course of your investigation are to be kept strictly confidential, unless they have been in your possession prior to disclosure by a Company of our Group or have become public knowledge through no fault of yours. You shall communicate them only to members of our Company and to the other members of the above mentioned Advisory Board, provided, however, that they undertake in writing to us a confidentiality obligation substantially in the same terms as set forth herein.

It is further understood that you shall not disclose any confidential data and information supplied to you in the course of your investigation or any processed versions thereof in technical publication of any sort, even in anonymous form, without our prior written consent, or unless such data and/or information becomes public knowledge, or has been in your possession prior to disclosure by us.

If you agree with the above, please return the attached copy of this letter after having indicated your acceptance by signing it in the place provided.

Very truly yours,

_____

Date

Dear Sir:

Further to our verbal agreement, we would like to confirm our decision to avail ourselves of your professional services in the area of company strategic planning.

Your services will be considered exclusively as outside consultants entailing no employment relationship.

As per our mutual understanding, your cooperation will take place both abroad and in the —————location.

For your above mentioned services, you will receive for each full day of actual work, the gross amount of USA $——— to be paid quarterly upon presentation of an invoice.

Said amount does not include expenses incurred for travelling, lodging, and the like, which are connected with the accomplishment of your task. These expenses will be reimbursed in USA $ against presentation of pertinent documentation.

During your consultantship, you will be bound by the terms of the secrecy agreement which you signed.

If you are in agreement with the above, please be so kind as to return duly signed the enclosed copy of this letter.

Sincerely yours,

NOTES

1. Publicly available memo analysis by Alliance Insurance Company, "Availability, Directors and Officers Liability Insurance" (January 1986).

2. Permission granted by Patrick J. Head to quote this perspective from his presentation April 30, 1986, to the Garrett Institute.

11

ADVISORY VIEW OF CORPORATE STRATEGY

It is helpful to consider the perspective that an experienced group of advisors is likely to share about the strategic transitions and future conditions into which corporations fall as they approach the 1990s. This view is based on personal experience on advisory boards and advisory councils of large and small corporations, publicly and privately held firms, domestic and international companies, industrial and service organizations, and not-for-profit institutions.

When I look at the way that many companies are managed, I'm reminded of the last performance by Karl Wallenda, the patriarch of the famous family of high-wire circus performers. Not long after four members of the Wallenda family were killed or permanently injured in a single accident, Karl, who was in his seventies, agreed to walk a high wire ten stories above a city street. As usual, he carried his sixteen-foot pole for balance, as he had since childhood. He had always been told to hold on to his pole—that it would keep him safe and balanced.

It was a windy day, and as he moved onto the wire he started to lose his balance, but just as he had been told, he used his pole, quickly regained control, and continued across. Then a sudden gust came up, and he started to fall. He could have caught hold of the wire as he fell past, but he didn't, because he was holding on tightly to his pole as he had always been taught to do. When he struck a taxi below and was killed, he was still holding that pole.

As advisors, directors and managers, we are all on a high wire. And, like Karl Wallenda, we are determined to hold onto our "pole"— our technology and our concepts of management and governance—as we have been taught. We think that in them lies our only safety. But like Karl Wallenda, we may not survive believing that.

What we have to do, so to speak, is to learn when it is better to let go of the "pole" and not just catch hold of the old tightrope wire but jump to a new and safer tightrope. A sophisticated, experienced, and expert board of advisors can have a great influence on adjusting attitudes, thinking, and planning for tomorrow. Independent, external objectivity and professional perspectives can be engaged through careful selection of advisors.

What follows offers some thoughts about how to let go and how to avoid a fatal fall. To do so, first consider the four basic notions of general systems theory: boundary, equilibrium, tension, and feedback. Advisors can use these concepts to examine present corporate state of affairs and to conjecture a future state—the Target Model of Strategy and Organization—which will be needed to adapt in an interactive/interdependent world. Finally, this chapter examines how to get there from where we are, what we may term learning to walk the tightrope of strategic transition.

THE PRESENT STATE: A BOUNDARY PROBLEM

Two strategic challenges are apparent for the 1980s and 1990s: (1) how to cope with external events such as international political entity restructuring and positioning, inflation, energy, military crises, environmental crises, world competition, Third World impacts and opportunities, surviving in maturing industries, renewed growth, cost competition, and keeping technology relevant, and (2) how to manage organizational transition innovatively in order to adapt to an interactive, interdependent world. Strategic thinking is required for both challenges.

In simple terms, the basic problem is that corporations tend to hang on to the traditional ways of *systems management* without fostering the innovative side of *management of human systems,* which is so important to transition strategy.

There are two significant strategic notions about the boundary of any organizational system. The first notion might be termed the shrinking frontier. If we think about what we already know and do as a field that is systematically cultivated and think of the universe of innovation as an unstructured wilderness surrounding this field, then, to innovate, institutions must reach and cross the boundary of our operational field to bring more land under cultivation, so to speak.

Looking at economic, social, or technological innovation from this point of view, we can, from the mathematics, begin to get a glimmer of the difficulties we face in trying to innovate continuously. When the length and width of the "field" are doubled, the area is multiplied by four, while the perimeter is multiplied by only two. Similarly, as an organization becomes larger (increases its perimeter), the proportion of its members who are surrounded by the familiar (the "area") increases even more. The proportion that has access to the unstructured wilderness of innovation opportunities decreases. Our frontier has shrunk. A complete corporate strategy recognizes this.

The second notion about boundaries is that our physical world and physical systems are energy-bounded. In contrast, our social and political systems are information- and knowledge-bounded. Just as the energy level determines the mode of organization in physical systems, the knowledge level defines it for political and social systems. But an even more significant point is that knowledge, unlike energy, is not subject to the first law of thermodynamics (the law of conservation of energy). Knowledge is not lost by sharing it with others. On the contrary, the knowledge level of a social system is *increased* by disseminating knowledge.

There is also an important capability in the creation of knowledge—a social (and political) system can constantly recreate its structure. A change of phase in the social system can take place through a reformulation or reconceptualization of the variables involved.

RECASTING THE STRATEGIC APPROACH: EQUILIBRIUM WANTED

This reformulation and reconceptualization of the variables requires sober thinking and strategic planning for the future. In planning corporate strategy we must seek to establish an equilibrium between (1) the conventional command, control, and communication hierarchical doctrines, and (2) the human, innovative side of business systems management. Corporate strategy must address uncertainty, disequilibria, and system dynamics both in the external environment and inside the corporate organizations.

This balancing is seldom easy to do, as this anecdote illustrates. The Boston Ballet, with the exception of a few traditionally popular offerings such as the *Nutcracker Suite,* usually loses money each year. In one budget review, the choreographer and art director wanted twelve toe dancers for a scene in *Romeo and Juliet.* The business manager's solution was "use seven and make them move around a lot." The management dilemma was how to retain the aesthetic and artistic "fuel" that drives and distinguishes the ballet, while still retaining management control of costs. This dilemma is like a mermaid, not enough woman to love, not enough fish to fry.

Nevertheless, it behooves management and the board to try to resolve the dilemma. If the strategic plan incorporates a balanced consideration of the behavioral side of the transition state, the organization will be in better shape to withstand turbulence from outside the corporation.

The classical strategic planning doctrine for corporate development is often expressed in debates concerning punctuated versus graduated evolution. We have seen this in the academic disciplines that articulate patterns of order emerging from chaos. In mathematics, for example, it is manifest in structural dynamics and in representations of growth cycles, maturing, and renewal. Cultural anthropologists and political scientists are watching networking movements and groups identified with political confrontations. The rhythms of growth, disruption, and revival of social transformations are readily perceivable in these network activities. Well-placed advisory directors can connect with these networks as part of their advisory role in scanning the environment.

Scholars are looking at issues of (1) structural change, adaptability, and learning of complex systems; (2) interactive procedures for conflict analysis and resolution; and (3) policy designs that recognize historical, cultural, and institutional dimensions and their strategic role in defining problems and implementing solutions.

The external environmental situation reminds me of Chinese baseball. Chinese baseball is played almost like American baseball; it uses the same players, same field, same bats and balls, same methods of keeping score, and so on. The batter stands in the batter's box, as usual. The pitcher stands on the pitcher's mound, as usual. He winds up in normal fashion and zips the ball toward the batter's box. There is one and only one difference. After the ball leaves the pitcher's hand, as long as the ball is in the air, anyone can move any of the bases anywhere! The result is that the context of the game is continuously changing. Uncertainty, some confusion, and some errors occur on the playing field. The behavior of complex systems and the development of techniques to bridge gaps between areas of "soft" and "hard" knowledge, between institutions, and between people are the most vexatious challenges before those of us who would strategically plan for the future of our organizations.

The International Institute for Applied Systems Analysis in Laxenburg, Austria (IIASA), is a nongovernmental, multidisciplinary research institution that brings together scientists from a network of 452 institutions around the world to work on problems of common concern. The IIASA advisory board, established in 1985, serves as a vital link with potential users of IIASA research results. It represents a forum for an expanded East-West dialogue among scientists, industrialists, and members of the policy community. The advisory board consists of sixty leaders from twenty countries.

Dr. C. S. Holling of the University of British Columbia, former director of IIASA, points out that the organization has demonstrated that, given a neutral environment, people from different cultures, ideologies, and nations can work together toward a common goal. I am certain that this is also true for large corporations where the stakeholders have different cultures, values, goals, and attitudes.

ISSUES AND NEEDS: TENSION AND CONFLICT

Corporate planning professionals are thinking about the fundamental paradoxes and tensions in corporate transformations from isolation to adaptation. These tensions and conflicts are much the same as those facing our world society.

Vulnerability of People and Their Natural Endowments

This is manifested by the vulnerability of climate and agricultural systems to high atmospheric levels of carbon dioxide (CO_2), the increased concentration of organic and inorganic elements such as freon, asbestos, acid rain, the threat of toxic substances, and the depletion of and alienation of biology, land, mineral, and energy resources. A corporate plan must appropriately acknowledge this vulnerability.

Strategic planners recognize that diverse managerial competencies are needed to cope with environmental uncertainty. For example, a threat condition favors control systems; shifting conditions favor adaptive systems; diversity in the environment favors internal differentiation of the organization to suit each market context. Uncertainty in the environment generally favors vertical and horizontal layering of the organizational structure.

Lags in Organizational Response to Interactive Environments

A series of major changes in management have occurred from the time of Frederick Winslow Taylor to the modern management period. Not until 1950, however, did we witness a serious business application of computers, although computers had at that time been in operation for more than a quarter of a century. In 1947 only 20 percent of U.S. corporations used computers for business forecasting purposes.

Today, most U.S. businesses forecast three or more years into the future.

Eric Jantsch, management theorist and historian, pointed out that there is a cycle of about six years in the initiation of different management innovations. In the early 1950s, corporate long-range planning, systems analysis (Wiener, Shannon), managerial psychology (Simon, Leavitt, Schlaifer), management by objectives (MBO, Drucker), and motivational Theories X and Y (McGregor, Likert) were introduced and remained in vogue for roughly six years. In 1956–1966 we saw the start of technological forecasting, planning, and orientation of functions along with early management information system (MIS) thinking.

The next six-year cycle (1971–72) embraced the systems concept of management, innovative organizational structuring, strategic (vs. long-range) planning, the strategic business unit (SBU) concepts, and the management of ideas or intellectual property. Among the more recent management innovations (1977–78) are networking, strategic management of technology, strategic management of mature business, intrapreneurship, alternative futures, environmental assurance, conflict-resolution mechanisms, and open systems planning.

We are now moving into a period where the systems approach is at the core of the next wave of management thinking. This notion is not new in concept but is new in the sense of implementation in business administration.

Resistance to Change

This is like a Hindu volleyball game. There is only one team. The challenge is to keep the ball in the air; the opposition is gravity. Our opposition is tradition, resistance to change, and the ability to manage ourselves and our institutions.

Management and Tolerance of Conflict

Conflict is purposely designed into the architecture of most corporations by the way the roles of board and management are defined. This conflict should be viewed as constructive tension, a positive dynamic in the life of the enterprise. It can stimulate creativity and innovation as well as provide a check and balance, if the conflict is not out of control or is reasonable considering the inherent ambiguities of corporate existence. Conflict is one parameter of a strategic plan.

Political Changes in the World

These include changes in political systems, boundaries, and alliances. Communications and business relationships are becoming truly global.

Given these crucial issues, certain needs are intrinsic to the strategic planning process for corporations in the future. Informed advisors can provide a valuable resource in respect to coping with the changes, constraints, discontinuities, and opportunities in the future. There are specific needs in response to this challenge:

Understanding the Complicated Patterns of Change

A change in phase in social systems occurs through reformulation or reconceptualization of the variables involved. As we noted earlier, the creation of knowledge enables a social or political system to re-create its structure constantly to fit the new knowledge level. This capability is true of corporate organizations, for they are social systems.

Our conventional organizational models feature hierarchy; they are goal-driven, rational, and mechanistic, and tend toward bureaucratic management of human systems.

New models are needed that include a balance of networking and a minimum of hierarchy. These new models require visionary, metaphorical human management of systems. They will function largely by information exchange both through lines of command and through human networking with and around the hierarchy and bureaucracy. The ancient operational tenets of the clans, guilds, and family models of organization are reappearing, often existing sub rosa in our larger organizations.

Understanding Dynamics of the Variables Involved

At least 200 orthogonal variables have been identified as significant in the management process and system. If we think about corporate development, we can consider this phenomenon from either a function, a process, or a systems perspective. Historically, most thinking dwells on the first two viewpoints—the functional and the process orientation of a company, including structure, that is, management of corporate structure. By functional orientation, I mean such activities as marketing, finance, planning, research and development, and human resources. Process includes such activities as organizing, decision making, auditing, monitoring, command and control, and information exchange.

These perspectives provide viable models within a set of relatively steady-state conditions. Because past steady-state and evolutionary trends have been interrupted, however, there has been a consequent symmetry break in management concepts, which not everyone has yet recognized. In great part this break occurred because of the uncertainties, transformation and restructuring we face in the future. In systems language, quite generally, the breaking of symmetries generates variety and leads to increasing complexity. We often lack both control and the systems to alert management instantly to every evidence of incipient instability and the management conditions that, according to past practice, were supposed to display equilibrium. Artificial intelligence/expert systems will play a part here. Strategic planners will need to understand artificial intelligence applications.

Development of the Knowledge to Use This Information to Release Human Creativity

The elements of this are the philosophical attitude and role model performance of top management, patience with the time and money that may be required in the functioning of an enterprise, reduction in hierarchical and bureaucratic constraints, and a revamping of motivation and reward schemes.

Understanding the Process and Role of Innovation

Innovation is like love, humor, or sex. Innovation, broadly, is useful change, and it differs from creativity or invention in that it must be adopted to be an innovation. It can suffer from overanalysis, overorganization, and overcontrol. Innovation is a uniquely human quality. Therefore, a strategic plan that does not address cultural conditions within the corporation that are required to foster innovation does not qualify for my transition model strategy.

An Understanding of Risk Analysis

Strategists are forced to deal with a mass of information that is often contradictory, incomplete, and even speculative. Cost/benefit analysis methods are available for comparing alternative futures, assessing the difference between uncertainty and probabilistic risk. The approach allows a net value to be assigned to each alternative, taking into account all the known impacts upon the corporation and other affected parties, dealing with this, and using alternative future scenarios.

Doctrines and Concepts for the Strategic Management of Various Functions

Technology, human resources, finance, and their congruence and integration with the strategic management of the entire corporation are some of these concepts. Only relatively recently have strategic planners forged a linkage between functional and corporate strategic plans.

New Social Geometry

New strains of organization are forming in contemporary human activity. Traditional institutional structures, processes, and concepts have failed to keep up with the demands for survival, interdependence, growth, and improved effectiveness of many of our organizations. While this is a normal evolutionary phenomenon, it needs special attention from top management, directors, and advisors.

Some traditional organizational forms are, in fact, mutating, and novel institutional architecture and social geometry are already evident. The challenge is to recognize these evolving organizational strains and capitalize on their effectiveness. In this regard, the "first in, best dressed" management system will have a competitive edge.

Some of the things that are happening are: (1) various stresses affect interpersonal relationships and performance of groups of people; (2) these are causing the formation of intricately connected, elusive, and perpetually changing (formal and informal) networks; (3) they take the form of coalitions, clusters, voluntary federations, and intraorganizational-owned systems; (4) in some instances, these are free-standing "centers" of intellectual, cultural, social, and technological focus; and (5) others are "tribal" group systems, matrix and collateral structures, cliques, or individual entrepreneurial initiatives. These new geometric or structural models of organization force us to reexamine the interpersonal relationships of people, the sociometry of the new organizations.

A Need for Sensing Social and Economic Traps

These traps arise when organizations start in directions that ultimately prove unacceptable, but cannot be reversed without causing even greater problems, for example, exploitation of limited resources, reliance on technology alone, disposal of waste, socially acceptable conduct of the corporation, and so on.

Changes in Culture to Adapt to the Future State

These are discussed in the following sections.

THE CULTURE SHIFT: BEHAVIORAL FEEDBACK

Large complex organizations usually include more than one type of culture. Strategic feedback from these internal cultures with their separate theologies should be accommodated in a corporate strategic plan. This is particularly true when striving for a change from an isolated position to a more adaptive, innovative target-model culture.

Four mental frameworks are useful here:[1]

The *structural* frame, which emphasizes formal roles and relationships, hierarchies, goals, technology, business administration policies, and controls. Strategic plai ning was born in this milieu and has a Pavlovian response to this orderly fiamework of thought.

The *human resource* frame that tailors organizations and interdependence of people, their needs, attitudes, and beliefs. Linkage between the corporate strategy and human resource management is lacking in many companies.

The *political* frame that views organizations as an arena of scarce resources where power, conflict, and influence are constantly affecting allocations. Bargaining, coercion, and compromise are routine. Coalitions are formed; solutions are developed through political skill and acumen. Strategic planners' use of alternative futures scenarios, computerized risk analyses, opinion research surveys are among the techniques that illuminate the political frame of strategic planning.

The *symbolic* frame, which abandons assumptions of rationality and treats the organization as theater or carnival. The rationale is that shared values and peer relationships as well as goals and policies can hold organizations togeviner. Organization is looked at as drama; improvements come with good actors and through images, symbols, myths, and magic. This notion is alien to the conventional strategic planning process. It is one of those new "balancing poles" we must learn to use as we walk the tightrope of strategic transition.

It is interesting that a 1980 study based on interviews with ninety senior executives at General Mills, Pillsbury, Exxon, Continental Group, Xerox, Pilkington, General Motors, Chrysler, and Volvo revealed an explicit rationale for leaving strategic pronouncements in a somewhat fuzzy state. The respondents preferred ambiguity in strategic declarations to avoid undesired centralization, focusing on otherwise fragmented opposition; rigidity that closes down options and makes explicit goals hard to change; and breaches of security on sensitive plans.[2]

The theory of cultural propriety suggests that a monoculture is wrong for most organizations. The organization of the future will have to have a blend of cultures. For example, part of the organization may have a *tribal culture* that permits entrepreneurial style, rapid decisions, and informal squire-archies with strong leaders. It has a spider-webbed center with radial lines of power and elitist influence.

Another part may have a *role culture*, with functional structure linked at the top by systems, rules, and procedures. This culture is all right when there is a steady-state business. The problem with role culture is that people strong enough to make it work are usually not strong enough to make it function as a support to other cultures. The role culture becomes an army of ants, and the grasshoppers must emulate or be eaten.

A *task culture* is sort of a commando unit approach. Expertise is the basis of power. An *existential* or *commune* culture is a flexible culture in which "stars" work for their own professional sake. Professional organizations use this culture where individual talent is at a premium. No single boss is recognized; a peer process based on expertise dominates. It is useful in research-type organizations.

An example of innovative use of different cultures is in the low-tech field of ocean shipping. The Norwegian merchant marine uses three organizational structures on its ships. The first is reserved for emergencies and is 100 percent hierarchical. Everyone knows what to do and takes orders. The second structure is used for special maneuvers such as bringing the ship into port. A matrix job rotation system is employed to achieve this. The third structure is used 90 percent of the shipping time. Hierarchy is put in cold storage, and small teams rotate the task of running the ship.

Inability to cope arises from cultural conflicts or the absence of "good" alternatives rather than from cognitive differences, conflicting objectives, uncertainty, insufficient information, or ambiguity in a choice situation. It has been pointed out that only individuals, not boards, corporate planners, or corporations have objectives. In this sense, the notion of conflict or organizational warfare never leaves the realm of conflict among individuals. This means that role conflict, role ambiguities, stress, tension, anxiety and the risk uncertainty spectrum, quality of working life, hierarchical differentiation, nepotism, titles, and political factors are representative sources of motivational forces or conflict between individuals. This depends on how they are positioned in a company-specific situation.

The challenge for corporate planners and corporate advisors is not only to identify conflicts (and opportunities) but to learn to lay plans for how to cope with them. The social scientist techniques can be helpful in dealing with this. Some of the techniques include the use of authority, responsibility, and accountability matrices; specialization; delegation, protest-absorption devices, political trade-off formulae; and the use of superordinate or aspirational level goals as a means of transcending conflicts and lesser goals. In even more abstract terms, the management philosophy and style will employ alternative ways of resolving behavioral and other conflicts such as introducing the notions of competing, accommodating, avoiding, and compromising confrontations, smoothing, forcing, withdrawal, and collaboration.

Four processes commonly used in conflict management are problem solving, persuasion, bargaining, and political structuring in which third-party intervention is often useful. These are tried and true processes with which most of us are familiar. Advisors should think about and use them more often.

OPEN AND CLOSED SYSTEMS

Strategic planners often tend to draw boundaries around the corporate domain with more certainty than experience or good conduct warrants. Examples are the boundaries between R&D and marketing, between financial planning and corporate objectives, between the corporation and its environment. When we strategically plan, we often use a closed-systems mentality similar to the command and control characteristic of the conventionally structured management system.

A closed system assumes that the organization is defined in terms of those who belong to it, and with that goes control over the situation by some authority system acceptable in any organization. However, the closed system is losing its relevance as the world becomes more interdependent and as external acceptance of the way corporations must adapt becomes an issue.

The context in which corporations will exist appears to be much more fluid and changing; as a result, adaptation and an open-system point of view in strategic planning seem to make a more appropriate model for the strategic planners' approach today. Our strategic plans should allow the corporation to adapt and cope with multiple, sometimes conflicting objectives and organizational goals as well as multiple interfaces with the environment. Open systems allow information, beliefs, intuition, attitudes, aspirations, value systems, and needs to flow continuously across any boundary which identifies a system.

While the traditional boundaries of corporate strategic planning are shrinking, they have also become more fuzzy. Beliefs, attitudes, and values may enter the strategic planning process and appear to be in conflict with the planner's traditional, internal rationality.

Changing social patterns in the environment have an impact on the strategic future of the corporation only if the system is open to such input. In the past, strategic plans have been concerned mainly with self-control of the organization and with competitors. The relationship with the environment was somewhat independent and a relatively stable situation prevailed.

Under new pressures from the societal environment and the ferment inside our larger organizations seeking more self-expression (an opportunity for the individual), we have to go back to the basics of general systems concepts to plan ways to deal with boundary, tension, equilibrium, and feedback. This can be done by change in philosophy, policy, and new social geometry to cope with interdependence, collaborative relationships, and objectives linked with outside and personal factors. The mechanistic closed system concept of a strategic plan or a company as an organization in a box (as listed on the back of the annual report) does not have much chance of dealing effectively with the future environment.

A NEW ROLE FOR STRATEGIC ADVISORS

The paradoxical nature of strategic success is that a corporation matures and develops certain norms and rhythms. It also acquires a history, identity, and life of its own. In effect, a corporation becomes a somewhat closed system. In order for new norms, beliefs, and values to become incorporated within the framework of existing company patterns, the system must become open enough to relate to the forces and changes taking place. This openness can be strategically managed during the transition time planned to move the corporation from an isolated to an adaptive state.

I believe that most corporate advisors are intellectually aware of and are ready for giving advice on strategic management of an organization in transition. Top management and boards of directors are often hung up politically, perhaps even emotionally, in suggesting fundamental "soft" changes that need to take place. They may intervene with the personal philosophy and career plans of the chief executive or top management or the attitude of statutory board members.

It's humanly difficult to retain the detachment necessary to make these behavioral changes and not upset the interface and relationship of corporate planning with the organization. Therefore, strategic advisors must be sophisticated skeptics, so that they can assess and make suggestions effectively. Line management, on the other hand, should not be skeptical. Managers must believe in change and have the will to carry out the responsible charge role under the broad concept of an innovative, strategic plan.

We began this chapter with the downfall of Karl Wallenda caused in part by his training that told him to hold onto his balancing pole to remain safe and balanced on the high wire. Some uncontrollable external forces in the form of a sudden gust of wind caused a "symmetry break" in the conditions under which he had to perform his high-wire act.

In walking the tightrope of strategic transition, corporations need to be prepared for, and to plan for explicitly, the uncertainties that will be encountered. Many contingencies will be out of company control.

An advisory board can be a comforting and effective resource to a statutory board of directors and top management. In order to achieve this relationship from the corporation's side of the connection, it is helpful to appreciate some of the perspectives a sophisticated board of advisors may possess. This chapter offers one slice of such advisory expertise.

NOTES

1. Lee G. Bolman and Terrence E. Deal, *Modern Approaches to Understanding and Managing Organizations* (San Francisco: Jossey-Bass, 1984).

2. James Brian Quinn, *Strategies for Change, Logical Incrementalism* (Homewood, Ill.: Richard D. Irwin, 1980).

12

ADVISORY BOARD PERSPECTIVES: STAKEHOLDER STRATEGY

When Paris sneezes, Europe catches cold.
—Clement Metternich, Austrian Diplomat and Chancellor, 1830

"When corporations sneeze, societies catch cold," modernizes Metternich's metaphor. It acknowledges both acute and chronic consequences of corporate conduct, although it may stretch the analogy a bit. Numerous parties may be impacted, prey to, or beneficiaries of resultant external forces over which they have no control. External advisors can offer valuable perspectives on value-laden issues that arise among various constituencies.

Components of our societies are increasingly interdependent. For example, the domino effect on the world's bourses after the October 19, 1987, Wall Street plunge commanded headlines because of worldwide reactions to potential business repercussions. Shares of six companies accounted for more than 50 percent of the $60 billion volume on the small Dublin Stock Exchange in 1987. Eight months after Black Monday's plunge, the Dublin Exchange was still more than 30 percent below its peak reached just prior to Black Monday's shock wave. The reason: each of the six companies depends on the international market for much of its profit. Each expanded abroad rather than rely on the stagnant debt-laden domestic economy for growth.

Corporate affairs are interwoven in our societies and sometimes reveal the most unlikely people in bed together. In mid-1987, the Communist party in Finland invested almost all its assets in shares of stock and lost a bundle when the October slump hit Finland's stock market. The party's stock picking was poor compared to Finland's share index, which outperformed other countries. As a result of this investment scandal, according to *The Economist*'s Nordic correspondent (June 4, 1988), the entire Politburo offered its resignation, the party leader quit, and half of the thirty-member staff were fired to save money.

Comparatively limited concern or spotty attention has been paid historically in Finland, Ireland, or elsewhere to impacts of other non-share-value manifestations of corporate conduct beyond the long-established codetermination role of labor in Europe. Impacts may be due to corporate structural or directional changes, expansion, contraction, or ordinary operational activities of a company.

One of the earliest models of institutional theory views institutionalization, per se, as infusing value and creating a complex of relational networks and exchange processes which have impacts far beyond the conventional corporate internal focus. The external components enveloping the corporate business world are numerous. Social, political, consumer, economic, technological, and ecological interests may be involved. It is difficult for a top management and/or a board of directors to stay knowledgeable and current on all of these external trends. A properly selected (and rotated) adjunct group of advisors can provide a unique and valuable perspective on the externalities affecting a corporation's future.

Next to share market value fluctuation and employment stability, environmental assurance is a current publicly sensitive issue. To illustrate, Danish industry is expected to be forced to spend twice as much on environmental protection as it does on research and development over the next few years, according to Otto Christensen, chairman of the Federation of Industries, as reported in the *Financial Times* of June 2, 1988.

Many individuals and institutions can have an indirect stake in various corporate happenings or in a corporate situation. For example, when a corporation restructures, or as with some large firms, merely shifts its weight around, many external interests may be affected. It reminds me of the story of the circus elephant that tripped and pulled the tails of three other elephants.

In discussing these issues in Belgium recently, I found that there is as yet no French or Flemish word for stakeholder, despite the nation's long sensitivity to and protection of labor, social, and employment linkages to corporate conduct. While such stakeholder consciousness exists in many regions of the world, the broader stakeholder concept has yet to be fully developed as a normative element of corporate strategy.

THE STAKEHOLDER CONCEPT

In times of feudal dynasties, the privileged class granted *stakes,* or a partial sharing of the agriculture yield of land area made available to tenant farmers, persons whose livelihood depended on tilling the landowners' soil. There were both positive and negative aspects for dependent farm workers. Stakeholders were also identified in those times as persons who held stakes for others until ownership was determined as in a wager or a business transaction. Later the serfdom and gambling heritage led courts to define a stakeholder as a person entrusted with the custody of property or money that is the subject of litigation or of contention between rival claimants in which the holder claims no right or property interest.

With further growth and complexity of societies, the stakeholder notion now embraces all those interests—including equity shareowners—that are affected directly or indirectly, positively or negatively, by activities of corporations and other economic institutions. Importantly, various classes of stakeholders include parties with no equity ownership, who have little or no control over the corporation but may be affected by its conduct or presence.

Roots of the stakeholder concept spring from historical ideas of Adam Smith (1759), Adolf A. Berle, Jr., and Gardiner C. Means (1932), and Chester Barnard (1938) with their socioeconomic research and writings. Apparently, the use of the term stakeholder in the management literature originated in an internal 1963 memorandum at the Stanford Research Institute as part of the corporate planning process involving systems theory, corporate social responsibility, and organization theory. Business school case studies (as at Harvard and Colgate) have focused on the stakeholder interlock between multinational corporate strategy and host government control over markets. The cases illustrate defensive restructuring by joint venturing in other national markets. They characterize issues of corporate conduct and stakeholder interests in the local national employment and economic scene.

Another classic business school case is that of the autonomous French national champion computer company, C21. In the 1970s, despite continuous government subsidies, C21 could not compete without economic subsidies against integrated multinational computer companies. In 1976 C21 was merged with Honeywell's French affiliate forming C26-Honeywell Bull. The French group required continued substantial government subsidies until late 1979 when IBM had a 30 percent share in the public market against C26-Honeywell Bull's 50 percent. It is significant that for years IBM has engaged distinguished nationals in various world regions including Western Europe to advise the multinational on its regional strategies.

The 1981 election of a Socialist party majority continued the support of the national joint venture company against foreign competition, demonstrating the pattern of international competition and the power and limitations of host-country stakeholder market control.

Restructuring to cope with this issue of multinational corporate strategy versus host government control has been employed in other industries: notably automotive (Ford in Spain); jet engines (U.S. General Electric, and SNECMA joint venture called Compagnie Français des Moteurs); microelectronics (MATRA-Harris Semi-conductors); and the European Airbus Industrie group. Stakeholders in the respective countries have benefited by the economic strength provided through international joint venturing.[1] The value of an advisory group reflecting the local national scene is obvious in strategic planning.

Bayless Manning, former dean of Stanford Law School, former partner at Paul, Weiss, Rifkind, Wharton and Garrison, and currently corporate advisor to Aetna Life Insurance Company observes, "Strictly speaking, a corporation is not an economic enterprise; it is a form in which some enterprise is organized. . . . In sum, a corporation is simply an organizational form, a legal carapace that surrounds infinite varieties of enterprises and institutions. That generalized, organizational form, not the conduct of the varieties of enterprises that adopt it, is the subject of our corporation laws."[2]

Manning positions the small groups of ideological critics of the American corporation as one species of corporate law reformers. This species takes as an immutable axiom the proposition that, for all institutions and for all times, the only institutional decisions which are legitimate are those arrived at on the basis of a consensus of all persons having an interest in or affected by the outcome. This is the stakeholder concept and calls for expert advisory input from disinterested, unaffiliated, objective advisors who have no conflict of interest or legal accountability in regard to offering their advice.

While social controls on conduct of corporations are needed to a certain extent, the role of the common shareholder as the ultimate constituency of the corporation makes a great deal of sense in Manning's view. Only this constituency—unlike workers, creditors, tax collectors, suppliers, and other stakeholders—the common shareholder plays only for the "entrepreneurial margin." Any arrangement that keeps a noneconomic activity of the corporation continuously going for purely stakeholder relationships redistributes the loss to others and burdens other parts of the economy.

The appropriate methods for dealing with trade-off decisions involved are political and social techniques including adjunct advisory councils or boards. The methods are not solely corporate decision rules for the long pull. This dilemma calls for better governmental and social means to be developed, rather than resorting to corporate law reform. Corporate leadership is the initiative needed to minimize social and political impacts. An experienced, outside advisory council or board can be a valuable asset to the chairman or CEO of an enterprise in determining the role of the corporation, if any, in effecting the changes needed.

In this regard, a normative strategy (described later) would not deal insensitively with adverse potential social or political impacts of corporate restructuring. Rather, responsible explicit advance plans would be made by corporations; for example, to cushion negative impacts on community tax revenue, provide assistance in relocating or retraining redundant employees, and ensure protection and cleanup of hazardous environmental plant emissions when or before a restructuring takes place. For that matter, any dislocation or discontinuity of corporate activity would be carefully considered in the trade-off decisions that must be made to keep the corporation economically viable and competitive.

OBEDIENCE TO THE UNENFORCEABLE

A modern stakeholder is one who holds that which is placed at hazard. In a corporate context this may go beyond holding ownership shares in the company. Thus, in thinking about a stakeholder strategy, it is necessary to be clear about the issue of legal accountability. We should not entangle the pyramid of power that governs our profit-making enterprises with those powers that govern nonprofit, charitable enterprises or governmental entities.

The courts are at the top of the pyramid of power of a charitable enterprise, whether it be in the legal form of a trust or a corporation. The board of trustees is the fiducial custodian holding legal title to the property for any charitable use. The authority and power of trustees to manage the charitable property for the public good is vested in their enfranchisement. This privilege is granted by custom, charter, and donative instruments. These say in effect, "the greatest good for the greatest number." Ultimately, what is "best" is the matter for the court, not the trustees, to decide. The determining adjudication is not necessarily what is morally right or wrong, but what is judicially acceptable or unacceptable.[3]

The board of directors sits at the top of the pyramid of power of a profit-making corporation. The directors are fiducially concerned, among other things, with legal accountability, generally described by the courts as the obligation of the duty of care. This duty is expressed in the form of the decision-making concept of the business-judgment rule. Courts have generally refrained from questioning the wisdom of board

decisions, even though such decisions may seem unrealistically simple when viewed at a later date. Business judgment inevitably involves economic and social risk evaluation and risk assumption. A
good outside advisory group provides a realistic sounding board for
assessing the risks involved.

These business judgments may involve "obedience to the unenforceable." Directors do what their sense of fairness, ethics, values, and
personal integrity tell them, even though they may not be obliged to
do so by law, regulation, or custom. Neither law, nor regulation, nor
free choice controls. Conscience, beliefs, morals, personal attitudes,
and ethics dominate. In board deliberations, ethics are concerned with
clarifying what constitutes human welfare and what kind of conduct
is necessary to promote it.

The ethical issues are perhaps those where accountability tends to
get most entangled in devising any stakeholder strategy. The board
of directors of a profit-making enterprise must possess the proprietary
mentality of a "good, business-like" approach. This often means making sensitive trade-off decisions between economic and social benefits
or impacts. The business purpose of a for-profit corporation is what
the board of directors is held legally accountable for. The for-profit
corporation is not an instrument for social purposes or social reform.
The directors are elected representatives of the owners of the corporation, not the general public. An outside advisory group can supplement the statutory board's concern for stakeholder interests without
assuming accountability or liability.

Consideration of any stakeholder interests of employees, customers,
suppliers, or communities where the corporation operates is not generally indicated in the legal accountability of the board of directors.
A sense of proper social responsibility of the corporation, however,
should prevail from a commonsense governance standpoint. Corporate conduct is an important issue in the public mind. Perceived or
actual corporate abuse of the charter granted by the state, as viewed
by the public, may only bring litigation, increased regulation, and
decline in business reputation, esteem, and image if social responsibility is not carefully considered when making business decisions.

The stakeholder theory rejects the Victorian idea of profit for the
owners as the sole or primary consideration. However, reducing this
theory to practice must recognize where the legal accountabilities
currently lie. Any realistic stakeholder strategy would acknowledge
the differences in role, power, and purpose between a for-profit business corporation and a charitable enterprise or governmental institution.

Given an understanding of these economic-social-political equa-
tions, a stakeholder strategic perspective will include social respon-

siveness as an element of corporate conduct. This inclusion may be driven not only by legal accountability but also "obedience to the unenforceable" or "manners" as cited by Lord John Fletcher Moulton, a high official in the British Munitions Ministry in World War I. This domain of human action is the sphere where we do what we should do, though not obliged to do so by law.

THE NOTION OF STRATEGIC PROPRIETY

The more recent sociological formulations in institutional theory that bear on the stakeholder concept, view active institutionalization as (1) a process of instilling value, (2) a creation of reality to a class of elements, or (3) even the notion that institutions are distinct societal spheres.[4]

Institutionalization in the form of a corporation produces common understandings about what is appropriate and fundamentally meaningful behavior. For example, restructuring of corporations in a suitable manner, which at least recognizes the existence and significance of stakeholders, is a strategic matter dealing with the societal sphere. This involves conflict resolution and trade-offs in social and economic responsibility. The parameters are three: economic-noneconomic human resource dimensions, ethical considerations, and consequences to relevant interest groups. There is not necessarily harmony among these various institutional complexes. But the logic and behavior of corporations that affect other factors of the overall system constitute repertoires available to individuals and organizations to employ in pursuit of their own interests. Outside advisors can provide an objective viewpoint on this complex of interests.

As we further examine this notion of strategic propriety, the control and management of corporations is considered beyond its economic dimensions. Unfortunately, such social, political, or ecological consequences are not always managed components of strategic action unless required by law as in the case of antitrust constraints.

Corporate social responsibility as an issue has become an activists' target in the last decade. The mood in America has some individual and institutional investors divesting their portfolios of companies that they do not consider socially responsible. A number of so-called socially responsible mutual funds have come into existence to meet the demands of more socially minded investors.

The Calvert Social Investment Fund is one with an impressive financial track record. Every potential investment is first screened for financial soundness. Then the investment is evaluated according to social criteria in which the corporation (1) delivers safe products and services in ways that sustain our natural environment, (2) is managed with participation throughout the organization in defining and achieving objectives, (3) negotiates fairly with workers, (4) creates a supportive environment, and (5) fosters awareness of a commitment to human goals. Companies doing business with oppressive regimes, manufacturing weapons, or producing nuclear energy are not acceptable to the fund.

The Calvert approach does not identify stakeholders as a group, but is clearly concerned with the social contract corporations have with society. This contract permits a corporation to pursue its prime economic function by governmental chartering of the company in the interest of long-term economic growth of the society.

The recent spate of mergers, acquisitions, divestments, asset stripping, and other restructuring has been too often dominated by self-interests. Proactive raider-restructurers give limited concern to strategic impact beyond antitrust constraints and economic benefits and losses. These raider actions often ignore any implicit obligations or recognition of the rights and interests of others impacted by corporate restructuring. Corporate restructurers of the raider variety have shown an insensitivity to the impact on other affected parties, despite the role of our legal and political system of chartering corporations in their social context.

Attorney Leigh B. Trevor is president of Stockholders in America, a coalition devoted to reform of federal law relating to hostile takeovers. He proposes certain reforms to restore the ability of directors to direct the legal system and repudiate the "blitzkrieged approach" to takeovers, demilitarize the takeover process, eliminate the dominant role of lawyers in the contest for corporate control, and acknowledge the complexity of the modern corporation. His viewpoint is that the American public corporation can no longer be viewed as existing solely for the benefit of trading profits on the part of short-term holders of its securities. Directors must, in response to a hostile initiative, be fully authorized to give fair and thoughtful recognition to the legitimate interests of all corporate constituencies, that is, the stakeholders.[5] A number of states have enacted such legislation, and others are considering doing so.

One reason for restructuring may be simply to overcome antitrust problems. This type of problem is especially acute and threatening when a proposed joint venture involves an American and a foreign partner who are otherwise competitive in the United States and overseas. Such joint ventures may affect various stakeholder interests. An advisory board with international expertise can provide a needed touchstone to the issues that may arise.

In 1984 when General Motors Corporation sought regulatory approval for a joint venture in California with Toyota Motor Corporation of Japan, the telling argument in winning approval of the Justice Department and the Federal Trade Commission for an initial twelve-year period was that the venture had a limited objective. The 50-50 joint venture assembles low-cost small cars which, in 1984, had a $1,000 to $2,000 cost advantage. GM was limited to purchasing 250,000 cars per year from the joint venture.

GM contributed sixteen people and Toyota, which managed the Fremont, California, plant, contributed forty people. The remainder were hired by the joint venture, which was capitalized at $300 million. Much of GM's contribution was the once-idle assembly plant. This responsible restructuring respected the properties. It created jobs, used idle fixed capital facilities, and had a generally positive stakeholder impact on a community and international trade balance even if this occurred as a consequence rather than a target objective. General Motors has used the advisory board concept for years, particularly in Europe and Australia.

The process of revectoring a corporation (or industry) may be perceived by some to rattle the cage of the status quo unfairly. However, it can be beneficial or destructive when viewed over the long term. Revectoring may violate or conflict with (1) social norms such as employee agreements, pension provisions, or local community and workplace customs, (2) environmental, health, and safety protection assurance, (3) political practices or realities such as sovereign rights, legal, or tax conventions, and (4) consumer or supplier interest caused by discontinuity or change in business relationships.

Certain stakeholders may receive no benefits—only damage to their position—from a corporate restructuring process. On the positive side, shakeup of a corporation may be necessary for survival or realization of a greater return to equity owners and benefits to other stakeholders for the long pull. Detached, objective perspectives from outside advisors can provide valuable input for the decision making and trade-offs that must be made.

The drive for competitive advantage is one major source of corporate transformation. The dominant criterion for success is total return to shareholders, including stock appreciation and dividends compared to competition. The impacts on employees, customers, and suppliers, divested and acquired businesses, factory communities, reshuffled managers, company bureaucracy, the environment, and corporate culture and style are often harsh from a human resource viewpoint. These components of our overall business system are seldom a formal part of corporate strategy.

Such a strategy is the ambition-driven transformation of the balance sheet by the restructurers. This is characteristic of American business pursuit of economic superiority of the private enterprise system. The drive for competitive advantage is, however, measured or traded off against long-term benefits and disadvantages not only to shareowners but to all stakeholders. The social accounting books stay open a long time. It often takes history to balance these books against the obvious economic gains and losses, which are primary factors in a corporate strategy.

A prime example of a controversial strategy is the transformation of General Electric, led by John F. Welch, Jr., who took over as chief executive in 1981. His personal objective was to prod the country's largest diversified corporation, with some $40 billion in sales, into acting like a growth machine. Advisory boards have been used by General Electric for years on a selective basis. The company's activities in Brazil, for example, have the benefit of the Brazilian advisory council.

Jack Welch trimmed the corporate staff from 1,700 to 1,000, installed eleven new managers in G.E.'s fourteen major business units, moved G.E. out of old standby businesses into broadcasting, investment banking, and high-tech manufacturing, and introduced an invigorated management development program at the Crotonville, New York, training center. Revenues have grown 48 percent since 1981, while return on equity of 15.6 percent for the twelve months ending September 30, 1987, surpassed the 10.9 percent average for companies in *Business Week*'s Corporate Scoreboard. However, G.E. still lags behind many of its smaller, more focused rivals. Westinghouse Electric Corporation turned in 22 percent return on equity, for example. The bottom line on economic performance supports the ambitious, tough, competitive G.E. strategy. Since 1981, total return to shareholders is 273 percent versus 126 percent for the S&P 500. The G.E. culture has changed dramatically to what G.E. Medical Systems' chief calls a "winaholic" team. I would bet the social side of the G.E. equation will follow the economic recovery in the long run.

An unchecked or unbalanced attitude on the part of those who control and restructure corporations can lead to adverse public reaction, litigation, regulation, or further legislation. In a free enterprise, market-driven economy the relocation or shutting down of facilities and the assumption of other political-social-economic risks in a corporation become trade-offs in return for potential economic and positional reward to the owners, managers, employees, and/or restructurers. Rules of the game suggest self-control of actions having anti–public interest consequences. Otherwise, there may be government intervention.

The target notion of a stable, economic-social system free from surprise discontinuities, disruptive enterprise restructuring, system changes involving dislocation of job and career futures, or business opportunities requires astute political balancing. This is constantly demanding and vexatious to achieve. Strategic propriety is one more perspective to be considered. An advisory council or board can offer an independent perspective to top management and a board of directors and does not have the vested interests of top management or the statutory board.

AMBITION- OR CONDITION-DRIVEN STRATEGIES

Restructuring is only one of the menu of corporate growth and life-cycle phenomena that are either ambition-driven or condition-driven. The ambition-driven species is the current target of public concern because of the surge in "hostile" restructuring taking place as a companion process to merger, acquisition, and divestment transactions. The ambition-driven strategy takes place under the beckoning banner of promising maximum shareowner value by achieving competitive advantage. Improved conduct of the strategist appears in order here. A "good," socially responsible strategy would include strategic components that explicitly deal with stakeholder conflicts and synergies no matter how indirect and peripheral they may appear to be.

Nationalization or privatization of business and industry are condition-driven species of strategic transformation. Political and social will create the conditions. Usually careful consideration of all stakeholder interests is the first order in such public consideration. How to deal with the transformation is a management problem.

In the early 1970s, the systems concept of management was introduced by scholars along with environmental concerns and the introduction of conflict resolution mechanisms. The systems approach to stakeholder interests is conceptually useful in developing a stakeholder strategy involving restructuring a corporation. Perhaps a major hurdle is that our legal, regulatory, and social norms, ethics, and policies have yet to catch up with the sensitivity, political realities, and issues needed to guide to corporate conduct for (1) this stage of world complexity, (2) the rate of change, (3) interdependency, and (4) interactivity of corporate and public interest.

There is need to also sense social traps, which arise when organizations start in restructuring directions that ultimately prove unacceptable but cannot be reversed without causing even greater problems, such as exploitation of limited resources, reliance on technology alone, disposal of wastes, and others. Asset reshuffling is often explained by the determination that operations are sold because they no longer fit with management's long-term strategy. Examples abound: NL Industries' spinoffs, Beatrice Foods Company's divestiture of over twenty operations in recent years, Borden's selling of over twelve operations in the early 1980s, and a host of other companies that divested over 450 distinct asset groups in the first six months of 1988.

Strategic transformation has rekindled strong interest by some corporations in their stakeholders. NCR Corporation most recently took an unusual public relations view of openly indicating that it does not think there is any fundamental conflict among stakeholders. NCR's chairman and chief executive officer, Charles E. Exley, Jr., addressed the First International Symposium on Stakeholders in Dayton, Ohio, on June 9, 1988, promoting NCR's image as a good citizen by offering the notion that the great wide world in which the company operates deserves as much consideration as corporate owners.

NCR is not alone in the American corporate world where directors of publicly quoted companies are becoming more concerned with corporate responsibility to a wider public than its shareholders. Companies currently seeking to serve the interests of their stakeholders are known as "vanguard" companies and include NCR, Control Data, Johnson & Johnson, Deere & Company, McDonald's, and Motorola. "Vanguard" companies start from the assumption that there is no general distinction between individual and corporate ethics. Professor James O'Toole of the University of Southern California's business school has recently written a book titled *Vanguard Management*. His research indicates that companies obsessed with profits to the exclusion of everything else may do better over a few years but not over the long term.[6]

Clearly there are conflicts of interest and differing expectations among groups of shareowners and stakeholders. An equity holder may perceive too great a risk over that of a bondholder for an investment in plant and equipment. However, the only direct clear legal obligation of corporate fiduciaries beyond that of obeying civil law and contractual constraints in general, is to the corporate owners who pay them. Thus, only a certain class of stakeholders seems legitimate, those with the long-term view that happens to coincide with management's desire to continue the operation.

USX Corporation's chairman, David Roderick, has been an eloquent champion of the national stakeholder's interest, particularly in his testimony in support of Senator William Proxmire's antitakeover bill. The main impact would be on corporate boardrooms where legislators, regulators, and public opinion have imposed on directors higher duties than representing corporate owners, that is, the fiducial responsibility to other stakeholders. Stakeholders may become disenfranchised by corporate actions such as restructuring.

In thinking about stakeholder strategy-driven impacts, it is useful to review the rationale and multiple reasons for restructuring (not in any rank order).

1. To alter ownership patterns; either public and private spinoffs, mergers and acquisitions, consolidations, joint ventures, and divestments.

2. To provide access to capital by going public with separate decoupled businesses; selling off business units, mergers and acquisitions, or in order to get favorable credit terms locally as in a multinational corporation's strategy.

3. To improve protection from liability exposure of a part of the business by separating assets into different corporations having different risk elements.

4. To change corporate climate, for example, to create an innovative environment by restructuring and reorganizing.

5. To refocus structure around a new business or strategy so as to minimize conflict with a prior business strategy.

6. To deal with tax and currency exchange fluctuation considerations.

7. To change the image of a corporation by transformation and reidentifying a new corporation.

8. To change the nature of the corporation, for example, into a holding company versus an operating company for business or legal purposes.

9. To deal with antitrust and/or legal constraints.

10. To cope with organized labor threats by separating operating units and labor contracts.

11. To downsize headquarters staff, decentralize, or centralize through reorganization.

12. To respond to market needs with a competitive advantage by providing better services and products via a completely separate corporate configuration of manufacturing and/or distribution.

13. To achieve flexibility of management, permitting different compensation policies, human resource systems, and career opportunities in separate restructured organizations.

14. To be responsive to differing sovereign nation hosts of multinational corporation operations, and to increase multinational corporate bargaining power by having independent corporate structures.

15. To control and protect transfer of intellectual property such as technology, and have access to local R&D through separate corporate legal entities.

16. To provide regional or national corporate entities with local directors and trustees for cultural, political, environmental, and business reasons.

17. To provide process mechanisms for separate joint venture arrangements, alliances, cooperatives, partnerships, commercial contracts, bartering, swaps, and others.

18. To respond better to competitive activity via a subsidiary in different countries where integrated foreign competitors did not initiate such competition, but where the competition could be hurt most. Example: IBM could not only fight the Japanese computer manufacturers in the United

States, but could also use its IBM Japanese subsidiary to attack in Japan. IBM is outstanding in its formal use of regional advisory boards in Europe, Latin America, and Asia-Pacific areas.

19. To achieve economic scale by specializing plants across borders in separate subsidiaries. A multinational corporation may be able to achieve larger production volume at a single site for a particular product or component. National companies are likely to have a small overall market and be unable to achieve economies of scale in a single location. A multifocal strategy competing with integrated competitors can provide both an economic scale and distribution in services in favor of national firms. The economy of experience for a company starting up a duplicate subsidiary has an advantage of lower cost of subsequent startups.

20. To establish export channels with independent agents and importers by altering a distribution system.

21. To provide geographical differentiation and market segmentation.

These are examples of strategic transformation with their impacts on stakeholder interests. While the corporate decisions on these transformations are the province of the statutory board, advisory councils can often act as an objective resource to the board and top management providing a stakeholder perspective on these strategic changes.

Yves Doz gives an example where an integrated multinational book publishing company coexisted with a local publishing firm. The coexistence is in such products as art books for which there is a small worldwide market and little material differentiation, but significant expense in photography, research, and reproduction common to any language edition. By contrast, in high school textbook publishing, complete differentiation is necessary across borders. There is no joint expense, but wide local markets for school books. An autonomous national company can prevail. An advisory council in the respective national markets can assist in the multinational strategy. Markets involving residential housing present the same issue and product life-cycle factor although the product cycle varies affecting corporate strategy and perhaps restructuring.[7]

Corning Glass Works is one of the foremost among the strategically driven corporations with forty joint ventures since 1934, only five of which did not succeed. Similar goals and values in the alliance, autonomy, and equalizing of risk were the key factors. The increase in business and employment resulting from these joint ventures is impressive and a model for responsible corporate transformation via the joint venture route. Corning Glass Works has five directors emeriti who provide an advisory resource to the board of directors. Corning also has had a European advisory board for years.

American Hospital Supply Companies emerged from a four-year slump in 1988 by extensive reconfiguration. The benefits in profitability, increased demand for investment, and employment despite only a modest increase in hospital admissions, are testimony to the positive impact on stockholders and stakeholders of restructuring responsibly.

The slide in hospital admissions began in 1984, hastened by tighter Medicare reimbursement rules. An upturn occurred in 1987 along with hospital occupancy rates which reached 64.4 percent, a 1.1 percent increase from 1986, according to the American Hospital Association. The positive impact on the industry was impressive albeit driven by economic forces.

Baxter Travenol Laboratories, Inc., Becton Dickinson & Co., C.R. Bard, Inc., Abbott Laboratories, and Johnson & Johnson were better positioned to benefit. Becton Dickinson's sales jump of 20.6 percent in fiscal 1987 to $1.6 billion resulted from its strategy in recent years of dramatic restructuring. Digitran, Endero, and its respiratory systems units were divested. Acquisition of Deseret Medical strengthened its hospital segment. Minority investments in Applied Biosystems, Inc., Quidel, Inc., Oncogene Science, Inc., Cell Analysis Systems, Inc., and Gibco U.S. Microbiology built a formidable presence in diagnostics. Becton Dickinson anticipates double-digit growth for the near-term future focusing on the business of health care. Impact on stockholders and stakeholders has been positive. Many of these high-tech firms gain advantages from advisory councils of distinguished scientists.

By 1988 Colgate-Palmolive Company had one too many businesses that needed substantial resources to be competitive. Electing to stay in consumer products, it used the approximate $1 billion proceeds from the sale of its Kendall Health Care Supplies unit to redeploy in consumer products and reduce debt. This restructuring followed two decades of diversification and subsequent divestitures, which brought the consumer products component to 75 percent of the firm's $5.6 billion business. In this case, the parent company prospered and retained the "entrepreneurial margin" of its core business, freeing others of its business units to compete on their own terms and with due regard for their own stakeholders.

STAKEHOLDER CONSCIOUSNESS

The overall philosophy of a stakeholder strategy involves three stages of consciousness-raising about stakeholders. One way of viewing this progression is to look at the broadening scope of the stakeholder concept which a company chooses to address.

In the first stage a company strategy can be characterized by the desire to tread water and stay out of trouble. Such a strategy focuses on immediate economic impacts of corporate actions on stockholders. The objective is to avoid unnecessary litigation and gives limited concern to adverse impact on stakeholders. This strategy is a nonformal one with any consideration of stakeholders lying with the lawyers and addressing only the necessary laws and regulations in the local environment. This stage deals only with those public constraints that leave no room for interpretation.

In the second stage the strategy complies in a more formal way with legal or regulatory constraints and public-social concerns. This approach includes a desire to manage better selected stakeholder relationships prescribed by company policy, laws, or regulations. The principal focus is on the stockholder, the employee, the environment, and community relationships. The strategy maintains a desired level of compliance with various social and legal requirements. It includes some recognition of potential impact of corporate decisions on various stakeholders however they may be perceived by the restructurer. Stage two is a strategy-with-compliance model.

There is a third stage: strategy with stakeholder assurance. The basic philosophy is that the full range of potential impacts of the strategy (and tactics) of the corporation is identified and carefully considered, and trade-off decisions are then made. This stage includes both internal and external components of the broad economic, political, and social system in which the corporation is restructured and addresses such from a strategic standpoint. Regulations and statutes impose certain compliance-related requirements, and thereby identify risks to be taken. However, there are other relatively remote risks and potential impacts, both beneficial and adverse. These may not be adequately covered by regulatory or statutory requirements or existing social norms but are also carefully recognized in the business decision process.

One of the purposes of developing a third-stage stakeholder strategy is to minimize surprises. Each situation is specific to the organization and its environment, both external and internal. Because the external environment is increasingly complex and hard to evaluate, new tools are needed to avoid the consequences of failure to act or consequences of uninformed actions. Various scholars and consultants have proposed more sophisticated approaches to detecting, defining, and understanding the implications of external forces and developments for any type of corporate activity. The impact of a sophisticated advisory council or board is one obvious approach to addressing these issues.

The basic approach is a stakeholder analysis for effective issues management. This is a logical, step-by-step process to identify all stakeholder groups and consider the reasons why a group affected might mobilize around any element of the issue.

The principal focus of "third-stage strategy with stakeholder assurance" is creating an initiative that embraces the perspective of the entire environmental system. The decisions are trade-offs in the light of economic, social, and political realities. The decisions acknowledge the fact that the corporation exists primarily as an economic entity and is not an instrument of social reform or means to achieve sociopolitical objectives.

This focus requires anticipating both the positive and negative impacts, as well as managing any risks involved in the process. Not many corporations take such a normative approach described as stage three. This strategy may involve the following sequence: issue identification, risk evaluation, risk management, and compliance with subsequent verification. One stakeholder analysis tool for effective issues management involves a systematic modular approach to detecting, defining, and understanding the implications of external forces and developments. The stakeholder analysis module uses a matrix approach to depict probable responses to each issue.[8]

STAKEHOLDER TYPOLOGY

In order to consider a practical and realistic strategy, it is helpful to view stakeholders in separate classes:

Class I—Direct equity ownership. These owners are securities holders, individuals and institutions having title to stocks, bonds, and other such instruments indicating direct ownership.

Class II—Indirect equity ownership. This class of stakeholders is represented by the pension funds, mutual funds, broker-custody accounts, trusts or foundation portfolios, and networks of investor groups holding shares in various corporations. An investor holding shares of such funds has indirect equity ownership.

Class III—Customer and client stakeholders. These are commercial entities dealing with the purchase of the organization's products, equipment, services, or real property; or acting as distributors, agents, licensees, debtors, or borrowers.

Class IV—Embraces all human resource components within and external to the corporation that may be impacted by a change in the nature of the corporation's business. This class includes the directors, top executives, managers, and nonmanagerial employees, retirees, and contract service employees.

Class V—Suppliers, commercial entities such as those providing advertising, tax expertise, certified public accountancy, medical, transport, legal services, plus suppliers who provide goods, real property, money, insurance, communications, and maintenance services, and others.

Class VI—Public services. Stakeholders in this class include those in the communities where operations of the corporation are conducted. Many supporting public services—utilities, education, protection, health care, transport, government administration—can be involved or affected by a corporation's conduct.

There can be a wide range of stakeholder influence on corporate behavior depending on the class of stakeholder. Shareowners, for example, have the power to change the board of directors and thus alter corporate strategy by electing directors with a different approach to management policy. Thus, in stakeholder Class I (the direct shareowners) there is some measure of owner control but low potential for commercial/social control.

Indirect shareowners in stakeholder Class II generally exert a rather low degree of influence except where large blocks of shares are held by certain investment institutions. Large institutional shareholders can exert an impact on boards of directors and thus affect the policy and philosophy of a corporation. The 1988 battle by the Italian and French Benedetti interests to gain seats on the board of the Belgian giant Société Générale is a case in point.

Stakeholder Class III concerns commercial customers who have no direct or indirect ownership control. But they may have a medium to high level of control from a commercial or political standpoint if the customers are, for example, state-owned as in many countries around the world, or where customers may be the primary outlet for a corporation's products and services. A new strategy, for its own sake, does not make sense if markets and customers are lost.

Stakeholder Class IV involves all human resources directly affected—employees, management, directors, pensioners—and all those whose employment by direct or indirect contract can be impacted by the corporate strategy. The 1988 controversy over the proposed U.S. Federal Trade Bill's requirement of a ninety-day notice on plant closings manifested employee concerns falling in this class of stakeholders.

Stakeholder Class V concerns commercial suppliers, those who are dependent on the corporate entity as a market. These stakeholders have no ownership control, but their behavior can have a medium to high impact from a commercial control standpoint. This occurs only if the supplies, goods or services are unique. Sourcing has to be taken into consideration when a corporation is restructured to avoid discontinuity due to lack of resource availability.

Stakeholder Class VI concerns the various public services impacted positively and negatively when a corporation changes its strategy. Plants and offices may be relocated, or sources of materials and services obtained from other locations. In the case of multinational corporations many of the problems of national sensitivity and good citizenship in one country are affected by a worldwide integration strategy involving shifting of assets and/or personnel to other locations. Multinational corporations are becoming more sensitive to this class of stakeholders.

STAKEHOLDER STRATEGIES

A project begun at the Wharton School in 1977 resulted in a stakeholder approach to a full-blown method of strategic management. It provides a framework, philosophy, process, and tools for implementing and monitoring stakeholder strategies. The issues raised, the analytical tools, formulations, and optional considerations apply to corporate strategists who elect to think about stakeholder consequences.

R. Edward Freeman, professor of business administration at the Colgate Darden Graduate School of Business Administration, followed this Wharton research, offering a stakeholder model of eleven categories of stakeholder groups as one way to analyze impacts of corporate activity including restructuring. These groups are: owners, consumer advocates, customers, competitors, media, employees, special interest groups, environmentalists, suppliers, governments, and local community organizations. Freeman's focus is on how executives can use the concept, framework, philosophy, and processes of his stakeholder approach to manage their organizations more effectively. This model is adaptable for the benefit of these restructurers serious about stakeholder strategy.

Freeman formulates strategies for stakeholders using four generic strategic programs: (1) changing the rules, that is, through government, decision making, or transaction process; (2) offensive programs of changing the beliefs about the firm, stakeholders' objectives, or adopting stakeholders' position, or changing the transaction process; (3) defensive programs reinforcing current beliefs about the firms' goodwill and intentions, linking issues to others that the stakeholder sees more favorably, or letting the stakeholders drive the transaction process; or (4) "holding programs" whereby nothing is done but monitoring of existing programs, reinforcing current beliefs, and guarding against changes in the transaction process. The concept of mapping stakeholder constituencies is also introduced.[9] Outside advisors can be of substantial assistance in this mapping exercise.

Former business school professor, Frederick D. Sturdivant, now senior vice president of The MAC Group, Inc., approaches stakeholder management in another, more pragmatic way. Because stakeholders often have conflicting needs and expectations, he recognizes that we are unlikely to possess either the ability or the will to find optimal solutions. Sturdivant proposes a four-step process: (1) objectively assess senior management commitment; (2) generate a comprehensive list of stakeholders; (3) shorten the list by grouping stakeholders based on similar needs and expectations; and (4) assess each subset's power. Step 4 is the disciplined, tough-minded sorting out of stakeholder subgroups on the basis of their power and, therefore, the degree of attention/responsiveness they will receive. "Ultimately, it is an economic concept; and, like it or not, unless stakeholder management can be cast as a process which enhances the economic viability and performance of the enterprise, it will never be a widely employed concept."[10]

One key criterion in corporate strategic management is the relative attractiveness of the environment along with consideration of competitive position, industry maturity, and level of risk. Comparatively little consideration or weighting is given to preservation or respect for the physical environment. Political, social, and legal environmental considerations are regulated to various extents. Ecological, consumer affairs, public opinion, and other stakeholder issues, however, too often appear in last place on the sensitivity scale except in certain developed countries.

Codetermination statutes in Western European and East European countries require labor or public officials to be represented on supervisory boards, enterprise councils, or other governing assemblies. This arrangement provides one mechanism for addressing employee and public interests in corporate or enterprise activities. As such it addresses many stakeholder problems in classes III, IV, V, and VI. The codetermination model has not gained much support in the United States. A guest multinational corporation can benefit substantially from the input of a host country advisory board. Many successful corporations have regional advisory groups in the various world sectors where they conduct business.

Scholars in universities, research foundations, institutes, and government departments are devoting increased effort to stakeholder matters in multinational and national company activities. A previously cited leading European scholar, Yves Doz, at INSEAD, Fountainebleau, France, has studied industry and multinational company strategy in the European Economic Community for some time. His findings are helpful in framing industry characteristics and multinational business strategies, and in identifying the issues in which some stakeholder interests can be considered.[11]

Significant issues are raised by a multinational company's integration strategies from the perspective of host governments and can be interpreted objectively by sophisticated regional advisory councils or boards. Governments may limit integration and force strategic considerations within local responsive rules. The key issues are:

1. Strategic decision control by internationally organized labor unions, such as in the case of French, German, Belgian, or Scandinavian.

2. Disappearance of national decision centers when multinational corporations integrate their worldwide strategies.

3. Market power of state-owned customers protecting a national industry.

4. Cost of citizenship in exchange for host-government continued license to a multinational corporation to maintain its integration. Sharing the "economic rent" derived from the monopoly power that integration creates is referred to as the "cost of citizenship." These costs may limit or dismantle multinational corporate integrated manufacturing and trade networks by differential regulations, taxes, royalty constraints, employee permits, or diversion of manufacturing or R&D facilities to distressed locations.

5. Financial transfers in view of local accounting regarding inflation, exchange rate, and intersubsidiary fund flow manipulation.

6. A positive issue arises in countries where training opportunities are few. Multinational corporate subsidiaries can be training grounds for good international managers. Restructuring to improve national responsiveness may bring training opportunities and resources to a host country. A company's competitive position must therefore allow payment to a host country (economic rent or citizenship costs), which involve an exchange of values between the multinational corporation and the host government. These costs are more or less explicit and cover, in most cases. stakeholder interests.

The stage-three level of stakeholder-consciousness, restructuring with stakeholder assurance, is clearly represented in socialist countries where, in theory, state ownership addresses each stakeholder class: owners (direct and indirect), customers, management and labor, suppliers, and public community services. In capitalist countries, the direct and indirect owners are usually protected primarily by securities laws and regulations with varying degrees of coverage and penalties for noncompliance.

Class IV human resource stakeholders are increasingly protected by both commercial contracts and some statutory or regulatory protection. Many other stakeholders in classes V and VI rely on negotiation, persuasion, public opinion, and the power of activists and political lobbying to have their stakeholder interests represented when restructuring takes place. Too often, however, this involves damage control rather than a preventive approach.

I doubt that management or directors can or should have to act as fiduciary to stakeholders in the real business world. Stakeholder capitalism as a rising power of ethics and accountability in corporate affairs is a seductive goal for those who are not in responsible charge of operating corporations. Moreover, it confuses legal accountability and the power of boards of directors to pursue economic goals with the power to pursue the broader public good.

The dismantling of corporations in the name of shareholder value—junkyard capitalism—can abuse the corporate system if only short-term economic interests are recognized. Managerial capitalism can be enriched by prudent consideration of realistic and practical stakeholder interests. However, the notion that legal or regulatory mandating of managers in responsible charge of economic-driven organizations *must* act in the interests of all stakeholders does not make practical sense for the long term.

I believe that the answer involves a change in attitude on the part of corporate boards of directors, management, and would-be corporate strategists. Together they can effectively consider and manage almost all stakeholder issues. This requires becoming more conscious of the ethical and moral dimensions of stakeholder interests and voluntarily mapping out plans to ease any adverse impacts which a corporate action initiates. Perhaps recognition of a basic teaching of Buddhism applies—the philosophy of interdependence. If something happens, then someone else is affected. Everything is linked and must be recognized.[12]

The role of the board of directors deals responsibly with the inevitable stakeholder conflicts to minimize negative impacts. R. Edward Freeman of the Colgate Darden Graduate School of Business Administration said it correctly: "Ultimately, the stakeholder issue must be resolved in the arena of distributive justice."[13] The sledding is rough, but the questions cannot be avoided. Advisory boards can, indeed, offer valuable perspectives that may not emanate from within a corporation or its subsidiaries and their respective local management and directors.

NOTES

1. Yves Doz, "Multinational Integration and Host Government Policies," in *Strategic Management in Multinational Companies* (Oxford, England: Pergamon Press, 1986), pp. 35–36.

2. Bayless Manning, "Thinking Straight About Corporate Law Reform," in *Corporations at the Crossroads: Governance and Reform,* ed. Deborah A. DeMott (New York: McGraw-Hill Book Company, 1980), pp. 11, 13.

3. James C. Baughman, *Trustees, Trusteeship, and the Public Good* (Westport, Conn.: Quorum Books, 1988).

4. For more on the many faces of institutional theory see W. Richard Scott, "The Adolescence of Institutional Theory," *Administrative Science Quarterly* 32 (1987), pp. 493–511.

5. Leigh B. Trevor, "The Blitzkrieged Director," *Directors & Boards* (Winter 1988), pp. 6–7.

6. James O'Toole, *Vanguard Management* (Great Barrington, Mass.: Berkley Publishing Group, 1987).

7. Doz, "Multinational Integration," p. 29.

8. Edith Weiner and Arnold Brown, "Stakeholder Analysis for Effective Issues Management," *Planning Review* (May 1986), pp. 19, 27, 31.

9. R. Edward Freeman, *Strategic Management: A Stakeholder Approach* (Marshfield, Mass.: Pitman Publishing Company, 1984).

10. Frederick D. Sturdivant, "Stakeholder Management: A View from the Bridge," First International Symposium on Stakeholders, NCR Corporation, Dayton, Ohio, June 9, 1988.

11. Doz, "Multinational Integration," p. 1.

12. This chapter is based on material that first appeared in *Corporate Restructuring: A Guide to Creating the Premium-Valued Company* by Milton L. Rock and Robert H. Rock. Copyright © 1990 by McGraw-Hill Inc. Used with permission of McGraw-Hill Book Co.

13. Freeman, *Strategic Management,* p. 249.

13

THE POWER OF ADVISORY BOARD NETWORKS

Some are born to connections; others work at it . . . if architecture is frozen music, then social networks are frozen gossip.
—Paul Barker, *The Guardian Weekly,* October 30, 1983

THE NETWORK ETHIC

The first two-thirds of my working life were spent in the international industrial sector—plant operations, technical marketing, the research laboratory, the executive suite, and "behind the boardroom door." The last third has been spent in contract research, consulting, and advisory board activities. That is to say, two-thirds of my work experience has been spent in relatively structured organizations and hierarchical cultures, and one-third in a relatively unstructured role with a diversified network structure and peer-dominated cultures.

The perspectives gained from these experiences underscore the value of networks outside an organization being served in a consulting or advisory capacity. There is an immense difference in the relative effectiveness and role of an ordered hierarchical organization and one empowered primarily by networking processes. How the two might be blended to meet the changes that are beginning to reshape our societal and business context is the subject of this chapter. An experienced and well-connected group of advisors can provide a unique perspective by tapping their respective personal networks of persons "who really know."

The blending offers an opportunity for advisors to supplement hierarchical and bureaucratic relationships. To grasp this opportunity, however, we need to think about professional networking and apply some of what we have learned in recent years from the anthropologists, behavioral scientists, and students of organization. That thinking, in turn, requires understanding the conditions and the changes taking place in the environment which afford opportunities for creating and applying network models in certain of our governance and top management endeavors.[1]

The principles of conduct governing an individual, a group or an organization—its ethic—are shaped by both the internal and external network relationships of persons connected in various ways or affected by corporate activities. Tapping these elusive networks requires professional effort. An advisory board is only one device to achieve this. It is a powerful source of information and experience.

THREE PERVASIVE CONDITIONS: A SHIFTING SITUATION

Our current and future environmental context can be characterized as one of changing turbulence. We can identify three significant components in this turbulence. The first is that most of our institutions are under attack. Government, education, business, the church, the military, our hospitals, and all large organizations are having trouble adapting to this turbulent context of adversarial activity.

The second major force at work in this turbulence is the flood of information, the impact of worldwide communications, and the political and social impacts that result.

The third force at work is more subtle. It comes from the decoupling of individuals and groups from large organizations in an attempt to seek identity and satisfaction through the formation of smaller groups— activist in nature, generally positive in objective. A new social geometry is developing, and access to these groups requires new connections.

Let's examine the three forces creating this shifting situation in the environment in which we must manage, govern, and advise our organizations.

Structure Under Siege

The conventional pyramidal form of organizing a company (or any institution) has often failed to satisfy the needs of the members of the organization. In many instances, the inflexibility of an organization keeps it from achieving its goals. The restructuring of the chemical, air transport, automotive, steel, petroleum, and financial services industries are but a few examples. The inability of many of our government organizations to cope with social, economic, and technological changes is another. For example, OPEC and the OECD are international entities under severe challenge. The EPA and FDA are prime examples of troubled U.S. agencies seeking to be more effective and responsive.

As a result of our structured institutional world being under siege, new strains of organization are forming in contemporary human activity. While this is a normal, evolutionary phenomenon, it suggests an opportunity to think about empowering human networks to compensate for some of the inadequacies of a hierarchical-type organization. At the governance and top-management level, a carefully selected board of advisors can help achieve this.

Organization, as we know it, is obsolete in the information society in which we now exist. Those in management who weave human networks have confounded both our own and our establishment's thinking.

These human networks are thriving while our staid and rigid organizations heave and struggle to be effective—or even to survive. Something fundamental is happening in organized society. The confounding is centered on the intuitive notion that somehow or some way networking may be basic to organizing and managing people in the future.

Networks are certainly need-driven and deliberate. We even sanction some of them. Tandem computer, Inc., of Cupertino, California, is a computer hardware manufacturer with a reputation for its enlightened management culture. The company functions effectively and routinely with almost everyone hooked up electronically. Tandem provides each employee with a personal computer. Direct dialogue is encouraged and practiced in daily business affairs. One goes direct via computer hookup to the person who can get something done. The normal hierarchy and bureaucracy is bypassed. Tandem supplements its electronic networking with a free beer and pretzel party every Friday night. All employees are invited to gather at the end of a computer-dominated workweek to engage in human networking. Management doesn't label these informal happenings as social networkshops, but that's precisely what they are. These optional meetings are fun-and-games time. They are vital ceremonies or rituals that have more symbolic significance than their informality would suggest. Four major functions are served by these parties. They provide the opportunity to socialize, to reduce anxieties and ambiguities, and to convey the message that the company cares about and values its employees. Exchanging information isn't enough. Some human, social networking is vital.

When Steven P. Jobs opened a multimedia extravaganza on October 12, 1988, to unveil his latest creation "The first computer of the

1990s," he hosted a crowd of 3,000 specially invited guests at Louise M. Davies Symphony Hall in San Francisco. The new Next Computer System launched an ambitious plan challenging his former employer, Apple Computer, Inc., as the industry's technological pacesetter. The happening was reported as the lead article in the October 13, 1988, *Wall Street Journal.*

Next had an advisory board of scientific and technical experts during the three years of development work after Steve Jobs resigned as chairman of Apple Computer, Inc. The advisory board members, mainly academics, were insiders during the development period and had a sensitive, confidential role in carrying out their advisory function. "You wouldn't believe the pressure we've been under to give people hints about the machine," stated Barbara Morgan, the director of advanced technology planning at the University of California at Berkeley. "I'm not sure I'd want to do this again." This case illustrates the obligations an advisory director assumes and shows why corporations are increasingly providing the same director and officer liability insurance coverage plus indemnification to advisory board members that they do to statutory board members.

The Advice Age: Deep Waters of Information

Those in the professional services business know the plethora of advice given most clients. Consultants, CPAs, and lawyers are becoming concerned about the quality of this advice. The corporate world is increasingly dubious about experts in general. This attitude has been carried to one extreme in the recently founded (1984) Institute of Expertology by Chairman of the Board Victor S. Navasky and President Christopher Cerf. The institute has 107 members dedicated to systematically cataloguing thousands of expert samples of misinformation, disinformation, misunderstanding, miscalculation, egregious prognostication, boo-boos, and occasional just plain carelessness with the truth, or simply put, lies.

At the other end of the spectrum is the recent brouhaha over the Commerce Department's concern about the massive giveaway of technical information to the Soviet Union. A hemorrhage of information considered damaging to the national interest is freely available under the American open system.

The dubious attitude also shows up in the burgeoning malpractice exposure and other liabilities encountered by those who give advice. These liabilities have reached a new peak in Britain's recent Insolvency Bill. Directors of companies that go into liquidation have two main fears from this bill. One is being found guilty of a new civil sin called "wrongful trading." This means letting the company keep going when a person "knew or ought to have concluded" that it would go bust. A person found guilty may have to make up personally for the company's debts and may also be disqualified from directing for a period of years. The other peril proposed was automatic disqualification for three years from all directorships, if a company goes into compulsory liquidation. This provision has been modified by parliamentary debate to refer disqualification to the judgment of the liquidator or receiver.

Corporations are also concerned about the need for better ways to handle advisory information so that it becomes a communication. Information by itself is of limited value. Only when it is received and absorbed and leads to behavioral or attitude change does it become a communication.

To sum up this point, we are in the "advice age." We have to learn how to navigate our corporations better through the deep waters of information. A sophisticated advisory board can be an effective clearinghouse for relevant information from external sources.

Undercover Movements

Informal social and business networks have always existed in and among large organizations and in society. That peculiarly British invention, the "old boy network"—or OBN—is a good example. The OBN is a club without premises, constitution, or life membership. According to the *Sunday Times,* it is not simply a clique, not quite an elite, not exactly a trade union, but with some of the qualities of all these alliances.

The OBN operates through contacts with a friend (originally from school) instead of through usual channels. It is a bureaucracy-buster, a queue-jumper, and red-tape cutter. Such networks offer the tribal security of an interconnected mesh of contacts not only in school, the military, business, government, and the professions, but in society in general.

Usually these networks have a vital role in the spread of organizational information culture. Recent changes in the texture of these networks have attracted considerable attention. The various stresses affecting interpersonal relationships and performance of individuals in organized groups are fostering formation of intricately connected, elusive, and perpetually changing (formal and informal) networks. They take the form of coalitions, clusters, voluntary federations, and intra-organizational-owned systems. In some instances, these are free-standing centers of intellectual, cultural, social, and technological focus. Others are "tribal" group systems, increased use of task forces, matrix and collateral structures, cliques, and individual entrepreneurial initiatives.

These new geometric or structural models of organization force us to reexamine the interpersonal relationships of people and the sociometry of the new organizations. These decoupled, undercover movements are usually based on decentralized power and personal growth, global cooperation, ecological harmony, and other "good things." They profess seductively attractive goals: resurgence of local leadership, self-reliance, and self-fulfillment. Networks seek to take back some of the power that has been relegated to impersonal governments and large corporations.

Undercover movements represented in the social and business networks with which we are particularly concerned are change-directed structures. They can affect future corporate effectiveness. They are the opposite of the OBNs, the elite university circles, royal alliances, private clubs, boards of directors and corporate establishment groups which still interconnect large numbers of people. In contrast, the emerging social, high-touch networks respond by weaving webs of awareness at various levels of activity. They are alive and well in most large organizations.

It's important to recognize and understand the network movements underway. Benefits can accrue in certain shifts from hierarchy and bureaucracy models of corporations to incorporate the more elusive network concept and in using the empowerment process of networking by management, directors and advisors. The challenge is not to stamp out the "new high-touch politic," but to engage it effectively within and outside our institutionalized organizations. A group of senior advisors with long-standing networks in industry, academia, government and international domains have built-in networks which can be accessed when a realistic perspective is needed for corporate purposes.

It is not happenstance that in a 1984 Arthur D. Little study of ten companies noted for their innovativeness, we found these companies to have a common, positive attribute of easy communications and human networking as an organizational style, both within and without the company organization. The art of innovation depends, in part, on the changing series of champions of the projects. The champions network directly with different elements of the organization and external environment in which they exist. Bureaucracy and hierarchical power flow are short-circuited by collaboration with others who really know. Innovative corporate cultures abound with human networking.

STRAWS IN THE WIND

Here are a few recent happenings that lead me to believe we must learn to better empower networking. An advisory board can offer perspectives on these trends.

A 1984 report from the International Monetary Fund presents a dramatic international comparison of the numbers, pay, and conditions of civil service bureaucracies. Britain has more bureaucrats in relation to its size, population, and living standards than any developed country (except Sweden). The peak was 746,168 in 1972, but was reduced following the Thatcher election to about 630,000 at present. Indices of government employees per capita (number of public sector employees per hundred inhabitants of developed countries in 1983) showed Sweden at 16.3; Britain at 13.2; Denmark at 12.6; Australia at 11.0; New Zealand at 10.4; Belgium at 8.8; the United States at 8.1; Canada at 7.8; West Germany at 7.7; and Japan at 4.4. These bloated bureaucracies are part of the force that telescopes individuals into smaller groups where the organization embodies the relationships necessary to be more effective. Networking exists amongst these governmental units and can be tapped by persons knowledgeable about such channels.

Hierarchy does not exist only in formalized organizations. For example, the human ecology in New York's Times Square is at least as elaborate and as fascinating as the ecology of the tropical jungle or that of a multinational organization. Different territories in Times Square mark not only different occupations, but different levels of status as well. A hierarchy exists.

Street people stake out regularly traveled routes where prostitutes, drug dealers, and bottle gangs preside. "Fixed spots" or "hangouts" are places where street people, such as male prostitutes or elderly male residents of single-room-occupancy hotels gather near subway stops or shoeshine stands. The third type of turf is the "hustling" spot, set up like a nomad's camp by those running con games, selling phony jewelry, shoplifting, or pursuing a host of activities that require good street sense and an aptitude for calculating the risks of arrest, injury, or being taken in by someone else's "game."

Each of these territories has hierarchical levels of occupational status. Street people have a hierarchy in which the mentally ill and alcoholics occupy the bottom rung, young male hustlers are farther up, and pimps who set up shop in bars—safe from arrest and other dangers outside—are an admired elite at the top of the street world hierarchy.

Each of these status groups shares norms and rituals learned in prison and in the ghettos. When the Times Square redevelopment plan cleans up this area, the street people will relocate to other areas, but their hierarchies will survive as a socially established ordering of human relationships.[2]

Peru's free market overturns the prevailing wisdom that capitalism is a dirty word in Latin America, and that an imported economic model helps only the rich and holds no promise for the poor. Over a two-year period, a study group accumulated 22,000 documents chronicling the extent of an informal sector. The economy is shown not to be the province of the upper class. Illegal busses provide 85 percent of Lima's public transportation, and illegal taxis provide 10 percent more. Underground activity accounts for 90 percent of the clothing business and 60 percent of housing construction. Sophisticated structures up to six stories high are built by the underground network of construction firms and workers. While bribery is part of the system and access to capital markets is denied, crude loan pools with high premium rates substitute.

The message is that the people of Peru have already chosen a market economy without foreign interference and despite the hindrance of their own government. The Peruvian government has a hard choice between honoring the existence of these powerful underground networks or continuing to carry out the strange charade in which millions of the poor are outlawed from earning an honest, productive living.[3]

For a company operating in Peru or considering it as a host country, knowledge of the way Peru's economy really works can determine success or failure of a venture. Assessing this condition via the services of an advisory board member who is tuned into this situation is one way to help determine a strategic approach.

With the changes in our basic value systems, a strong drive toward egalitarianism is resulting from the growth and affluence of developed nations. Both individuals and institutions are searching for a stronger sense of identity. The human potential—personal and spiritual—network is peculiarly American, and a child of the postindustrial information age. Examples of such networks are the American Humanist Association, Cooperative Communities of America, Women Outdoors, Esalen Institute, North American Network of Women Runners, World University, and Society for Human and Spiritual Understanding.

The social reform networks have arisen because of social complexity, social pressures and political imperatives. Examples of these networks include the National Indian Youth Council, NAACP, ACORN (Association of Community Organizations for Reform Now), SANE (a citizen's organization for a sane world), Institute of World Order, MNS

(Movements for a New Society), Institute for Social Justice, Amnesty International, and Common Cause.

These are only a few "straws in the wind" of the shifting situation in which we find ourselves. An understanding of professional networking offers a partial solution for dealing with this complexity and rapid pace of change.

ANTHROPOLOGY AS A PATHWAY

Sociologists and anthropologists have used the concept of networks and networking as a metaphor for over a hundred years. It was not until 1965 when anthropologists were studying charismatic movements in churches and black power that other movements (such as civil rights, environmental, antiwar) were found to show similar patterns of behavior.[4]

These patterns can be used constructively in corporations, other institutions, and affinity groups such as professional organizations to improve creativity, motivation, individual fulfillment, and performance effectiveness—if the nature and dynamics of the change-directed networks are understood.[5]

Universities, learned societies, and consultants are trying to develop this understanding through research on social networks and networking processes. The goal of this research is to develop algorithms, software, new applications, and relevant data sets. For example, a recent social network conference produced papers on emergent network properties, statistical network models, organizational networks, social networks, and ethical relations, exchange theory, network analysis, and historical research, social support networks, communications and computer networks, network measurement and other network-related topics. Corporate advisors who understand the dynamics of networking can be a special asset to a board or top management.

We have discovered that seven major channels of linkage make social and business transformation networks function: (1) overlapping membership from different groups; (2) linkage based on friendship and personal relationships which derive from shared values and visions; (3) exchange of leadership among groups; (4) geographic movers who spread the word; (5) conferences, seminars, colloquia, telecommunications, and joint activities of networkers with a common interest; (6) grapevine communications; and (7) split-level ideology that forms the glue with a few common themes and a wild array of variations. Networking may be free-forming, free-standing, personal, spontaneous, casual, self-organizing, overlapping, and ever-changing among individuals regardless of organizational role, structure, or process. A network is a people-power line and a communications pathway. Networks empower individuals rather than organizations.

The chief products of networking are information processing, pattern recognition, and societal or organizational learning. The importance of computer and telecommunications technology is obviously vital in social and business networking.

The process of networking is a changing matrix of weak ties. These consist of:

Relationships, shared friendship, trust, and values.

Fuzziness, indistinct borderlines between interests and stages of development.

Nodes and links, entries or receiving points that serve to link and convey information.

Balanced worth of individual and subgroups.

Coherence of some critical values that bind network members versus reward and punishment systems.

The systematic study of networks and the process of networking have shown certain virtues and limitations as well as paths from one attitude or culture to another. These were only dimly realized before.

Informal but powerful groups, attitudes, beliefs, values, degrees of freedom and barriers against, and options for conducting our affairs can be identified. These can be empowered or managed to a better degree by networking. Networks can thus improve organizational effectiveness, innovativeness, and creativity. The challenge is to learn to identify, empower and guide (rather than control) informal and emergent networks without overorganizing or institutionalizing the network. Top managers need to know about these processes. A corporate advisor knowledgeable about such mechanisms can be a unique asset.

Another feature is that informal networks are seldom independent centers of power. Thus, they are very dependent on social and business context. This means special management attention must be paid to corporate climate and texture, company philosophy, organizational structure, management and governance processes, ethics, values and general company culture.

Cliquishness, elitism, power groups, "the establishment," and conservative political characteristics are common in many informal networks. These attributes may be counterproductive to attempts to change complex organizations or systems. Networks need to avoid or minimize these typical attributes if they are to cope with hierarchy and bureaucracy.

Columbia University's sociology professor Ronald S. Burt suggests one network theory of action. He believes that we all use our resources to realize our personal or group interest. We seek to do our thing. A second belief of his is that we all pursue our self-interests in a social context. The intersection of these beliefs provides a premise for structural theory of action in the network model.

The belief in purposive action postulates that each person has the right to the products of one's own private property whether in the form of goods or labor. In turn, this right is solely controlled by the property owner. Any other actors, therefore, value this property as a resource rather than a right. Given this idealized relationship, each of us is motivated to improve our well-being. Economists would say we act to improve our utility. We then evaluate the utility of alternative actions and perform those we perceive as yielding the greatest reward; that is, enlightened self-interest. Sociologists call this empowering our networks.

Social constraints can be modeled in three ways. The first is through the status of individuals and organizations—power, prestige, and position—and the role sets interconnecting these as they form a network of social structure. The second model is that of a network or individual self-interest. And the third model concerns the autonomy with which each of us has to act without constraint, in other words, our degrees of freedom.

Burt's structural theory of action suggests that actors can take action independently using their resources solely to realize their self-interest. Books have been written on the merits of "looking out for #1." However, since we do not exist independently in organizations, a more normative perspective calls for an interdependent evaluation by each of us as a function of the socializing process. The action is ideally motivated by values and beliefs and by our being part of an organization.

The structural action theory of networking and networks bridges the extremes of such atomistic and normative behaviors. Thus, power and autonomy together underlie transformational change and social structure. The balance of these opposing notions may be powerfully achieved by multiple networking around and along with hierarchy and bureaucracy. There must be a quid pro quo for those doing the networking, so that the institution is not destroyed. A mutually beneficial exchange of information or property takes place within a social structure of an organization (and in spite of it).

THE NETWORK ETHIC IN ADVISORY PRACTICE

A new characteristic is manifest in many organizational endeavors whether in counseling, operating, or governing an organization. This *network ethic* is a useful, professional perspective on how to get things done in a complex, hierarchical, bureaucratic society. Our society is struggling to be more effective and adaptive in an environment of changing turbulence. The purposes of networking illuminate this advisory network ethic:

1. Networkers can accumulate influence or power by control of information and by learning. Hierarchy can mean a monopoly of information with the leader, leading in turn to a decision monopoly. Hence inequality of opportunity occurs because the leader does not have the same regard for everyone, and not all pieces of information are equally important. Network relationships with direct person-to-person communication bypass these barriers.

2. Common interests and sharing of common ideology, a common position in a social or business situation can build a power base.

3. Personal chemistry, friendship, fellowship, trust, respect, and peer relationships are powerful forces in human situations.

4. A common response to leadership—an outlet for personal enthusiasm—is a force enhanced by networking.

5. Achievement of adequate communication density across interfaces, between people, is the result of the connecting power of networks.

6. Networks can be viewed as culture carriers or developers. For example, the diplomatic corps carry their country's culture flag professionally to all embassies and offices around the world.

7. Networking can be considered a precursor or forebearer of formal organization. Once a formal structure is created, the network disappears unless special arrangements are made to preserve it. Smart managers leave networks alone as much as possible and consider them lubricants for the formal organizational structure.

We must learn how to think networks and networking. Such thinking requires that we expand our mind-set from the hierarchical, bureaucratic model of the past (the Orwellian-type structure and order) to include the elusive network model (the Renaissance perspective) in which the individual is the center of power even though this person must exist in some type of ordered context.

If we do not recognize this network ethic, we may find ourselves like the group of South Pacific islanders in the late 1940s. On an abandoned military airstrip, these primitive Melanesian islanders marched in formation before a control tower wearing tattered uniforms. In the tower, a man wearing earphones carved of wood spoke into a wooden microphone and made marks on a clipboard. Other islanders squatted patiently searching the skies, watching and waiting for a silver airship to arrive and deliver cargo. These people in Papua New Guinea believed that if they went through the same motions as soldiers did during World War II, it would call down bounties from the sky.

The anthropologists who studied these "cargo cults" have also offered us a way to deal with our current changing turbulence and increased complexity for our contemporary institutions. Social networking can provide people-power and bureaucratic bypass—that is, different patterns of thought and action to make our organizations more effective in our complex society.

The relatively recent discovery of the technical nature, dynamics and significance of social (high-touch) networks within and outside our institutions and in society, in general, previews how progressive corporate organizations will learn to work more effectively in the future. Research and development departments, human resources, marketing, and corporate relations functions are obviously beneficiaries of networking applications.

NETWORKS AND ADVISORS

Here are some possible uses of networks that could interest corporate advisors:

1. Remedying particular organizational problems, for example, lack of innovativeness, bureaucratic barriers, pockets of discontent, misunderstandings, political cliques.
2. Transforming public, membership, or employee opinions toward different value systems, social or political orientations, for examples, consciousness-raising on global problems, acid rain, Third World connections, and others.
3. Inter-institutional coalition building. Work done at Arthur D. Little on strategies for health services, clinics, hospitals, joint cooperation on university/college consolidations to avoid duplication, excessive investment, and destructive competition are examples where networking is key.
4. Achieving organizational change is a natural process for networking. Moving a company culture from an existing state to a target-model state can be facilitated by human networking.
5. Strengthening and empowering professional societies through peer communications, scheduled events, meetings, publications, and the building of status roles.
6. Miscellaneous uses in the fields of communications, morale building, and consensus building.

7. Tapping outside expert resources not readily available to the top management or statutory board.

Innovative leaders and others will explore this intriguing dimension of human resource management for their corporations. It is important to track the trends of emerging research and development in social networking and the phenomenon's impact on our corporate organizations. Progressive corporations are constantly seeking improved relevance to their environment and their stakeholders. To do this, companies need to improve the physics of their organization plus the climate and texture of company culture which contribute to creativity and innovation.

In conclusion, let me characterize the *network ethic* as a working hypothesis, as follows:

1. A new paradigm is emerging in the contemporary form of social and business networking, that is, personal empowerment and individual growth rather than subservience. These individual "nodes" are not easily accessed. Special effort is needed to tap these resources.

2. The driving forces of this paradigm are changes in basic value systems. The search for the human potential manifest by social reform and transformational movements has created numerous activist social networks. These are self-organizing, overlapping, open-ended and fluid. They bypass hierarchy and bureaucracy and are human-centered, information-intensive, and often idealistic. They are usually disenfranchised from the establishment.

3. This decoupling process can be variously interpreted as a retreat from complexity, a return to tribal security, a change-directed restructuring, a personal search for fulfillment with more degrees of personal freedom, entrepreneurship, and creativity; or management sensitivity to that which "should be tolerated to promote health" that cannot in any case be literally controlled.

4. Elegance in management traditionally implies symmetry—a power-driven hierarchy with ordered command, control, communication and surveillance. The conventional corporate way of life is the only option offered to employees despite inevitable conflicts with personal values and goals as these change with personal experience, maturity, economic situations, and individual central life interests. Networks can relieve some of this tension without destroying the necessary organizational structure.

5. An inelegant dysfunction often results with individual and corporate career conflicts. This is reflected in reduced organizational effectiveness at a time when external stress, pressures, and complexities also challenge management of most institutions.

6. An opportunity may exist to combine an overlay (or underlay) of networking concepts and practices with the hierarchical, bureaucratic paradigm of traditional organizational functioning.

7. The trick is to manage the relationship between insensitive, power-driven hierarchical models and individual-centered networks. This calls for a new education or learning about empowerment models for both individuals and organizations, and means to readily tap these sources of information.

Anthropology has shown us a way to achieve a balance of dealing with hierarchical, bureaucratic and networking organizations by interweaving both of these model structures and empowering them when appropriate. It also shows ways to access far-flung centers of information not readily accessible by conventional business channels. Engaging well-positioned advisors in various external networks can extend a corporation's access to valuable perspectives. Networking is perhaps the ultimate in local autonomy action. It is a one-on-one theory of action and it is becoming a recognized model in organizational and advisory work.

Austria's highest military decoration—the Order of Maria Theresa—is reserved exclusively for officerships for those who turned the tide of battle by taking matters into their own hands and actively disobeying orders. Maria Theresa can teach us how to turn the battle tides of complex organizational work by empowering the hidden networks that are "waiting in silence for the moment of expression."[6] Advisory directors can be of significance in accessing their networks outside the corporation.

NOTES

1. See H. Igor Ansoff, "Conceptual Underpinnings of Systematic Strategic Management," *European Journal of Operational Research* 2, 19 (1985), for an interesting discussion that guided this thinking on the environmental changes underway.

2. Vernon Boggs and William Kornblum, "Symbiosis in the City," *The Sciences* (January/February 1985), pp. 25–50.

3. Claudia Rossett, "How Peru Got a Free Market Without Really Trying," *Wall Street Journal* (January 27, 1984).

4. Virginia Hine, "The Basic Paradigm of a Future Socio-Cultural System," *World Issues* (April/May 1977); also coauthor with Luther Gerlach of *People, Power and Change* (New York: Bobbs-Merrill, 1970); and of *Life Way Leap: The Dynamics of Change in America* (Minneapolis: University of Minnesota Press, 1972).

5. Portions of this chapter have been adapted from the author's *Corporate Networking: Building Channels for Information and Influence* (New York: The Free Press, Macmillan, Inc., 1986).

6. Michel Foucault, *Les Mots et les Choses,* translated as *The Order of Things, An Archaeology of the Human Sciences* (New York: Random House, Vintage Books Edition, 1973; original edition 1966 by Editions Gallimard), p. xx.

14

ADVISING THE FAMILY BUSINESS BOARD

A fund-raising letter from the Niagara Lutheran Home in Buffalo said in part: "The building and grounds committee has presented a rough estimate of $75,000 for needed repairs to the board of directors." Perhaps adding some outside directors or advisors, at less cost, could remedy this situation. I know from many years as an active director and advisor to boards in both family and public companies that experienced outsiders can often perform preventive maintenance on the hidden stresses inherent in governing a business. In family companies in particular these stresses stem from the ever-existent clash of goals and values of individual family owners also serving as directors and managers.

The outside director or advisor can perform a distinctive service by enabling the board of a family business to give the right priority to the important things to worry about. Effective outsiders provide objectivity in key relationships, transitions, and interactions. Closely held corporation boards usually have closely knit membership, often family members, the family attorney or banker, other relatives, and long-time friends. This makes up a coopted group which, at times, is unable to effectively deal with the business issues objectively. This hangup is due to the social contracts that implicitly exist between board members. Recently, I was asked to serve as an advisory director to such a family-dominated firm's board. After a lengthy get-acquainted exposure to allay fears of the family directors that such outsider contribution to their governance process would be acceptable and professionally offered, an arrangement was made that proved very helpful over a three-year crisis period.

The conflicts between emotional, social, and economic attitudes, be-liefs or expectations of family board members are normal albeit vex-atious human problems. They are complicated by role ambiguity; family politics, power struggles, and conflicts of interest; family tribal loyal-ties, bonds, and sibling rivalries; different attitudes toward risk, so-cial accountability and long- versus short-term gain; dynastic and ne-potistic tendencies in matters of succession, organization, and professional management.[1]

PERSPECTIVE OF A NONFAMILY DIRECTOR

Many family business boards exhibit the Garden of Eden syndrome: Since we live there, we can't afford to be objective. Many also believe that being in a family boardroom is a game the whole family can play. Some act as though the only real purposes of a family board are to exclude others from membership, to fulfill a statutory requirement, and to husband the family jewels.

Such an insular, inexperienced view can lead to debilitating im-pacts on company and family assets and upon personal relationships. If you are invited to be on, or advise, a family business board, be sure that it's not the type of situation where directors shake hands and then go off and count fingers.

Of course, many, if not most, family business boards are very effec-tive. They are able to cope with the conflicts and stresses inherent in the nature of family relationships and business goals, regardless of the size of the enterprise. Such boards often have outside directors defined as peer-respected, independent individuals who have no direct or indirect connection with the firm or the family other than serving as a director.

Closely held and family company boards of directors march to dif-ferent drummers than do publicly held company boards. The identity, location, and "musical training" of the family board member "drum-mers" are often not well established or perceivable outside family cir-cles.

Becoming and remaining an effective, well-respected outside advis-ory director to a family business board requires some doing. Personal gratification and trusting relationships can be rewarding. But you have to like to work with tension-filled, emotional human relationships as well as with business excitement. This reminds me of graffiti I saw in London, "Work for the Lord. The pay is terrible but the fringe benefits are out of this world!"

Sometimes one has to be tolerant about the length of time a culture change takes in a family business boardroom. No matter how little impact you expect from your advice and presence on a family business board, it's likely you will be disappointed. Except in crisis, changing family attitudes, values, and goals take a long educational and annealing period of time. A trusted, competent outside advisory director can sometimes provide the glue that holds the board and family firm together during such metamorphosis.

Distinctive Governance Roles

While there are general criteria for outside statutory directors of both public and family companies, there are also criteria that are family-firm specific. No two family business problems or opportunities are alike. These criteria are also relevant to the advisory director role.

Conventional criteria for appraisal of governance for all closely held corporations encompass the well-articulated criteria for boardworthiness set forth generally for corporations in the Model Business Corporation Act and the *Corporate Director's Guidebook* by John M. Nash and Alexandra R. LaJoux (1988). These cover the standards of conduct, duty of loyalty, duty of care, and orientation of new directors. The responsibilities and attributes of individual independent directors are also set forth.[2] Over and beyond these legal and regulatory criteria, I believe there are special roles an outside advisory director can play on a family business board. These are the role of:

Arbitrator—capable of counseling on family disagreements, hostilities, and other emotional stresses or conflicts if called upon to serve in such a role.

Gap-filler—when owners lack time or expertise to cope with the difficulties of managing a family firm in a dynamic environment.

Resource—to the board or top management, supplementing internal resources available and providing freedom from group-think, concinnity, and lack of objectivity. Such complications can occur when the advocates of a decision are involved in its justification or are beneficiaries of the action.

Father confessor—Family owner-director-managers occasionally need someone to talk to confidentially and to share concerns, hopes, or troubles. A good listener who is trusted can be a stress reliever or personal counselor.

Devil's advocate—Family firm boards need an occasional champion of the worst cause or case for the sake of argument. Defects in the evidence or presentation can be properly outlined by a skilled outside advisory director.

Catalyst—An experienced outside advisory director can be a change agent for the board or the family company itself by provoking the need for significant change in conduct or objectives of the enterprise. Going public, making a divestment or acquisition, or change in top personnel are examples of catalytic action.

Image asset—Talented and/or distinguished persons who serve as outside advisory directors can add credibility to a firm by their association and willingness to be identified with the enterprise. This may be particularly important in the firm's banking relationships.

Corporate networking—An independent outside advisory director often has a network of potential sources of capital or new business, technology sources, economic trend information, international contacts and connections in industry, government, and educational centers. These outside networks can be of benefit to the family firm.

Given all these talents, even such a "water-walking" outside advisory director will be stretched to cope with the unusual blend of family-type problems that exist in many family-owned companies.

Distinctive Governance Contributions

During the last forty years, I have served as an outside director, an outside advisory director, or counseled boards of family firms, both here and in Europe. The following situations illustrate contributions from an independent perspective when facing a complex challenge unique to a family or closely held firm. Names of the companies are disguised.

*Case #1: CEO of the Month.*This business was started over forty years ago in upper New York State by three college sophomore classmates as a full service, general retail store serving students and townspeople. The three founders formed a corporation owned by them and eventually their families.

One founder provided financial smarts, one provided innovative marketing input, and the third handled personnel. The senior was nonexecutive chairman, the second oldest was vice chairman, and the youngest was president. They could not agree on who would be CEO. The team approach and plural management served the enterprise well as it developed regionally. Approaching an $80 million revenue level in ten years, the company went public. The three families retained 40 percent ownership—sufficient to control the firm effectively, to elect three business friends as outside directors, and to engage two outside advisors who served as professional counselors to the board.

The chain of stores diversified geographically under this talented management trio. However, plural management leadership came on hard times. Each founder-principal pressed hard on his functional interest somewhat to the exclusion of the whole business strategy. Earnings drifted; competition took its toll. The outside directors and advisors were critical, unhappy but powerless to persuade the founder-director-managers to let go and reorganize to fit managerial requirements of the business.

The three owners tried vainly to assume proper control by taking turns being chief executive officer for a month at a time. This shifting leadership caused subordinate management to play the game of waiting until the proper founder-director was in the CEO seat to make a proposal. Financial requests were delayed until the expansive, marketing-oriented founder was CEO. Major executive personnel decisions were scheduled to catch the people-prone founder in responsible charge, and so on.

Profitability drifted to such a point that the outside directors and advisors threatened to resign unless the three founders faced the reality that (1) their founding team model no longer adequately served the public corporation requirements for professional management, (2) management succession planning was nonexistent, and (3) the founders had to relinquish their confusing managerial roles and confine their input to the director level.

The good news came tardily but effectively. The founders gave up executive roles and served only as founder-directors. A new outside, nonexecutive chairman was elected. A new CEO with demonstrated success in the retail business was recruited, and a turnaround took place. The advisory directors were replaced with statutory directors who were professionals.

*Case #2: The Candy Store Problem.*This family business in organizational communications consulting faced a variety of options from which to select with little basis for picking one "candy" or another. The young founders were husband and wife with advanced college degrees plus aggressive talent in marketing. They became intrigued with electronic mail, on-line information systems, computer conferencing, video training via multi-mode, and a periodical covering a range of value-added communications media. Three years after they engaged two outside advisory directors, the impact of independent, experienced advice saved the fledgling enterprise from bankruptcy by realistically facing the candy-story syndrome that beset them. Flexibility in their attitude allowed them to cut back plans gracefully and refocus with somewhat sobered enthusiasm on their original area of expertise, communications consulting. My last contact with the founders indicated they were back on a narrower strategic track and had good chances of building a viable business.

*Case #3: Feudal Family Wardship in the Boardroom.*This is a case of governance practice from the Middle Ages alive and well in contemporary Europe. I first became aware of this anachronism on a task of strategic assessment of a financial intermediary public company in northern Europe.

The board of International Investments, Ltd., faced a strategic need to change geographic investment patterns in order to reestablish profitability and growth. This meant partially abandoning the country where it was founded over a hundred years ago. The family members were reluctant to make any changes but agreed to engage two experienced persons as advisors to the top management and board.

As one of these advisors, I attended what was a painful board meeting for all seven directors, four of whom were elder statesmen and immediate descendants of the founding families. The three younger directors, who were also related, had graduated from schools of business administration at Stanford, Harvard, and London School of Economics, respectively. An enlightened twentieth-century view of business strategy had been inculcated into the younger directors. The fiducial responsibility of directors to *all* the shareowners when making strategic decisions was clear to the younger board members. In practice, this was emotion-laden but business-driven.

Another issue was on the same agenda; election of two outside directors not associated with founding families although these families controlled only 14 percent of shares outstanding. The impasse was relieved some meetings later when poor corporate results forced family-dominated directors to elect two outside directors whose independence and integrity reinforced the decision to unlock the strategic business hangup by facing the relocation issue. The advisor's role was taken over by the new statutory directors. Moral: Outside advisory directors can often sort out and help resolve key issues where accountability, role ambiguity, and obsolete strategy are causes for unsatisfactory corporate performance. Professional governance talent is not necessarily inherited.

*Case #4: The Outward-Bound MBA.*This was a case of applying business administration skills in a family-owned niche service business. The founder's objective was to create a technology transfer capability for specialized patents, technical information, and know-how lying on the shelf or in laboratories of out-of-the-way universities and technical institutes. Two family members who incorporated Hi-Tech Development, Ltd., were scions of a wealthy family. Their father had created an investment firm and sold it before his death a decade ago. The sons were well educated and had postgraduate experience respectively in publishing and governmental international commerce.

Business problems arose: technical credibility, cash-flow limitations, control systems, unfocused strategy, and too many corporate goals for the resources available. The principals knew the textbook rules for business but were not objectively monitored by their family-dominated board.

I became involved as an advisory director. The enthusiasm of the entrepreneur founder-director-manager was contagious. But the realities of actually starting a business as opposed to knowing how it is done was the Achilles heel. The smart founders had the necessary education but no field experience in the commercial trenches. The business plan and control of new project formation bore little relation to realistic timeframes to completion or availability of working capital.

The resolution, although based on conventional wisdom, unfolded more slowly than the founding brothers expected. An achievable set of goals, a sound business strategy including fallback alternatives in case the chosen market was not there, and a control system were key to the solution. Moral: Business survival is the first stage of a new family-owned business. Educational merit badges are important, but experienced guidance can be critical to success of a new corporate venture, providing family directors will accept such input.

*Case #5: The Great Man's Legacy.*The Adams Construction Company was founded in 1946 by Henry Adams, a civil engineer. His family business employed two sons and a daughter in managerial and ultimately director roles. The untimely death of the founding-entrepreneur and paternal leader left ownership in family hands with unresolved problems of company leadership or roles for each sibling. None were ready or qualified to take over the reins.

For six years momentum carried the company satisfactorily before the firm became fragmented and overextended. Banks forced the family board to bring in a financially expert outside director. After one year he was trusted sufficiently by the family directors to appoint him CEO and elect him chairman.

I became involved as an advisory director along with three other experienced outsiders. We acted as a resource to the chairman, the board, and individual family directors as we gained credibility and trust with the owners.

This case had a positive outcome. Personal and family goals were separated from company goals. Succession plans and an executive development program were introduced. Plans are underway for a private placement, which will dilute family equity. Prospects are excellent for this family enterprise to make the transition to a professionally managed and eventually publicly held corporation.

DISTINCTIVE GOVERNANCE EXPECTATIONS

As a company develops, it is affected by external changes in the political, social, legal, environmental, and cultural conditions in addition to changes in family member roles and interests. Accordingly, the attributes, criteria, and standards of competence for governance change.

When serving as an outside director to a family business board, an advisor needs to appreciate the special attributes of governing family businesses. These may be less "glamorous" or of lesser "star quality" than what a public company may seek in building the image of its board. Further, the expectations of an advisory director should include ability to cope with emotion-laden issues of the family interests.

Recently, certain governance dimensions have become increasingly evident for publicly held corporations. They also have limited value to some family business firms. In general, large public companies are seeking board-level advice to provide the following perspectives:

Multinational focus;

Representatives with constituency board members, for example, women, blacks, consumers, or labor representatives;

Social responsiveness, or the selection of outside directors or advisors having special sensitivity to social issues;

Public directorships. These are now a fact of boardroom life in many European countries. Here the movement has been limited to restructuring of some U.S. boards to include directors and advisors who can especially represent the public interest; and

Comanagement, not yet a topical boardroom issue. This generally means employee participation in corporate governance through an employee representative on the board. It is not particularly relevant now to the closely held corporate board in the United States, nor has the concept been generally accepted for publicly held corporations.

For the family or closely held U.S. company, some of these changing dimensions will have relevance in the boardroom as the family firm develops. On the other hand, there are three emotion-laden crises that transcend all other issues in the boardroom of a family company. The key words are "relationships, transitions, and interactions." These concern three crisis areas for family owners: the crisis of letting go; the crisis of reorganization; and the crisis of succession, or the dynastic tendency. The key crises and issues facing family corporations' directors have nearly always existed under the corporate governance bed covers. Five issues appear to have immediate impact on the family corporation director. The outside director should be keenly sensitive to these issues for they are where an independent perspective is often needed.

My experience leads me to select five key issues of prime concern in the governance of family businesses. They are particular, troubling, demanding tensions, dilemmas, and complexities of being an advisory director to a family business board.

Issue #1: Ownership Control

Case #3, Feudal Family Wardship in the Boardroom, briefly described in the preceding section, was an example of a once-controlling group of families failing to recognize their responsibility to all shareowners after the family holdings had shrunk to 14 percent of outstanding shares. The ownership control issue has at least four aspects.

The owners' de jure or de facto control and influence affect the board's independent deliberations, board process, responsibilities in a statutory-fiduciary sense, evaluation of company and executive performance, role in CEO succession, participation in the governance and management processes, and ability to act as a resource to the company. An outside director can objectively sort out these respective governance processes for the benefit of family directors.

Separation of ownership from directorship and management roles is often a problem and may not be realistic or appropriate. For example, the roles can overlap in areas of director nominations, CEO succession, and maintenance of realistic compensation arrangements that deal equitably with salary compensation compression tendencies. Independent perspective of an experienced advisory director can often keep a faithful competitive view before the board on these sensitive matters.

Identification and resolution of conflicts can be troublesome if owner objectives differ from developing institutional objectives or performance criteria for the enterprise long term. Sometimes a credible view from an ad hoc advisory council can help family directors evaluate alternative consequences.

Estate planning considerations can dominate the strategic future of the enterprise and its dividend and financial policies in certain family corporations. Impact on nonfamily employees, strategic positioning, and long-range future of a family enterprise can often be assessed more objectively by nonfamily directors.

Issue #2: Board Role

The following points bear examination:

Effectiveness and scope of the board of directors. How separate is, or should be, the governance process from ownership private influence on sound conduct of the corporation. Advisory directors can often help family director-managers distinguish between running a corporation and seeing that it is well run.

Influence of the advisory directors on corporate strategy, growth objectives, goals, diversification, and divestment options.

Objectivity and independence of the nomination and renomination process for statutory directors.

Management of conflict-of-interest problems of director-founders, owners, and director-legal or director-financial counselors.

Flexibility of the board role to accommodate crisis stages and significant changes faced by the company. Advisory directors often can help the board weather the three emotion-laden crises mentioned previously.

Delegation and retention of power to professional management. A qualified outsider can help the board select top professionals and insure the proper power flow as the company organization develops.

Minority shareowner protection if and as appropriate. Effective outside directors and advisory directors are especially sensitive to the board's fiduciary responsibilities.

Takeover protection—the outside board member or advisory director role with a family corporation board can be significant in evaluating options and surmounting difficulties of fair appraisal.

Issue #3: Individual Advisory Director Role

Advisory directors have certain matters to address on a personal basis. They should consider the courage, confidence, and ability necessary to act independently in fulfilling the various duties of a fiduciary; to risk rapport and collateral with owners and colleagues in taking an independent position; and to relinquish their advisory role rather than be considered captive.

I served for three years as an advisory director on a family-owned company board in the Midwest. The company had no outside nonmanagerial directors. Along with two other advisory directors, we offered our resignations because the family members refused to face the reality that none of them were qualified to occupy the senior management position they placed themselves in. The matter was resolved by three of the four owners relinquishing managerial roles and confining their positions to nonmanagement directorships. The fourth family member took a less responsible management post.

Advisory directors should understand the difference between advice or counsel as an advisory director and fiducial accountability of a statutory director. They should embody exemplary codes of behavior, morals, and ethics. Prospective advisory directors should make some assessment of the ethics and conduct of directors, officers, and employees, relating such to the special obligations a private firm has before accepting an engagement as an advisor. Finally, they should evaluate their own expectations and personal needs as advisory directors, such as: adequate indemnification and protection, proper compensation, intellectual stimulation, identity and recognition, service opportunity and gratification, time requirements, and social relationships.

Advisory directors are uniquely positioned to assist the family firm in providing continuity at the governance level, particularly when ownership is being transferred to younger members of the family. Often, they can negotiate differences between generations or between groups that may be represented on the board.

Issue #4: Management and Director Succession

Case #1, CEO of the Month, described previously, illustrates how outsider counsel effectively guided the founder-director-manager-dominated board when the founders failed to relinquish managerial control and select competent successors. The crisis was resolved under the pressure of drifting corporate performance by the intervention of outside advisors on the root problem.

Advisory directors can play a vital role by providing an objective perspective on three sensitive subissues:

Control of nepotism, concinnity, and group-think in major matters of management development and succession and candidates for directorship.

Separation or combination of chairman and CEO roles and staffing of other organizational roles to ensure competent incumbents regardless of family relationships.

Exposure to CEO and top management back-up candidates both from the family and from outside the family.

An unpublished doctoral study of management succession in family business at Harvard Business School analyzed data taken at thirty-five field sites and from published sources. A model of the transition process was developed. Transitions from first to second generation were compared to those from second to third generation. Managerial strategies were classified according to the nature of the transition and the relative priority of family and business issues. The Y.P.O. and Smaller Company Management Program at Harvard Business School cooperated.[3] The study validates the directorship requirements for family boards and the opportunity for qualified outsiders to contribute in serving on such boards.

Issue #5: Stakeholder Concept

Enlightened boards of directors are examining this notion as a more socially responsive perspective. Advisory directors to family business boards can offer an objective viewpoint on this trend.

The stakeholder concept implies that shareowners are not the only corporate constituents who have a vested interest in the conduct and performance of a given firm, that all parties interested in the welfare of the company and affected by its policies and practices have a stake (hence "stakeholder") in the business. This includes owners, employees, customers, state and other government bodies, competitors, environmentalists, suppliers, and community neighbors. Stakeholders may be defined as any group whose collective behavior can directly affect the organization's future but which is not under the organization's direct control.

Understanding how the free economic system provides the goods and services which are the essence of this country's standard of living varies widely among the various stakeholder groups. The main difference between stakeholder and other dealings is that interactions with stakeholder are rarely a one-time or transaction-oriented event. They occur within the context of enduring relationships; stakeholder constituencies remain.

These are but a few of the distinctive issues of concern when advising family company boards. Many more issues are in the pipeline of the regulatory and legislative bodies and in the data base of the public opinion pollsters. The advisory director to the board of a family business can contribute in important ways by helping the family directors anticipate and address these troublesome issues.

REWARDS FOR ADVISING A FAMILY BOARD

There are joys and benefits of being an independent, advisory director to a family business board. The foregoing emphasizes stressful directorship experiences and specific troubled conditions encountered by some family companies. Why, then, does anyone want to advise a family business board given the pressures, exposures, and emotional climate that can prevail? I can think of at least eight potential rewards on the basis of my own boardroom experience.[4]

Exhilaration of challenge: Advisory directors tackle vexing issues in their serving owner's and public interests. The exhilaration of gaming to overcome conflicts and challenge is ever present in the family company boardroom.

The service ethic: Most of us are initially driven by the ethic of competition. However, I suggest the ethic of service is equally, if not more, rewarding to many of us.

Eliteness motivation: There is an eliteness pattern of identification with successful organizations. In a social-economic sense, boards can have far-reaching power. By their approval or disapproval, they direct flow of capital and start new businesses.

The ethical algorithm: Ethics in corporate governance implies a process of deliberation and debate among fellow directors and advisors who share concerns for the social consequences and social fabric. Great satisfaction can be derived from developing an ethical algorithm or pattern for a family company.

The ego factor: This is one of the few elements of advisory directorship that can grow without nourishment. However, serving as advisor to an effective board can provide a form of self-confidence, a satisfying sense of identity, and a measure of power to one's psyche. The social networking benefits of advisory directorship can share rewarding experiences and contacts both inside and outside the boardroom.

The rituals and ceremonials: We all like parades, parties, and performing. Being privy to boardroom drills can be very satisfying to some persons.

Team play: Peer acceptance on a family board "team" gives many of us a social contract with interesting persons we might not otherwise have a chance to work with or meet. It is rewarding to be part of an effective governance team.

Perks and pay: Pay for giving advice and being accountable in a boardroom can be significant. Advisory director compensation is made up of not only the psychic rewards previously listed but real income in the form of fees and of indirect income in the form of perquisites.

To conclude, advising a family business board contrasts in many ways with service on a public company board. The difference in governance focuses on the special sensitivities required of an advisory director to face the issues, dilemmas, and emotional climate that often accompanies family company boardroom service. While the human scale and tenor of a family-controlled board is company-specific, there can be great opportunity to advise the family company and its owners responsibly. The rewards of service are there if you can remain detached and professional in offering your personal contribution to making the board and management more effective.

NOTES

1. With permission from Jossey-Bass Inc., Publishers, this chapter draws on the author's article "Differential Directorship: Special Sensitivities and Roles for Serving the Family Business Board," *Family Business Review* 1, 3 (Fall 1988), pp. 239–47.

2. See Robert K. Mueller, "Governing the Closely Held Corporation: A Special Stewardship Challenge," Part I, Vol. 7, no. 6 (June 1983), and Part II, Vol. 7, no. 7 (July 1983), *Director's Monthly,* Official newsletter of the National Association of Corporate Directors, Washington, D.C.

3. Simon A. Hershon, "The Problem of Management Succession in Family Business," Doctor of Business Administration thesis, Graduate School of Business Administration, George F. Baker Foundation, Harvard University, Cambridge, Mass., 1975.

4. See Robert K. Mueller, "The Joys of Directorship," *Directors & Boards* (Fall 1986), pp. 7–10, for a more extensive presentation of rewards for board service.

15

CULTURAL REALITIES FACING ADVISORY BOARDS

Like the happy centipede, many people get along fine working with others without thinking about which foot to put forward. But when there are difficulties, when the usual methods do not work, when we want to learn more, there is no alternative but to examine our own behavior in relation to others.

Joseph Luft[1]

Within its boundaries, a corporation develops its own culture, which is related to the economic, social, and political climate, industry, technical nature of the institution, and the persons involved. The key persons include the owners, directors, management, plus the entire work force. A corporate etiquette, or sort of ethical system, evolves. It is set by the moral and ethical tone at the top. In turn, this is affected by tradition and certain canons or codes of behavior. These canons concern values, beliefs, attitudes, style, business practices, private communications, and intellectual honesty. Important, too, are the air of stability or instability, and degree of social contracting between individuals that characterize the corporate culture and corporate climate. The climatic conditions are those concerned with the nonpurposeful milieu in which the company exists. This contrasts with the purposeful texture or structure employed by institutions and organized entities, that is, the formal networks and hierarchical relationships.

HONORABLE WORK

Wilhelm Roscher, nineteenth-century Leipzig professor of political economics, believed that "the higher the culture, the more honorable the work." To be in a privileged position of advising a top management or board of directors carries an obligation to find out about the corporate culture—both its "high" and "low" attributes and their relation to one's own culture—in order to provide meaningful counsel.

One corporation, a medium-sized, multinational manufacturing company headquartered in the East, engaged a three-person advisory council. I had the "honor" of serving on the council. An interesting behavior pattern and consequent etiquette was evident at the board level. It evolved out of a long, troubled history of company performance and the dominance of founder-sibling directors who owned the controlling portion of company stock.

As an advisory group to the chairman-CEO, we quickly learned that the philosophy of the board on the future of the company was split cleanly between the owner-directors and the independent outside directors who were detached from historical factors and family ownership. The board meetings were friendly enough with some performance issues out in the open. However, the helplessness of the independent directors in forcing a realistic assessment of the future and a major change in strategy was so frustrating and tension-producing that even the social contracting at the informal postmeeting board luncheons was often avoided.

The corporate etiquette was observed to deteriorate during the five years the advisory council performed its "honorable work." At one time, it reached a point where the few nonresident outside directors essentially ate alone with the inside directors while the resident outside directors found some excuse to go back to their company offices on other business to avoid socializing. You could almost plot the earnings per share by the luncheon attendance. The etiquette pattern displayed the rift in philosophy of how to direct and manage the company. The advisor's challenge was to assist in resolving the basic philosophical conflict that underlay the behavior pattern. This took almost five years of counseling by the advisory board.

Existing theories of corporate culture generally fail to take the nature of the culture to be changed into proper account. Different cultures behave and change through different processes. The challenge to an effective advisory board is to understand the nature of the culture of the corporation being served. Beyond the philosophical or ideological conflicts which may exist, this challenge embraces the stages of development, the competitive position and the environmental situation which are determining factors in the specific cultural condition of the corporation.

The thrust of this chapter is to offer to corporate advisors a limited repertoire of perspectives needed to appreciate the different roots of good governance and good management. These perspectives have their respective criteria for success, values, sanctions, norms, beliefs, articles of faith, symbols, dominant themes, and manifest behavior. This is obviously too vast a field of theory and practice to address in one chapter or in several books because of the multiple learned disciplines of natural and social sciences and the business situations involved. But we can offer several specific guides.

SOME PRIMAL GUIDES

As a primal guide for directors and officers considering, or dealing with, advisory boards, there are many useful perspectives available in short form on which to reflect. These are baseline touchstones when, as an advisor, one is faced with the realities of a particular corporate culture and climate. These selected viewpoints include: (1) the strategic equation of balancing multiple cultures existing in one organization; (2) the archetypes, and (3) the systems perspective, to select only three.

Another recently popularized model of culture suggests using what a Theory Z company or an "excellent" company possesses. Some scholars suggest this use of the ideal company as a role model and then following certain processes.

The strategic equation model, however, suggests that culture, environment, and strategy should be congruent. If the external conditions change, a new cultural balance and new strategy are called for. This requires a corporation to change its culture to meet the new demands.[2]

Any of these changes in corporate culture requires dealing with the paradox of the management of human systems and of human systems management. The management of human systems is the *science* and technology of managing, striving for productivity, efficient performance, and technological competence through innovation. Human systems management is the *art* of linking human beings into purposeful teams and catalyzing their full creative growth through leadership.

Before attacking the science versus art paradox, advisors must first face up to the problem of defining culture as used in an organizational sense since this definition is common to whatever perspective is chosen. A simple definition of culture is: Culture is an integrated behavior pattern. The essential core of culture is the traditional ideals and, especially, their attached values. These ideals include thought, speech, action, and certain artifacts. Culture depends upon individuals' capacity for learning and transmitting knowledge from one to another. Culture is concerned with norms or rules for "right" behavior. The values and aspirations of individuals further make up what is called culture and its derivative, multi- or polyculture.

On the surface, this definition seems straightforward enough. But in it are seeds of confusion that hamper attempts to deal with multiple cultures that commonly exist in an organization. As Ashley Montagu pointed out in the 1960s, "Man alone among the forms of animated nature is the creature that has moved into an adaptive zone, which is an entirely learned one. This is the zone of *culture*, the manmade, the learned part of the environment."[3]

Because cultures are learned, their expression and their interaction sometimes lack harmony and clarity. Cultural propriety, for example, suggests that there are organizational advantages to having different cultures and styles. A monoculture is wrong for most large and diverse organizations. Differences in culture are generally healthy. Choice and blend of cultures should be designed and managed rather than allowed to occur haphazardly. But we lack the tolerance and ability to deal with conflicts and tensions that infringe on our conventional way of conducting ourselves.

Montagu summed it up well in an earlier book: "The culture of the human mind is the finest of all the arts and one of the most neglected. Neglected, not because we are uninterested; but because we are confused. Confused about the direction we ought to take and confused about the goals we should pursue. And so, with the best will in the world, we busy ourselves perfecting means to realize a confusion of goals."[4]

Taking Advantage of Contradiction

One approach to "unconfusing" corporate goals lies in the *contradictoriness* that is one of the characteristic properties of people, groups, organizations, and institutions. An organization, for example, can be both big and small, weak and strong, beautiful and ugly, bureaucratic and innovative, centralized and decentralized, risk-giving and risk-taking, proactive and reactive, tightly controlled or loosely controlled, and so on, all at the same time.

One theory of cultural propriety suggests that in our multicultural organizations, we should use this contradictoriness to maximize the advantages of having different cultures and styles. The thesis unravels like this.[5] Ineffectiveness, slack and incompetence in an organization are due to mixed management philosophy, styles or cults. (Different philosophies work against each other.) Most organizations develop their own composite cultures, which are a mix of such cults. This is not necessarily bad. Having a blend of cults is usually desirable. However, individuals have their preferred management philosophies, which may or may not be congruent with the organizational culture(s). Therefore, analysis of the cultural approach to management is a useful diagnostic aid, especially for advisory directors or councillors. It provides clues about the comfort and discomfort of individuals within the particular cultural propriety of the organization, clues that can be used to enhance the desirable characteristics.

One way to take advantage of this thesis is to recognize three types of jobs to be done. Steady-state, programmable activities can be handled by systems, routines and prescriptive rules; they usually make up 80 percent of most organizational work and the prime domain of management. Development efforts deal with new situations or problems that require new systems or routines which adapt to change. Exceptions or emergencies require instinct, speed, and creativity rather than logical analysis and personal intervention.

The Strategic Equation of Balancing Cultures

One useful theoretical approach to understanding corporate culture suggests four frameworks for thought. Each is a theology that offers scripture and preaches its own version of the "gospel" to managers, directors, and advisors. This has been described more fully in Chapter 11, "Advisory View of Corporate Strategy."

Large, complex organizations usually exist with more than one of these frames of reference: The structural frame, the human resource frame, the political frame, or the symbolic frame. A healthy multicultural organization will have at least these four frameworks aligned with one another in such a way that they are mutually supporting, for each perspective has a unique competitive advantage. Culture, environment, and strategy are aligned. Structural elements will be in the foreground under conditions of high consensus, low rates of change, high certainty, and relatively young organizations. Human resource phenomena will be particularly evident when there is high abundance, high consensus, or rapid change in a relatively older organization. Political processes surface when resources are declining or scarce, disagreement is widespread, change is rapid, uncertainty is high, and the organization is older. Decentralization can minimize this. Symbolic processes are most evident under conditions of disagreement, rapid changes, ambiguity, and uncertainty.

Rites and Rituals as Cultural Elements

If we analyze the deeper sets of symbolic meanings in complex social systems that humans develop (of themselves in relation to such systems), we address the concept of human emotionality. This manifests itself at the level of the individual, the group, the organization, and ultimately at the level of society or institutions. Symbols are treated as highly personalized factors.

Rites and rituals are often the most prominent symbolic elements in a culture. But there are many other cultural elements to be considered. Anthropologists would include ceremonies, myths, sagas, legends, stories, folktales, symbols, language, gestures, physical setting, and artifacts. The two important elements of a corporate culture, rites and rituals, are readily observable by experienced advisors. Advisors will be sensitive to the notion that corporate cultures have two basic components: *substance* or networks-of-meanings contained in the corporate ideology, beliefs, norms, and values; and *form,* or the company practices whereby these meanings are expressed, affirmed, and communicated to members of the organization and the stakeholders of the corporation. Cultural realities can serve as sensitizing mechanisms to show how certain behaviors—which may be perceived as irrational, nonrational, or unproductive—are functional for some members in organizations. Individuals tend to march to different drummers even when they are gathered into a corporate organization. Observant advisors can spot these different behaviors and cluster them into the various cultural frameworks.

If we carefully observe the rites and rituals of a corporation, we often find at least six types of expressive social consequences to consider. The consequences are evident in multicultural organizational dynamics and need to be managed or guided for an organization to be effective.[6]

Rites of Passage—These facilitate transition of persons into social roles and corporate statuses that are new for them. Examples: business, army or fraternal functions, promotion, transfers, and others.

Rites of Degradation—These dissolve social identities and their power. Examples: demotion, removal and replacement of a CEO, outplacement, dishonorable discharge from armed or other government services, expulsion from a club, association, or professional society.

Rites of Enhancement—Social and business identity and prestige power are reinforced; for example, master salesman awards, senior scientist titles, *Time* magazine's Man of the Year, conferral of knighthood in Britain, Nobel prizes.

Rites of Renewal—This type of rite refurbishes social structures and improves their functioning. Examples: organizational development programs, Harvard's Advanced Management Program (AMP), quality-of-work-life (QWL) programs, quality circles.

Rites of Conflict Reduction—Conflict and aggression are reduced by deflecting attention away from solving problems by compartmentalizing conflicts and their disruptive effects. Examples: collective bargaining, arbitration, committee or task force formation, place role or organization formation, brainstorming, use of Delphi technique to tap peer forces.

A. R. Radcliffe-Brown in *The Andaman Islanders* (New York: Free Press, 1964) described the peacemaking ceremonies of North Andaman Islanders in which dancers from two contending factions mixed together randomly to form two groups. One group of dancers then expressed aggressive and hostile feelings toward the other, with each member of this group giving "a good shaking to each member of the other party." In response, the other group showed "complete passivity," expressing neither fear nor resentment. In this manner, collective anger was appeased, wrongs forgiven, and peace was temporarily restored.

Rites of Integration—These encourage and revive common feelings that bind members together and commit them to a social system. The rite permits venting of emotion and temporary loosening of various norms and may reassert, reaffirm, by contrast, moral rightness of usual norms. Examples: office holiday parties, company picnics, annual general meetings of stockholders (AGM), professional society meetings.

There is a message here for "managing" multicultural organizations such as universities, business conglomerates, hospitals, multidenominational churches, international organizations (political, social, economic, technical, and cultural). The message is to *be careful* about rites and rituals. Strong symbolic cultures provide security and sense of purpose. They also give meaning and direction to organizational members' efforts. "Pursuit of excellence" company-type cultures force individuals to "either buy into their norms or get out."

But rites and rituals can either impede or facilitate organizational change or adaptability. Consequently, they must be handled thoughtfully, recognizing the multiple consequences present. Effective management requires assessment and evaluation of rites and rituals, using them for continuity, modification, or discontinuing certain behavior.

It is doubtful that a popular rite or ritual can be suppressed. But it can be often modified and new super-ordinate symbols, rites, and ceremonials gradually substituted if that improves integration and effectiveness of the multicultural organization. These events are called "rites of creation." Otherwise, it is best to allow the social cultural behaviors to remain as valuable enhancements of past culture.

Archetypes

Perhaps the strangest human systems in the cultural makeup of organizations are those symbolized by archetypes. These patterns or models lie deep within the formation and operation of the psyche. Such general symbolic concepts are revealed in great myths, legends, fairy tales, and religions of the world. The archetype is the most symbolic, universal, psychological image of a character type know to humans. Perceptive advisors can recognize these if they are sensitive to corporate cultural frames of reference.

Scholars have demonstrated that in examining the great diversity of world cultures, the more one finds at a symbolic level, the more there is an incredible, if not astounding, amount of agreement among archetypal images. This agreement is too profound to be produced by chance alone. Therefore, it is attributed to a similarity of psyche at the unconscious level.

At this most basic image level, the purpose of archetypes appears to be to help people give an emotionally satisfying picture of the world. The world is so terrifying to the primitive person and to the child that we need some way of coping with it, of organizing it. The civilized world of government, business education, religion and society in the twentieth century can be just as overwhelming when we strive to manage and govern complex human systems. Thus archetypes come into play.

Literally every aspect of human existence is capable of being turned into an archetypal symbol, image, or character. An archetype, or image that presents it, contains the essence of a particular human experience that has been repeated enough to make it permanent, but not necessarily an unalterable print on our neural structure. Some of our experiences are so fundamental in existence that one cannot expect the human condition without them.

There are archtypes corresponding to every kind of authority figure, condition of chance or uncertainty, occupation, death, war, creation, and so on. In order to take advantage of their usefulness in guiding multicultural organizations, we need not regard our archetypes as literally "real," that is, actually existing. They can serve, however, as projective tests written large and naturally in terms in which one can understand himself, herself, or the organization.

Such images naturally and automatically crop up in modern organizational life. They afford a unique way of understanding multicultural organizations and their impact on individuals and vice versa. Many books have been written around archetypes, including *The Man in the Gray Flannel Suit, The One Minute Manager, The Gamesman,*

The Managerial Woman, The Organization Man, to name just a few in the business world.

One of the most systematic and extensive treatments of archetypal images can be found in the analysis of the twenty-two major symbols that comprise a deck of tarot cards.[7] The cards can be organized in a format that comes tantalizingly close to a "periodic table of human elements." However, we know that the number of archetypes is not fixed, constant, or static. Although considerable insight can be gained in the broad outlines of the full range of archetypes, complete and definitive knowledge of the full set seems closed to mortals. Indeed, such knowledge is open only to the gods, one of humankind's earliest and most enduring of archetypes. In principle, all archetypes are contained in all others. This does not mean, however, that they operate equally powerfully at any given moment for all individuals. Some archetypes overwhelm or overshadow others. A multicultural organization is a zoo of archetypes.

The symbolic (that is, expressive) patterns of archetypes that signify any organization are countless. However, four basic archetypal characters have been progressively refined and elaborated into impersonal institutionalized forms. They are presented as the basic building blocks of society and all institutions by organization theorists, particularly William Thompson.[8] Thompson selects the institutionalized archetypes for modern society as the *military,* the *medical profession, artists and entertainment,* and the *manager and managerial class.* As might be expected, these archetypal characters are symbolized as the hunter or warrior (for the military); shaman or medicine man (for the medical profession); clown or fool (for the artist and entertainment); and the chief (for the manager and the managerial class).

Thompson argues that institutions exert influence on people's inner personalities, in a way that causes new archetypes to emerge around the symbols that are in tune with the images of an age. If we are to use this concept in managing a multicultural organization, we need to identify the relevant archetypes. Ten archetypes are described in a more recent study conducted at McGill University.[9] The study focused around an understanding of the strategy-making process by examining the organization and environmental context of eighty-one undisguised cases on business organizations of which 80 percent were published in *Fortune* magazine and the balance in the Harvard Case Clearinghouse Series.

The companies were examined to see whether certain score patterns or interactions among environmental and organizational strategy-making variables occurred with uncommonly high frequency. Patterns were defined in terms of the relative strengths and weaknesses of the scores on thirty-one variables. Though there was some limitation to the use of factor analysis, the first proportion of these patterns was at least a hundred times larger than the second. The archetypes identified were thus considered significant under a binomial test of proportions.

About 90 percent of the sample is included in ten archetypes of which two are pertinent to our discussion of managing multicultural organizations. The first of these was "the giant under fire" archetype, symbolizing companies such as Heinz, duPont, and General Motors, operating in a challenging and a complex dynamic environment. Considerable heterogeneity and hostility were present due to competition, antitrust suits, markets becoming saturated, changes in customer tastes and buying habits, plus need for change in production technologies.

The "giant under fire" archetype is faced with an environment posing tremendous complex administrative tasks that successful firms have proved to be very capable at handling. These tasks are organizational intelligence in the form of scanning the environment, establishing sensitive controls, and facilitating internal communications. Furthermore, there is the requisite decentralization in the delegation of all but top strategic management to middle and lower management. Even some of the overall strategy making is done by divisional vice presidents. Power centralization at the top is quite moderate.

Task complexity dictates that many parties get involved in the top-level direction of the company. A firm adapts to its environments incrementally. In this modern archetype, institutionalized practices include decentralization, sophisticated organizational intelligence, and a very analytical mode of decision making. Traditions may impede any attempt at drastic change, but most of the moves that these companies do make tend to be in the right direction.

The second archetype of interest is the "entrepreneurial conglomerate." This type of company is run by a powerful, charismatic chief executive in control of strategy making and interested in expanding and diversifying. Often he or she has a high share of ownership. Strategy is bold expansion by acquisition, in either related or unrelated industries. This prototype manipulates its environment instead of reacting to it. Examples cited are Boise Cascade, Gulf and Western, Textron, and Hanson Trust.

The most immediate repercussion of a manipulative growth/acquisition philosophy is the increased heterogeneity of the environment. Management must cope with a multitude of industries, which may be very different from one another in terms of required methods of operation. Consequently, the new divisions may be positioned in different environments that are more dynamic.

This complexity creates the need for more external intelligence activity. Much emphasis is on monitoring the management process of subsidiaries via scanning controls and communication devices. The complexity of administrative tasks makes it necessary to delegate the operating functions to the managers of subsidiaries. Only the major strategic changes are dealt with by the entrepreneur and his or her headquarters staff.

Importantly, the constant preoccupation with acquisitions makes the need for planning (that is, the futurity analysis variable) acute and very obvious. Environmental complexity and intelligence activity insure that enough problems and opportunities come to the attention of corporate staff to constitute an incentive for planning and analytical activities.

These are not the only archetypes that symbolize management of modern multicultural organizations, but they are representative. While some successful firms adapt to their environments by changing themselves, such as the "giants under fire," others manipulate or change their environments by entering new markets. The "entrepreneurial conglomerate" may establish new technologies and innovate.

Most multicultural firms decentralize in response to administrative complexity while others apparently can afford to be tightly centralized if they have a charismatic strong leader sensitive to the criteria for success in overseeing a multicultural organization.[10]

Greek Guidelines

There are at least four culture archetypes that have been identified as representative of the plurality of models existing in multicultural organizations. Handy uses patron Greek gods as metaphors for these types: (1) the club, clan or tribal culture represented by Zeus; (2) role culture represented by Apollo; (3) task culture represented by Athena; and (4) the existential culture represented by Dionysus.[11] Without taking these too seriously, the metaphors intuitively identify the gods with certain preferred values.

I have added a fifth type model—the systems culture, represented by the Greek god Hermes—to cope with the challenge of managing a multicultural organization that may contain any or all of the four other models. Let's review each of these models briefly to identify their characteristics that are significant in governing, managing, and advising multicultural organizations.

Handy's theory of cultural propriety hypothesizes that a monoculture is wrong for most organizations. In cultures that are healthy there is always some choice. Certainly a blend of cultures can be designed to improve the effectiveness of managing a multicultural organization rather than letting a mixture of cultures occur haphazardly, and then worrying about governing the resultant organization.

The *club, clan, or tribal culture* is symbolized diagrammatically by a spider web. From the center, lines of power and influence are of a consultive and consensus nature, and they extend and reduce in importance as they become more distant from the center. Relationship with the "spider" is more important than title or description. Peer pressure is also a motivator.

Zeus, the patriarchal, irrational, benevolent, impulsive, and charismatic king of the gods was feared and respected. He is a metaphor for a strong leadership role present in most club, clan, or tribal cultures.

The main attributes of this model on the positive side are an entrepreneurial environment; speedy decisions and communications; informal, trusting, intuitive, personal, nepotistic, and long-term relationships. Some not-so-good attributes are shortage of documentation and control; tendency toward crony networks; elitist attitudes; individuals subordinate to the leader and the organization. In their early days, perhaps Xerox and IBM were particular examples of this type with firm, strong individual leaders. Some large corporations are successfully run this way at the present time.

The *role culture* represents the structured, ordered model. This is symbolized by a Greek temple drawing strength and beauty from its structure and functional pillars, which are joined only at the top (the boardroom or CEO's office). Pillars are linked by tension—the policies, rules, and procedures of the bureaucracy.

Apollo is the god of order and rules, with rational and logically prescribed roles for everyone. The most positive attribute for this hierarchical role model is its excellence for steady-state conditions with stability and predictability in the environment. Roles are fixed; security exists. Examples are regulated banks and life insurance companies (particularly in past years), monopolies, civil service, or state industries. Stable product and service lines prevail. Planning is based on the past in order to forecast the future.

On the negative side of the Apollo role-culture model, we see that it resists change. It often overreacts to environmental conditions after ignoring the changes, and it is a stylized culture. Individuals are subordinate to the organization, and any influence they have is up through the chain of command. Everything should fit into a rule book. Standardization is a goal, and the role culture is systems-oriented with division of labor coordinated by chain of command.

The *task model* culture is diagrammatically symbolized by a net or matrix, drawing resources from various parts of an organizational system. Power is at the interstices, not at the top. The task model is loosely connected with purposeful commando units (largely self-contained) having specific responsibility within an overall strategy to perform a specific task.

The Greek god metaphor for this is Athena. She was the warrior goddess, patroness of Odysseus, an arch problem solver, a craftsman and pioneering captain. The positive side of the task model is that it recognizes expertise as a basis of power and influence rather than age, service, or kinship. Creativity can flower. Intuition is valued. There are fewer private agenda conflicts than in the tribal or role cultures. Only a nominal hierarchy exists. There is an informal class system based on peer relationships. It is ideal for growth and new venture situations.

The negative attribute of the task model is that it tends to be an expensive model, effective but not necessarily efficient. Certainly it is unsatisfactory for steady-state plateaus or routineness. Communications and control are difficult. It lacks corporate standards and is nonconformist. The model may be vulnerable to external impact. Individuals are subordinate to the organization. Task cultures often invent fine solutions to unnecessary problems, in other words, the Concorde phenomenon.

The *existential* (or self-commune) *culture* is symbolized diagramatically by a cluster of stars in a circle. Stars are not mutually interdependent. Membership by negotiated contract (social, intellectual, and economic) is the theme rather than being "hired" or "owned" by the association. It is an organization of consent. In that sense, the market determines the nature of employment relationship.

Dionysus, the god of wine and song, was picked as the Greek metaphor, featuring individualism and the value of personal freedom. Most of all, obligation to the organization is a social contract. Permissiveness dominates with flexibility in a changing environment.

The positive aspects are that individuals can do their own thing, functioning without the organization. As in a marketing cooperative, individual talent is a premium. Examples of this culture model are law firms, physician groups, clinics, and artistic co-ops. The model is ideal where a guru individual with professional talent is crucial to success. Personal identity and freedom are preserved. It is a specialist culture.

Some negatives may be attributed to the fact that this culture recognizes no "boss." There is temporary liaison of individuals based on peer respect. There is a lack of mandated control. Management is by consent, with the individual having right of veto. This coordinated effort requires endless negotiation. The organization exists to help individuals achieve their own purpose. It is difficult to manage it effectively, as the peer process dominates. Security depends upon the individual's ability rather than any organizational protection. Most problems are the result of middle organizational conflicts, rivalries, private crises, crucial selection, allocation, or promotion decisions.

My fifth type is the *systems culture*. The primary notion here is that of general systems theory with its frame of reference of four basic concepts. Given the purpose for an organization, these systems concepts are the notions of boundary, tension, equilibrium, and feedback. Components of such an organization are normally concerned with interactivity, interdependence, conflict, synergy, and integration of parts.

Hermes is my nominee as the Greek god metaphor for this culture. Hermes represented trade, commerce, science, invention, oratory, eloquence, communications, and generalist attitudes amongst the gods of Mount Olympus. While Hermes had some questionable talents— including cunning, trickery, and luck in discovering treasure—he had style. He can be identified with governance culture and the Olympian view of the world, which is helpful in guiding a complex system of multicultures.

Systems Culture

Given the fact that many of our organizations are complex and multicultural, advisors can find help if they take a systems view. Ludwig von Bertalanffy's general systems theory conceptualized, among other things, organizational environment as made up of two components: climate and structure.[12] Repeating the distinction made at the beginning of this chapter: the *climactic* conditions are those concerned with the nonpurposeful milieu in which companies exist. This contrasts with the purposeful texture or *structure* employed by institutions and organized entities, that is, formal networks and hierarchical relationships. An open system climate allows members of the organization to relate to the outside world, so that information and energy exchange of values are constantly taking place.

There also exists a binary notion of organizational structural concepts. On one side is the social construct model of an organization, which is distinct from the other side—the rational structure with command and control systems. In dealing with multicultural organizations, the management and communications processes must accommodate both the "soft" and the "hard" concepts, that of the social construct and that of the rational model. The notion of multiple objectives, multiple criteria, and multiple standards is a requirement in a complex system.

Companies in business are gradually tending toward becoming what nonprofit institutions "always" were. Their organizational systems must fulfill the social franchise given the institution when it was incorporated by the state. At the same time, the system must provide for the adaptive survival of the institution in an economic sense. In a multicultural organization, the sourcing, coupling, and supporting norm concepts can enhance the strengths of the functional organization in relationship with the line groups, departments, and units.

Some years ago, Professor Mintzberg postulated some controversial concepts regarding organizations. They still characterize our multicultural organizations today. Among these postulates were: [13]

The more dynamic the organization, the more organic the structure.

The more complex the environment, the more decentralized the structure.

The more diverse the organizational markets, the greater the organizational propensity to divisionalization.

The more hostile the environment, the more the organization is driven to temporary decentralization.

Disparities in the environment encourage the organization to centralize selectively and to differentiate work constellations; that is, a multistructure is formed.

The market process model concept of an organization is a somewhat radical departure that is useful in dealing with multicultural organizations. From this viewpoint, organizations are seen as places where people exchange a variety of things. They thereby create their own desires. In the process, they create cognitive maps, perceptions of externalities, social relationships, norms, values, social and organizational standards, and collective organizational goals and behavior. This model is also known as the social construction model; the precursor was Chester Bernard's 1938 view of organizations as incentive and distribution devices. More recently, Paul A. Lawrence and Jay Lorsch popularized the transactional theory of organization in the late 1960s, extending the notion of the market process model.

In thinking about advising on the governance and management of multicultural organizations, we have a choice of valuable managerial competences, depending on the environmental conditions. For example, conditions of threat favor strong management control systems. Conditions of change favor adaptive systems and skills. Environmental conditions of diversity favor internal differentiation. A dominantly uncertain environmental condition favors vertical and horizontal layering of the organization.

From a practical advisor's standpoint, there are certain tenets to use to encourage and empower a company to be innovative in its nature and complexity. Some of these are obvious to an experienced advisor and are commonsensical in nature. Other tenets may be counterintuitive but have proven to be of worth by organizational experts.

1. Employ idea men and women who also have fun at their work. The existentialist culture is important here.

2. Have open communications throughout, and particularly with outside contact; the human resource cultural frame of reference encourages this. The nature of the communications and social links an advisory board has with the chairman, CEO, and top management reflect this attribute.

3. Tolerate heterogeneous personnel policies that deal with some marginal, unusual, nonspecialist types and permit eccentricity. Again, a human resource framework works for this culture. Sponsor and empower human networking.

4. Feature decentralized structure with planned minimization of administration and headquarters. The tribal or club culture possesses this characteristic.

5. Where appropriate, employ computer integrated administrative oversight (CIAO) to watch for excesses in managerial staff behavior. The structural framework and role culture can often provide this computer support, but it should not stifle the other "soft" cultures.

6. Employ ad hoc advice, such as advisory boards and ad hoc councils. Use brainstorming techniques within for the autonomous strategic business units. This works in a mix of existential and task cultures. Symbolic visions and super-ordinate goals can also stimulate the organization.

If a corporation does these things, advisors may find the organizational culture characterized as having irregular asymmetrical growth, not a steady growth pattern. Outside advisors can often judge the meaning and significance of such a pattern. Judgments are often suspended on emerging or incorrigible strategies; such delays could be viewed as indecisiveness. Here an independent board of expert advisors may be of value as a sounding board.

Increased allowances may be granted R&D divisions, particularly for what may be viewed by purists as undisciplined exploration, investigation, and thinking. The paradox of tolerance and open-mindedness must go along with conviction of a relentless business strategy. A curvilinear relationship with creativity first rises then falls with motivation. The trick is to maintain creative effort but not produce panic effects toward an immediate solution (for example, jumping out a window versus looking for a fire escape).

Organizational pressures often impede creativity. Inner drive and task involvement are prerequisites and must be preserved. A relaxed, even playful attitude allows some disorganization, undisciplined approaches to strategic problems until a selected alternate can be pursued with conviction.

These tenets and their likely fallout consequences are not easy to accept for corporate leaders accustomed to a monocultural organization. In a multicultural system a manager needs to possess what I call a high "M.I.T. factor," that is, mal-integrative tolerance for non-standard conduct of affairs. Otherwise, the "confusion of goals" which, years ago, Ashley Montagu identified as the major cause of cultural neglect, will dominate the corporate culture.

CULTURE REALITIES: A REPRISE

The happy centipede approach to governing, managing, or advising a corporation with no attention to which foot to put forward is an unsatisfactory model for dealing with changes in the environment, strategy, or corporate culture. Advisors should seek to understand the realities of a corporate culture before any strategic or tactical advice can be meaningful and usable. This requires insight and sensitivity to corporate culture and corporate climate.

The "stranger factor" is important for an advisory board in order to be effective. This means that the advisors are, and remain, independent ("strangers"), objective, expert, professional, and experienced. They cannot be captive to the chairman or CEO. Close personal friendship should be set aside when the advisor-advisee relationship is in play.

Being a "stranger," yet a confidant of the chairman or CEO is somewhat oxymoronic. But this contradiction is the operative key to being a good member of a corporate advisory board. The advisors must be aware of their own behavior in relation to the advisee, in addition to being insightful about the advisee corporate culture.

Corporate governance in the 1990s will unquestionably demand a wider repertoire of corporate cultures, processes and concepts. Some socialization of directors, advisors, and top managers seems inexorable as each sees their role. This means innovations in the boardroom and top management with more trade-offs, debates, experiments, and compromises; more brokerage, confederation, negotiation, networking, and arbitration of value exchanges taking place. Advisory boards have a special place in this complex.

It is interesting that a bipolar corporate learning process is at work already as we enter the last decade of the 1900s, involving venturing and centering. Corporations were already experimenting with new policies and structures at the beginning of the 1980s. The venturing opens up the corporate boundary to new experience, to willingness to confront issues, examine alternative futures, discover strategic options, accept expert outside advice, make trade-offs, and initiate actions when an advisory group assumes a change-agent role.

The centering process can integrate these newly acquired experiences, behavior patterns, values, and concepts while reassessing responsibility. The counseling function is taking place beside a more realistic monitoring of performance. Ideally, venturing and centering alternate during developmental transitions in a growing or maturing corporation. Directors and officers need to learn how to do this more effectively. External pressures that began fulminating in the 1970s are forcing many boards to learn to juggle these two learning processes in parallel for the 1990s.

Role change and reform for individual directors and officers are also taking place in these best of times and worst of times. Boardworthiness of individual directors is a particular issue. Independence, integrity, credibility, conflicts of interest, corporate morality, and sensitivity are high on the hit list for individual directors.

As directors and officers learn to govern or manage more effectively in conditions of turbulence and disequilibrium, they will also learn to synchronize venturing and centering in tractable alternating cycles. One thing is sure: some new learning processes will certainly unfold and flower.

Learning how to face the realities of a corporate culture is a requirement for directors, officers, and advisors. Cultural frames of reference can be used to interpret and predict events. Advisors will be able to recognize cultural patterns that form barriers or opportunities for improving corporate effectiveness. As Edward Sapir has said, "Forms and significances which seem obvious to an outsider will be denied outright by those who carry out the patterns; outlines and implications that are perfectly clear to these may be absent to the eye of the onlooker."[14]

NOTES

1. Joseph Luft, "The Johari Window/A Graphic Model of Awareness in Interpersonal Relations," *NTL's Human Relations Training News* 5, 1 (1967), pp. 6–7.

2. Alan L. Wilkins and W. Gibb Dyer, Jr., "Toward Culturally Sensitive Theories of Culture Change," *Academy of Management Review* 13, 4 (1988), pp. 522–33.

3. Ashley Montagu, *Culture: Man's Adaptive Dimension* (New York: Oxford University Press, 1968), p. v.

4. Ashley Montagu, *The Cultured Man* (New York: World Publishing Co., 1958), p. 14.

5. Charles Handy, *Gods of Management* (London: London School of Business Studies, Pan Am Books Ltd., 1978).

6. Harrison M. Trice and Janice M. Beyer, "Studying Organizational Cultures Through Rites and Ceremonials," *Academy of Management Review* 9, 4 (1983), pp. 653–69.

7. S. Nichols, *Jung and Tarot: An Archetypal Journey* (New York: Samuel Weiser, 1980).

8. William Thompson, *The Edge of History* (New York: Harper & Row, 1971).

9. Danny Miller and Peter H. Friesen, "Archetypes of Strategy Formulation Management," *Science* 24, 9 (May 1978), pp. 921–33.

10. This section draws on "Managing Multicultural Organizations," remarks by the author November 3–6, 1985, at CIOS XX World Management Congress, Kuala Lumpur.

11. Handy, *Gods of Management.*

12. Ludwig von Bertalanffy, *Modern Theories of Development* (New York: Harper & Row, 1962).

13. Henry Mintzberg, *The Nature of Managerial Work* (New York: Harper & Row, 1973).

14. Edward Sapir, *The Unconscious: A Symposium* (New York: Alfred A. Knopf, 1928).

16

ADVISING ON NONPROFIT TRUSTEESHIP PATHOLOGIES

More business people are joining college and university boards. They make up forty percent of all board members compared to thirty-four percent in 1977.
—*Composition of Governing Boards,* 1985 (Washington, D.C.: Association of Governing Boards of Colleges and Universities, 1986), p. 15

Increasing costs of hospital insurance programs are causing corporations deliberately to place more of their executives on hospital boards. Thus, it seems that corporate America is becoming even more powerful in the nonprofit boardroom whether as statutory or advisory directors who are especially sensitive to and knowledgeable about trusteeship versus directorship.

The danger here, of course, is that individuals coming from the profit-making sector may apply "the good business-like approach"—the proprietary mentality. It should be emphatically repeated that "business purposes have no place in a nonprofit boardroom or organization."[1]

Professor James C. Baughman of Simmons College further points out that the reason so many recent court decisions involving trusteeship of nonprofit institutions have caused fierce shock waves was not so much that they were novel, but that "the myth that trustees have the final say—the ultimate authority—was so accepted. It is frequently stated that trustees sit on the top of the pyramid of power. They don't. The courts do. The board of trustees, although it may be appealed to by staff, is not the final court of appeal."

Boards are only one link in the chain of governance and management. Ultimately, what is "best" for a nonprofit institution is a matter for the court to decide—not trustees. This is so because there must be an ultimate adjudicator—not necessarily what is morally right or wrong, but what is judicially acceptable or unacceptable.[2]

Expert advisors to a board of trustees or a chief executive of a nonprofit enterprise can help in understanding that the conventional business-like approach is out of place in a nonprofit boardroom. The extent of this is illustrated by the congressional committee's observation in connection with litigation before the Pennsylvania Supreme Court over the Barnes Foundation's museum's charitable tax status and operating practices. The committee commented: "Foundations should operate not only in a goldfish bowl, but they should operate with glass pockets."[3]

TRUSTEESHIP IN CONTEXT

The role of an advisory board or council of a nonprofit institution is substantially different from the advisory board role for a profit-making corporation. This is described in detail in Chapter 8. Guiding those who function as advisors to trustees presents a complicated challenge. It is necessary to reemphasize the following context, which adds to and includes the differential characteristics cited in the previous chapter. Nonprofits are driven primarily by the ethic of service; for-profit institutions are driven primarily by the ethic of competition. The great majority of nonprofits have no stockholders. What full responsibility means as a trustee of a nonprofit institution is often ambiguous. In the event of alleged dereliction of duty by trustees of nonprofits, there is a problem of how to determine precisely who the injured party is.

There are no beneficiaries of a nonprofit charitable organization in a comparable position to beneficiaries of a private trust or the shareholders of a business corporation who are sufficiently interested to call the charitable fiduciary to account. With respect to handling surplus or unexpended funds, if any, from operations, nonprofits are prohibited from distributing monies left over after paying expenses (so-called earnings of the institution) to private persons.

Nonprofit boards (in contrast to for-profit boards) usually have a larger number of incumbents, fewer insiders, and use the executive director title for the person in responsible charge. Many nonprofit trustees have limited managerial experience and support services available to them; they have fixed terms of service and demand less time of service devoted by volunteer trustees. Studies show that nonprofit trustees tend to ignore the task of discussing policies and normally accept decisions of the executive director. The volunteer relationship is a major cause for such mental set.

The legal function of governing by its board of trustees of a nonprofit institution is primarily to see that the property and funds of the institution are devoted to the purposes for which they were given. It incorporates the ethic of service. The following definitions from Black's Law Dictionary are relevant:

A *trustee* is a person appointed or required by law, to exercise a trust; i.e., to whom property is legally committed in trust. The fiducial accountability involves confidence or trust.

A *fiduciary* is a person having duty, created by his undertaking, to act primarily for another's benefit in matters connected with such undertaking. A fiduciary is required to have scrupulous good faith and candor and is required to act in character analogous to that of a trustee.

A *director* is one of a group of persons entrusted with the overall direction of a corporate enterprise . . . one who regulates, guides, or orders . . . a person appointed or elected according to law, authorized to manage, and direct the affairs of a corporation or company.

Pricing of services is a difficult operating problem for nonprofit institutions (such things as hospital services, below-cost tuition, offset formulae of investment income unrelated to services, and so on). Nonprofits have no automatic relationship between an increased demand for service and an increase in funding by public sources, gifts, contributions, or legacies. Most nonprofits deal with politicians and donors (now owners) and often with supplicants.

The root problem for nonprofits is how to improve organizational effectiveness. Profit-seeking institutions tend to postpone or neglect longer-term impacts on society in pursuit of economic goals (for example, environmental, social, consumers, human rights, equal opportunity, and so on). Nonprofits pursue the service ethic while often suffering from short-term crises of survival, political discontinuity, and the continuing task of maintaining financial integrity, viability, and retaining qualified leadership.

The distinction between nonprofits and for-profits is blurring somewhat. Despite their ethic of competition, for-profits are becoming closer to what nonprofits always were, that is, more socially responsive and service-oriented. A main distinction is a temporal one, along with a shift in accountability in the for-profit sectors from primarily that of shareholders to that of stakeholders.

Both nonprofit and for-profit organizations have multiple objectives, multiple goals, multiple criteria, and multiple standards. These are dynamic and change with the external and internal environment, needs, and resources. Changing expectations, attitudes, life-style, beliefs, values and goals are taking place in both the nonprofit and for-profit sectors. Overseeing these requires special skills and understanding on the part of trustees and/or directors.

ISSUES FOR NONPROFIT TRUSTEES/ADVISORS

It is a fair statement that in 1965 the trustees of nonprofit institutions were hardly prepared for what the next decade would bring. In essence, institutions ran away from and with them. From every constituency—students, patients, clients, members, employees, administrators, donors, local citizens, and even governments flowed a torrent of complaints and actions directly critical of the institutions, and indirectly of the trustees.[4] In more than a few cases, when irate publics took their own institutions to court, trustees were found negligent. The inflation of the 1970s and the subsequent government retrenchments continue to generate similar pressure. In the 1980s most trustees and governing boards, embarrassed by the past, have struggled heroically to stay abreast or get ahead of their expanding responsibilities. But there have been serious deviations from propriety or from assumed norms.

More pertinent to current advisors of nonprofit trustees is the puzzle: What is coming next? Will trustees of the 1990s be another *tabula rasa* to be passively written upon by the stylus of forces and events beyond their ken and control? Or will they, be anticipation and foresight, undertake to study the future and prepare themselves accordingly? An experienced advisory board or advisory council can assist trustees and top management of nonprofit organizations in addressing these vexatious issues. One way to get minds around the complex of conditions is to adopt a systems view.

The systems answer to whether a board of trustees will be able to cope with the future depends, in great measure, upon the spheres of concern, interest, influence, obligation, responsibility, authority, and accountability that are acknowledged and addressed by the boards' system of governance. This compass of the board system is changing. Outside advisors can be engaged to provide wisdom from new areas of concern to the trustees.

Survival, societal relevance, renewal or obsolescence, increase or decline in competitiveness and maintenance or change of purpose are conventional criteria for judging effectiveness of the board of trustees system. The growth and development of such a system is not a linear process. It is influenced by a host of political, economic, cultural, technological, and social forces. This dynamic situation sets the stage for cognitive view of what trustees and their advisors should worry about.

The paradoxical nature of strategic success is that a board matures and develops certain norms and rhythms. It also acquires a history, identity, and life of its own. In effect, it becomes a somewhat closed system. In order for new norms, beliefs, and values to become incorporated within the framework of existing board patterns, the system must regularly open sufficiently to relate to the external forces and changes taking place. An advisory board can trigger this outreach to externalities.

The trustees must operationally define a flexible boundary of awareness and concern around selected governance variables where there is less interchange of energy (or communication, powerflow, perceptions, value changes, or whatever) in order to exercise reasonable oversight and control. Then an examination is made of what is happening inside the institutional system. The boundary is sporadically readjusted as necessary to cope with the changing external forces at work, the threats and opportunities implied. This cyclical process allows the board to decide on appropriate governance matters of concern and relevance as time goes on. An advisory board can offer a valuable perspective on this pulsating concern and awareness.

The next ten years or so will see at least four trends gain momentum as we become a more polarized have-and-have-not world. In turn these trends will surface some old and some new issues and create a new pathology for trustees and advisors to address. From our industrialized, interactive, complex vantage position the foreseeable issues appear to flow from a number of trends including a blurring of the public versus private sectors; the role of institutions in the developing world, which calls for an entirely different perspective of governance; a shift in accountability of corporations from shareholders only to accountability to the stakeholders; and the changing nature of governing boards to a more open concept system of oversight and guidance versus the closed system of conventional management.

If an issue is defined as a point of debate or a matter of concern on which responsible, conflicting viewpoints may arise in the boardroom, the emergent issues can be clustered into three functional areas for trustees and advisory board consideration. Three of these areas of a board of trustees' role have intellectual content: (1) *philosophy, principles,* and *policy;* (2) *decision making;* and (3) *control,* given knowledge of the barriers, constraints, and realistic degrees of freedom. Emergent issues for the next decade then fall into the following patterns.

Philosophy-Principles-Policy Issues

Mission Command. Taking charge of the institution's strategic direction, ensuring the integrity and fulfillment of institutional purpose, preserving identity, and guiding the smooth conduct of the institution is the command mission of the board. The internal corporate environment, the resources, externalities, and constituencies involved require a board of trustees to take active responsibility for ensuring survival, achievements, continuity, and societal relevance. The board is the accountable body in command of the mission. It can often use experienced, independent, expert advisors as a sounding board or referent base in making decisions on its mission.

Boundary. The horizons of institutional competence and incompetence are changing. Yet auditing and monitoring within these horizons is a requirement for good stewardship. Clarification and definition of the boundaries of board concern is a continuous challenge and needs explicit attention. The lines between social, political, and economic accountability are particularly blurred as not-for-profit institutions interface with the private and public sectors and reach into the less developed world.

Interactivity. The increased frequency and severity of interaction between institutions of all types in society presents vexatious problems. Some buffering processes and entities (for example, coalitions, professional societies, quasi-government organizations, and so on) are needed so that trustees can maintain a steady strategic course for an institution. The personal outside networks of experienced, professional advisors can provide nonconflicting bridges to other institutions and domains of human activity.

Signals of Change. There are many signals of future change. Advisory boards or councils are particularly valuable resources to detect these signals. It is important that a board of trustees (or its advisors) reduce the noise level from these signals in order to concentrate on the ones that are important to the philosophy, principles, and policies of the institutions. This means that trustees need to take initiative action to deal with changing rates of change, the turmoil, conflict, discontinuities, and new strategic vectors of the institution. Reexamination of institutional roles, shift in attitude or culture, and assessment of mission relevance are examples of initiative response to change.

These four issues spawn many structural and functional changes. An institution may move from single service to institutional conglomerate. Once confined to patient-care service, the Massachusetts General Hospital has also become a degree-granting institution in every health discipline except medicine, a research corporation in contract with two German multinationals, and a consulting business, among others. Ten years ago, it was necessary to apply to the commonwealth for recharter as a holding company. Will these components remain compatible or will they become increasingly divergent?

Trustees of large-scale institutions will have to ask what business are we in? What business should we be in? Should not? What are the critical factors in the determination? Who are the parties to the decision? By what process?

Others face the inner conflict—the disgruntled employee. Nonprofit institutions are operated and administered by highly educated, independent, and strongly motivated professional "employees." Many find their personal and professional standards at variance with those of the institution. Professional groups, once considered a subspecies, now see themselves demeaned in status, compensation, and recognition. Unionization, strikes, time-consuming protests, resistance to change, and litigation are a present and growing activity. Are trustees satisfied that atmosphere and procedures are in place for rapport, communication, and due process for grievance, whistle blowing, and protest? Is there an early warning system? Should trustees insist upon a direct role in these affairs?

Nonprofits are not immune to mergers, hostile or friendly. St. Asaph's Episcopal Church in Bala Cynwyd, Pennsylvania, and St. Alban's Church, Merion Station, have, in many ways, their pasts behind them. In the late nineteenth century, surrounded by large and well-to-do congregations, substantial edifices were built for both, including parish houses and rectories. After World War II, population and economic shifts in the Philadelphia area brought about reduction of over 70 percent of St. Alban's congregation and 80 percent of St. Asaph's. Annual giving dropped comparatively. St. Asaph's found itself on so short a tether that it gave up a full-time minister. Property costs for both, fueled by inflation, became excessive. Under canon law, the property was under the control of both vestries. Pressure from the bishop and common sense exercised by the vestries led to the exploration of a merger. Recommended to the congregations, the merger proposal was turned down, despite recommendations by both vestries. Nonprofit institutions will face increasing pressures to consolidate facilities and services and to merge. Most merger recommendations will be plausible. Almost all will be resisted by a variety of constituencies. Can trustees improve the process of considerations and decisions?

Trustees must deal with resource generation, allocation, and control. The chairman of the Laclede Gas Company of St. Louis is a member of Civic Progress, Inc., an association of chief executive officers of the St. Louis area's thirty largest employers. He is also the chairman of a civic progress committee involved with health care cost containment. In the course of reviewing the strategy for cost cutting, it was discovered that members of the committee were reluctant in some cases to attack the budgets of their own institutions. Furthermore, it became obvious that reducing costs depended largely upon prior decisions about the allocation of resources, particularly priorities. Additional study indicated that if long-term and larger savings were to be realized, short-term funding and spending in certain instances might have to be increased.

Trustee and board members have always been under pressure to "give, get, or get off." Tomorrow's funding demands will grow in size and in competitiveness. There will be equal demands for controlling and reducing expenditures. Trustees will be in the center of this struggle. Trustees, to be effective, may have to master a comprehensive and integrative approach to all these aspects of the financial picture.

Trustees must deal with the changing face of ownership. St. Joseph's Hospital in Bangor, Maine, is owned by the Sisters of the Transfiguration—a religious order specializing in health care. Five years ago, St. Joseph's found itself in such serious financial difficulty as to threaten bankruptcy. The sisters agreed, under the duress of circumstance and prodding from the local bishop, to employ a management firm to unravel the difficulties. The firm was given a three-year contract with authority to appoint an administrator and oversee all operations. The administrator promptly organized an outside group of Bangor's leading citizens to join the sisters on the board. After two and a half years, St. Joseph's was well in the black, filling a large gap in the community's health care, and prepared to rehire the administrator, the management firm, or go it alone. The hospital was the main source of the order's revenue, and one sister, supported by several others, was anxious to move up from assistant administrator to CEO. After prolonged discussion, the order decided not to rehire the administrator. The outside lay trustees resigned.

It appears that ownership patterns in nonprofit institutions are undergoing change. Boards and organizations once under the domination of a few donors, a paternalistic religious affiliation, a founder, an omnipotent CEO, or self-perpetuating trustees are becoming restless. "Lay" boards in all fields are indicating less willingness to be purely advisory. Constituencies are agitating for board representation. Outside funders are insisting upon evidence of board involvement and commitment. Insiders, whether one or several, will, by force or their own design, accommodate themselves to new associates. Anticipated planned change appears preferable to confrontation and resignation.

Decision-Making Issues

Governable Risks. In the future, the board of a nonprofit entity needs to spend time discovering which uncertainties can be converted into governable or manageable risks. While this job is primarily the management's for the board, the discovery and assessment requires new sources of information—often less accessible to management, new perspectives, and new processes for ordering the array of uncertainties. An outside advisory council can supplement the management's assessment and determination of these risks.

Environmental Forces. The future environment will differ radically from the past. Trustees will need to know "what is happening out there" in order to keep in touch with reality. The challenge will be to make subjective, judgmental distinctions about what is relevant. An expert council of advisors can provide a valuable perspective on these environmental forces.

Priorities. The number of issues will be beyond the capacity of a normal board to respond to them adequately. Hence, priorities are needed in order to allocate attention and resources. Nobel laureate Herbert A. Simon's concept of bounded rationality helps to explain the rising need for qualified advice. Individuals as well as organizations often cannot comprehend problems that exceed a certain level of complexity. When the level is passed, it is difficult to have a rational response. An adjunct advisory board of experts can help in understanding and assist the board and management in setting priorities. Three previously cited decision-making issues may be illustrated by "the straw that broke the CEO's back."

Wall Street Journal, January 27, 1983—"Wharton's Carroll Quitting: A Case of Pure Fatigue," Philadelphia. At 10 a.m. Donald C. Carroll is sitting behind his desk with his eyes closed . . . and rubbing his eyebrows. Mr. Carroll is the dean of the University of Pennsylvania's Wharton School, and at the moment he looks tired. . . . a couple of faculty members . . . want to raise money. . . . their proposal conflicts with still another research center at Wharton that is already seeking money from about 25 companies. "Eeww, boy, this is complicated," the 52-year-old Dean says, burying his face in his hands. . . . Strains and pressures take their toll. Mr. Carroll is leaving the job at the end of the academic year. So are the deans at Stanford, Chicago, Dartmouth, Carnegie-Mellon, Berkeley, Indiana, Texas, Purdue, and many other universities.

How much can the best of CEO's stand? For how long? To the CEO is the board a ready help or another burden? How realistic are the expectations of the board and the organization? How realistic are his expectations of himself? How adequate really is the organization around him in view of growing demands? What is the board doing about management succession and continuity? About management training? About people development? An experienced advisory council can assist the chairman, CEO, or trustees in coping with these vexatious issues without taking on the statutory duties required of the board of trustees.

Control Issues

Board Compass. A broad scope or compass of awareness of the larger societal, technological, economic, and political context in which all institutions exist will be the hallmark of an effective board of trustees. Many future events that will impact institutions are likely to be outside the conventional cognizance and experience of present trustees. A basic change in target board composition or addition of an advisory board(s) appears in order to provide the trustees with capability to cope with these impacts.

Criteria and Standards. Events impacting the institution in the future will often be outside the organized managerial or governance focus of the corporation in terms of command, control, communication, audit, and monitoring systems. Governance criteria and standards—both objective and subjective measures and value systems—need reexamination.

A cognitive map of the general compass of concern and accountability of trustees on the board of the future includes speculation and knowledge of the barriers, constraints, and relative degrees of freedom which are expected to prevail during the next, say, ten years. The controllable actions may become fewer due to regulations, statutes, and activist pressures unless boards take initiative to self-police their conduct. Three case examples demonstrate the problems and challenge of future control of nonprofit organizations.

Adequacy of Information

The Orton Society, a national association, is dedicated to the diagnosis and remediation of dyslexia. Named for Dr. Samuel Orton, the pioneer neurologist in the field, the society has been successful in creating a forum in which a wide range of administrators, teachers, physicians, various learning professionals, and parents can exchange ideas and strategies. However, with the rise in the public's awareness of dyslexia, greater opportunities in neurological research, and government regulations mandating remediation of dyslexia along with other handicaps, the society is compelled to undertake more and more organizational responsibilities. Members of the board of the society are experiencing difficulty in making the transition. The biggest difficulty is shortage of information—numbers of dyslexics, parent and family backgrounds, school responses, defused markets for society services, sources of funds, and so on. The board is inevitably "hung up" on decision making because nobody is clear as "to what we need to know and where to go to find out." An experienced administrator with a personal stake in the society has turned down the CEO position on the grounds "nobody knows what is going on."

The problem of what trustees need to know to be effective will grow more intense as the winds of institutional demand and opportunity freshen. Trustees will be expected to "assure themselves that all relevant, pertinent, and accurate data are provided." If critical information is not forthcoming, the diligent trustee is obliged to request it or face charges of ineffectiveness at best or negligence at worst.

Institutional Integrity vs. Constitutional Rights

In 1957, in *Sweeny* v. *New Hampshire,* the Supreme Court of the United States protected the rights of a professor refusing to testify regarding the content of a course he was teaching by affirming the essential freedoms of the university as establishing who may teach, what may be taught, how it shall be taught, and who may be admitted to study as the prerogatives of the university. In 1978, 50 percent of all revenues received by public institutions of higher learning and 25 percent of all private revenues came from the federal government. In the same year, the courts and the Department of Health, Education and Welfare, in order to impose desegregation obligations, mandated a ten-state education system to merge campuses, to determine course offerings, and to distribute enrollments. Later, the U.S. Department of Labor mandated the University of California to release privileged material on faculty promotions. Still later, a University of Georgia professor went to jail rather than reveal how he voted in a tenure case. Trustees confront, and will continue to confront, similar issues in patient rights, collisions over gene-splitting and defense-related research, and competing claims of justice affecting the freedom and accountability of institutions with the federal "connection."

Board Organization

If trustees are to respond effectively to issues of the future, the organization of the board will determine their success. Of all the problems, trustees should be giving highest priority to the organization of the board. The reason is simple. Legal, appropriate governance is the activity of a unit, not an individual. A distinguished director once said, "A trustee is responsible 24 hours a day—the only way he can exercise that responsibility is at a duly constituted meeting of the board when a quorum is present." How many trustees are satisfied with their board's capacity to meet today's responsibilities? Studies reveal that few are comfortable with planning, monitoring progress, and incorporating new members.

Looking ahead at coming obligations, how many trustees are satisfied that the board organization is up to snuff? Some of the straws in the wind: reduction in size, elimination of the executive committee as "the board between meetings," full-time chairs, "professional" trustees, trustee compensation, staff services, expanded board budgets for board development, and so on. Increased environmental and institutional complexities will require equal advances in the organization and practice of the board.

The future trends, issues, and concerns of nonprofit institution trustees require a new understanding of and attitude toward the role of an effective board, the role of individual trustees, and the role of any advisors. Coping will require more experience, intuition, instinct, and subjective judgment. These human attributes may be reinforced by increased use of quantitative, logical techniques (such as strategic planning, alternative future scenarios, and others) available for dealing with uncertainty, complexity, and velocity of change.

The first step is increased consciousness on the part of the trustees and the management of the need for change. The second step is agreement on a target model board system for governing the not-for-profit institution. This model will be institutional-specific and subject to change. The third step is a transition model to allow change to take place in an orderly and acceptable fashion as trustees and top management face more sophisticated problems and heavier responsibilities in the future. A sophisticated advisory board can often help guide this three-step process.

The next section diagnoses the "pathological types" of nonprofit boards of trustees, suggests strategies for dealing with these pathologies, and discusses three of the CEO/board of trustee models in United States practice. Specific suggestions for top management, trustees, and advisory boards are outlined. These can serve as guidelines for dealing with the "pathologies" commonly found in the conditions of nonprofit boards of trustees. The guidelines suggest specific means of coping with the structural, functional, and control changes produced by trustee conduct. These changes may deviate from propriety or from acceptable practice—that is, become a pathological state of governance unless carefully directed.

IMPORTANT PATHOLOGIES IN BOARD/
STAFF RELATIONSHIPS

These notes categorize and address major imbalances and other stresses in the relationships of boards, staffs, and chief executives in a variety of institutions.[5] Most of our examples are drawn from acute care hospitals, academic medical centers, universities, and independent schools. The stimulus for this presentation comes from particular sources in the professional practices of the authors. One of these sources is the apparently inevitable and repetitious cycle of a board and its chief executives, from an initial "honeymoon" period to the angry board ultimatum to the chief executive to resign or be fired, a cycle that characterizes all too many institutions all too durably. Another source is the indecision, frustration and rage that are so often the concomitants of living and working in "world class" academic and medical institutions, where the senior professionals are individually powerful but collectively cancel the formal leadership of the institution as well as each other.

Pathological Types

Strong Board–Weak Head–Strong Staff. Academic Medical Center resists change initiative from the board. Staff incentive supports the status quo because the effect of the various changes advocated by different service chiefs and heads of departments and deans of research cancel one another. Head is professionally less powerful than many of his "subordinates," the board is ultimately willing to defer to the staff, and they leave the executive head high and dry when his own expertise and personal strength are being challenged beyond his capacity.

Weak Board–Strong Head–Weak Staff. The long-time school head of the classical mold whose success depends on a stable environment and an unfailing ability to command. When the inevitable decline comes, the board and the staff are unable to supply necessary direction, and the system goes into chaos.

Strong Board–Strong Head–Militant Staff. Sometimes associated with geographic separation between board and institution, this pathology is a power play to "win" control of the organization. The effort is to unseat the other party (board chairman or head) by gaining political support of constituents.

Split Board–Strong Head–Weak Staff. As the board fights, the head anticipates arbitrary action detrimental to him or her and secures protective power bases such as alumni support, embroiling the entire institution in the conflict. Whether the head can survive is questionable in the long run.

Board Serves as Temporary Staff, with Professional Assistance. Professional associations, for example, in which leadership character and quality change annually and quixotically, promoting a defensively bureaucratic staff structure and preventing long-term continuity and development.

Board–Head Relationships During Office Turnover. Cases of relatively stable relationships between board and head suffer traumatic change when the chairman is replaced and a new relationship has to be built. The head's need to feel in control during the transition may prompt the new chairman to exert authority and a cycle of distrust is born.

Strategies for Dealing with Pathologies

Reframing. This strategy involves creating new ways of thinking about the institution, its environment, and its component parts. The strategy, when employed, should have the effect of (1) breaking up or rendering inappropriate the old patterns of narrow self-interest, conflict, or isolation, and (2) inviting increased allegiance to the institution on the part of the major professional players.

A reframing can result from several activities: a strategic planning process, a mission and goals study, an organizational renewal effort, or as a reaction to a serious outside threat. The services of a third party can aid in any of the above. Reframing is probably most suitable in cases where there is some awareness in the institution that a new direction is needed.

Creating a New Locus or Source of Power in the Institution. This strategy is based on the premise that, under normal conditions, there is insufficient power concentrated in any individual, position, or group in the organization to compel the organization to move together in a new direction. The strategy would be to create a new source of power that, with board sanction and approval, can chart a new direction for the institution and mobilize the resources required to move in that chosen direction.

In creating a new source or locus of power, the board could: (1) establish a new mandate for the CEO, (2) hire a new CEO with a new or different mandate for leading the organization, (3) establish a strategic planning (or analogous) committee, made up presumably of board members, senior administration, and key department heads, and (4) other?

Negotiation. The strategy here is to identify the perspectives and interests of each department head, and discover areas of common interest as well as positions or interests that are nonnegotiable. The result would be a map of sorts showing the positions and situations of each principal player in the institution. A direction could then be shaped around this map, if participants agree to negotiate with one another.

The services of a third party to do the required mapping can be very useful. The third party would work with an internal group to shape a mutually agreed upon direction for the institution which would take into account the interests of all major parties, or would serve directly and primarily as negotiator. Effecting this strategy requires at least a surface willingness on the part of administration, board, and key professionals to seek a new direction, and a willingness on the part of all to be candid about their interests, plans, commitments and areas of possible negotiation.

Building Consensus Around a Plurality. The strategy here is to find a large enough number of professional leaders who are middle managers and who will agree on a direction for the institution, so that the remaining department heads will have to come along, in time, or be left out in the cold.

The consensual issue would have to be carefully chosen to be appealing to all (or most) of the department heads and permit them to join without appearing to "sell out." And, the choice of department heads among which to build the consensus would also have to be carefully made.

The advantage of this strategy is that not all key department heads would have to "buy in" at the start. Thus, the strategy could presumably be implemented more quickly than if a full consensus were sought.

A Planned Showdown. This strategy would involve a power play or direct confrontation between the administration (backed by the board) and (presumably) the most powerful department head, the purpose of which would be to shift the power relationship in the institution by reducing the power or stature of the professional staff. The idiom is win-lose; the end result is shifting power to the administration at the expense of a more docile but less fully engaged professional staff.

A Succession of Stronger CEOs. This strategy aims at gradually increasing the power of the CEO position by retaining successively stronger people and by the board's changing/strengthening CEO mandates. This is obviously a long-term strategy and would involve relatively short, probably explicit terms of office for each incumbent. It would also require a continuous board commitment. This, in turn, would require a board whose membership and leadership is quite stable.

Planning and Evaluation Processes as Steps in Recurring Goal-Setting Cycles. Review of board-executive relationships and procedures would be emphasized as a means for guiding and improving the interplay and collaboration of a board and its chief staff executive. This strategy, like the preceding strategy, is the result of long-term objectives to build self-correcting structures and processes, rather than a short-term result of crisis management.

Attainable and Valuable CEO/Board Models for Professional Institutions

There exist in U.S. practice at least three models that some institutional leaders pursue as their ideals.

The *traditional model* casts the CEO as authoritarian leader with the board supporting him and deferring to him. Most independent schools are, or used to be, in this model. Boards seem to like it, but reject heads who do not carry out the model perfectly forever. Many universities ambivalently pursue this model, but feel bad about the strength of authoritarian values. Many teaching hospitals feel bad because they do not pursue this model. This model is deeply embedded in American culture: business, church, school, and government.

The *board-interaction model* casts the CEO in the role of board educator, mobilizer, and facilitator, and commits the board to the role of knowledgeably holding the CEO accountable for explicitly agreed results. Some independent schools are now committed to this model. St. Paul's School, Buckingham Browne & Nichols, and the Park School are possible examples. It seems to be close to the Bok model at Harvard. Where this model is being intelligently pursued in professional institutions, it appears to lengthen the half-life of incumbent CEOs significantly, as for example in the independent schools named above.

The model depends on the realism of expecting the CEO to understand the professional substance of what's going on in the institution, being able to convey the issues to the board, bringing the board up to at least amateur standing in dealing with professional issues, and persuading the board to use the expertise its members come with. The effort required of board members is considerable.

The *CEO/peer model* casts the CEO in the role of consensus builder among powerful and relatively autonomous professional leaders whom he represents to the board; the board must either find the means to activate itself or revert to passivity. The Boston University Medical Center attempted to develop this model at the end of Arland Christ-Janer's tenure as president of Boston University, but successors did not value this model.

The CEO/peer model may not require that the board acquire unused devices (such as its own professional staff to educate it and help it formulate issues for itself), but it certainly cannot be both active and under control unless it finds feasible and trusted means for acquiring the information it must have. In a sense, this model is that of the Quakers (Religious Society of Friends). (Query: Is there some other balanced-power relationship that is not on dead-center?) Each model fits some situations better than others.

1. *CEO as authoritarian leader.*
    a. Crises requiring unilateral control and decision making.
    b. Inability of key stakeholders to accept or even understand any other model.
    c. Unchangeable circumstances that restrict a board to passivity for a period of time.
    d. Truly superior qualities of a particular person make him or her a de facto authority to whom almost everyone automatically defers most of the time.
2. *CEO as board mobilizer and facilitator.*

    a. Participatory values are influential in determining roles of stakehold-
       ers.

    b. CEO has skills to enable him to use the strengths of a mobilized board
       in assuring adequate issue confrontation and conflict management of
       the professional staff.

    c. Board members with enough energy and availability to hold up their
       end of the bargain can be acquired and retained.

3. *CEO as mobilizer of professional peers.*

    a. Complexity or breadth of institution precludes any one person being
       substantively in charge.

    b. Board values the differences as well as the consensus brought it by the
       peers, and is able and willing to move and not be paralyzed by this
       condition.

    c. Tradition of the institution can be interpreted to allow both the board
       and the CEO to be judged successful, even though they carry out only
       the roles appropriate to this model.

Each model can be accepted and put into practice if acceptable to
stakeholders. And this requires a generic process for deliberately
sanctioning a particular model once leadership has made its initial
choice.

1. Identify stakeholders.

2. Identify model in use.

3. Obtain stakeholder opinion on what model is in use.

4. Develop alternative approaches to test for preferred model.

5. Develop educational processes to familiarize stakeholders with pros and
   cons of available models and to persuade key influentials that a selection
   among models is possible.

6. Test for preferred model.

7. Work out and implement a process for assuring that all or most stakeholders will accept the same model.

8. Carry out a process for identifying gaps between model in use and preferred model.

9. Develop a process to modify procedures, roles, relationships and responsibilities if necessary (board, CEO, professional staff), that will fill the
   gap between existing and preferred models.

10. Carry out changes in procedures, roles, relationships, or responsibilities.

The actual content and emphasis in particular steps will be different at various institutional levels and among different stakeholder
groups.

Advising a nonprofit board of trustees and its top management must
not mix (1) profit and nonprofit activities, (2) legal contexts, (3) liti-

gation and protection considerations, (4) accountabilities, (5) power flows, (6) trusteeship versus directorship, or (7) enfranchisement of charitable trustees, that is, the privileges granted by government to nonprofit trustees to operate eleemosynary organizations for the public good with the conventional corporate charter to operate a for-profit organization for benefit of its shareowners.

Trustee advisors well informed on the special nature of nonprofit institutional governance are rare birds indeed. There is a career opportunity developing for experienced, qualified men and women in this *pro bono publico* advisory field. The ethic of service is the dominant driving force with the ethic of competition taking second place as long as the advisor is expert and peer respected in a relevant field.

NOTES

1. James C. Baughman, *Trustees, Trusteeship and the Public Good* (Westport, Conn.: Quorum Books, 1987), p. 159.

2. Ibid., pp. 153–54.

3. Ibid., pp. 94–95.

4. Adapted from "A Syllabus on Emergent Board Agenda," Seminar and Workshop jointly presented in Boston, October 25, 1983, by The Cheswick Center, Boston, and Arthur D. Little, Inc., Cambridge, Mass. Abstracts from remarks by Henry W. Sherrill, chairman of The Cheswick Center, and Robert K. Mueller, chairman of Arthur D. Little, Inc.

5. Abstracted from a paper presented by John Seiler, James Dunlop, and Homer Hagedorn at a Governance Consultation Workshop, Boston, Mass., October 25, 1983, jointly sponsored by The Cheswick Center, Boston, and Arthur D. Little, Inc., Cambridge, Mass.

Appendix

ADVISEE SEARCH: GETTING INVITED TO SERVE AS ADVISOR

In the spring of 1987, Doyle Graf Mabley, a New York–based advertising firm, asked 600 people with household incomes of $100,000 or more to rank twenty symbols of personal success and achievement, such as owning an expensive car or holding an important position in government. The top three answers: owning a business, traveling abroad frequently, and sitting on the board of a cultural institution.

The *Wall Street Journal* of January 7, 1988, quoted Adam Stagliano, who supervised the survey, as commenting: "Owning a car or a boat, anyone can do if they have the money, but (being on a board) requires something else. They (directorships) are more traditional elitist symbols." Or, as Suzy, the *New York Post*'s society columnist puts it: "You can be rich and powerful but not prestigious."

Being a director or trustee on a charitable or for-profit institution brings a cachet that cannot be ignored despite the liability exposure that may be involved. An advisory role may not be quite as prestigious, but it carries much of the same distinction.

PREPARATION STRATEGY

A preparation strategy for seeking an invitation to serve on an advisory board—or a statutory board of directions, for that matter—can be chunked into three categories: (1) personal attributes, (2) situational conditions, and (3) techniques or practices that may enhance opportunities for sitting on an advisory board. The range of valuable personal attributes is so broad and situation-specific that only some general qualifications can be usefully discussed. Most of the following is conventional wisdom.

Personal Attributes

Someone said a person's character is what he is when he isn't being watched. Although personality and character profiling is beyond the scope of this discussion, it is critical to any potential advisory career analysis. Fitness for the role at hand, intelligence, competence, experience, peer relationships, ideological orientation, philosophy of life, integrity, ethics, morals, values, style, diligence, enthusiasm, motivational traits, biologic and constitutional factors (age, sex, size, genetic factors), social and demographic factors (education, social class, culture, family, religion, reference groups), and other attributes shape the person and the future in his or her present setting or in an advisory role to which he or she aspires.

Although it is relatively easy to be objective about other people and subjective about ourselves, the tough problem is being subjective about others and objective about ourselves. Hence, outside counsel is often helpful in assessing our attributes.

For purposes of private mapping of a search for an advisory role, an attempt, to some degree, should be made of one's own character profiling. A good personnel program in a company will include resources to help individuals size up themselves. Outside analysts (including one's spouse or offspring) can often help us to come to grips with a reasonable fix on personal characteristics.

Central life interests or a lifetime commitment to an institution, industry, or profession is a strong signal of dedication, achievement, and determination. Central life interest requires acceptance (or tolerance) of a set of norms and values. These include the obvious variables of (1) job satisfaction; (2) cohesiveness of the employee unit or peer relationship(s); (3) a perceived job autonomy or the extent to which an employee or professional thinks he can use his own judgment on the job; (4) organizational or professional status; (5) perceived advantages of the organization or professional associations by comparison of this with other environments that might yield other advantages; (6) the perceived chances of promotion or peer recognition; (7) the paternalism or collegial climate; and (8) participative aspects of the extent to which one is involved in company, professional or learned society–sponsored activities and outside networks. Suffice it to say, personal attributes must be exemplary. A chairman or CEO seeking a corporate advisor will consciously or subconsciously assess a prospective candidate's personal attributes.

Prospective advisors should have substantial career experience relevant to the company seeking outside counsel. Industry, functional, or operating knowhow developed over a successful career provides a bedrock of practical knowledge and expert knowhow. In addition, street-smarts are often key to being a peer- and advisee-acceptable advisor. Successful line and/or staff experience can be impressive, even determining, when being considered for advisory board membership.

The mental set is the framework of thought comprising the unique internal politics of our complex of minds. There are two extremes to this framework's outer limits.

One way of looking at this bipolar set is as follows: The unselective, nonevaluative perspective accepts unordered totality as the mode. This natural approach of just letting the problems hang out and hoping that things will work out is surprisingly successful, on occasion. But it is an unreliable, unstructured process that cannot be counted on as an advisory technique.

The intuitive emphasis on association and response is not usually effective either. The other extreme is a quantitative, analytic type approach which emphasizes generalizations, conceptual hierarchies, formation of class concepts and comparison processes. Advisory boards need both types of mind-set.

Operations researchers suggest that as we advance from simple problems toward more complex issues. The optimum framework for the human mind changes from the LRSQ (logical, rational, sequential, and quantitative mind-set) to the PISQ (perceptive, intuitive, simultaneous, and qualitative set) approach. Using this transitional approach involves a shifting, interchangeably, from one continuum of thought to the other, depending on the step at which the thinking is taking place.

Effective advisors may have either an objective, logical, quantitative mind-set or a subjective, intuitive, qualitative, mental orientation. Talented advisors can switch from one such mental set to the other, or at least acknowledge the "unique politic of this complex of minds" in their counseling process.

Title, hierarchical or professional status carry the perception of relative success, power, prestige, and leadership. Obviously, these attributes are valuable assets for an advisor. Public identity in an active role either as a professional, executive, scholar, academician, or public servant count heavily in the desirable attribute category for prospective advisor candidates. Unemployed, inactive, retired status or similar identification is often a negative attribute, for obvious reasons, unless the candidate is active in some meaningful way, keeping his or her professional skills up to date.

We don't particularly need a theory to identify and empower our own friendship networks. But there are sociologists and anthropologists who have provided enlightening perspectives on the characteristics of people's network relationships and the process involved. See Chapter 13 for more on this important attribute.

From an individual candidate advisor standpoint, two models of network relationships are important: one is based on personal friendships, acquaintanceships, and connections; and the other is based on structural, occupational positions in one or more network systems such as a job in a corporation, government office, school, or hospital, or a role in a social club or association. The first model deals with "ego or personal networks" and the second with network position or "positional networks."

An ego network is usually measured by the extent to which it provides support for the people in it. Ego networks are "dense," meaning that all involved are connected by intense relationships with each other.

Personal or ego networks attend to the relationships in which a person is involved. These networks involve only the individual's direct relations to others and may omit or be oblivious of unreciprocated relations with persons who have no direct relationship, but may have an indirect connection. Saying this more simply, if we confine our networking to only those whom we know personally (or positionally), we miss the "other world" out there of contacts and friends of our contacts and friends. This is the exciting, potential scope which networking offers when conducted in a conscious and determined way.

Personal obligation networks are an offshoot of personal networks. In the business world one can only use personal collateral in a limited way; for example, in getting appointments or seeking special attention. This reciprocal exchange can be shared from time to time with those with whom one has connections on a transaction or business basis (as distinct from a superior-subordinate relationship).

The network position model describes a person's relationships with all other people in a system—an organization or industry, for example. It differs from an ego network principally because the relationships one does not have to others in the system are as important as the relationships one does have.

All these positional and ego relationships tend to foster network cliques. A clique is a set of people in a network who are connected to one another by strong relationships. Examples of cliques are family, playgroup, community, and friendship networks. These groups of people are characterized by having intimate face-to-face association and cooperation.

There are two challenges involved in the networking process. The first is to nurture and empower our ego model and position model networks. The second is to extend these networks to "another world" beyond our ken. This is where a theory of networking is useful. To be able and willing to use networking in large organizations, going beyond the traditional, personal acquaintance networks, offers a chance to improve organizational effectiveness.

A third model is the attribute network. These networks loosely link individuals who share a commonality, such as similarity of personal attributes, political affiliation, goals, sex, status, social causes, old school ties, or whatever.

Transactional networks, a fourth model, are those that focus on the exchanges that occur among two or more individuals, that is, buyer-seller, trading, client-supplier, legal, accounting, and other professional services.

Part of our networks are planned, organized, and intentional. Other parts develop by chance. This part needs diligent cultivation in order to enhance its value as a candidate advisor or director.

Possible channels of communication grow very rapidly as the organization grows. With two people you have two channels—one each way; with three people you have six channels; with ten people you have ninety channels. With 100 people you have 9,900 possible channels. Networks are reciprocal. For continuity, networks must be win/win. Find ways to help others. Usually they will reciprocate when you ask for help.

Networks are also dynamic. They are either growing or shrinking and will not remain static long. Keep a network growing on one end because it is probably diminishing on the other end. Networks thrive on courtesy. Return even marginal telephone calls. Do not get insulated from your networks. Listening, courtesy, and appreciation are enough reciprocality for many people. In the act of networking, the persons involved are in a peer relationship even if they have very different ranks in various organizations.

Networks have to be built before they can be used. Building requires patience, dedication, attention to detail, reciprocity, developing a track record, and more. Networking is like trying to cultivate wild flowers. You don't plant and hover over them. You permit or create an environment where they can come out and grow. Cultivation of networks increases the value of one's background and assets of interest when seeking an invitation to serve on an advisory board.

Situational Conditions

The career context, or environment, where we gain experience, competence, and network relationships may be viewed as multiple domains in which there may be potential to establish credibility as an advisor candidate. Forces beyond individual control vary by industry context, geographical or political regions, and functional professions. These forces are always situation- and time-specific.

The best of times or the worst of times can exist for any context. Importantly, identify with an environmental context where you are knowledgeable, experienced, and up to date, and have special expertise and peer recognition. Don't seek candidacy in areas where you are not well established.

Harvard Professor Rosabeth M. Kanter at a Colby-Sawyer College commencement in New Hampshire in June 1988, recited some of her secrets of being a leader. The first one concerns timing of your presence.

1. Showing up—Corazon Aquino was there when her husband was assassinated. "I can do that," she said. Prospective advisor candidates have to be where the action is: business conferences, seminars, professional societies, and associations, and the like.

2. Have cause to believe in a dream. Advisor candidates must have a vision and think about their potential role as an advisor.

3. Empower others; gain power and recognition by sharing. Developing our networks is a prime way to achieve this. Build networks before they are needed. Networking is the process for making contacts and achieving recognition which can be precursors to invitations to advisory boards.

A significant attribute is to get one's economic position to a point where you are not dependent on current income from an advisory board engagement.

Keep abreast of advisory director–prone companies. Competitors watch each other and often adopt competitive tactics. If possible, get acquainted with corporate advisors, and let your interest in candidacy be known.

Executive and director recruiting firms are always on the lookout for experienced business talent. Getting on statutory boards is one means of public exposure, which can lead to an advisory role with another noncompeting company. Past directorship experience is a valuable asset for a prospective advisor to have.

Techniques and Practices

Effort must be spent in understanding what advisory boards, councils, or panels do and don't do. Techniques used in seeking an invitation should be natural, consistent with personal style and professional behavior.

Personal attributes, situational conditions previously cited, plus luck, are keys to any invitation. In any event, be realistic about what you have to offer and where your talents might be useful. Given this caution, avoid unnatural acts of solicitation. There are commonsense pointers that may help.

Be currently informed—this is a particular challenge for those who have decoupled from their primary vocational position due to downsizing, merger or acquisition, obligatory retirement, or career change. I have served on an advisory group where a fellow advisor was not invited to stay on the council because he dropped out of the mainstream of his business. Further, he showed lack of effort to stay informed through various networks, publication reading, and professional activity. He really retired mentally, vocationally, and educationally.

Be a selective joiner and organization worker. Professional and learned societies, trade associations, educational programs, political, religious, health care, athletic, and social organizations afford exposure to other proactive persons. They may be a link to a prospective advisory position. Propinquity, personality, performance, and presence can favorably impress a colleague who has referral power or is in search of outside advice for an enterprise. Publication of papers, speech-making, program chairing and other practices are obvious ways to get exposure, demonstrate expertise, and experience. Like any professional organization, you must be willing to serve in various subordinate, support roles before you are asked to take any leadership or councilor position.

Opportunities abound for continuing education, "going back to school" on a part-time, convenient schedule. This hones professional or business talent, makes new contacts, and keeps you informed in your own field of expertise or a new area of interest.

Applying experience and talent in volunteer service for the public good is rewarding. It increases exposure to other talented individuals who may be a long-shot key to an organization seeking advisors.

Willingness to work with a small startup firm, association, or other group initiative in the throes of struggling to be successful is rewarding. It affords a chance to demonstrate a constructive role in advising and being observed by others—bankers, venture capitalists, lawyers, community, or industry leaders. This demonstrates willingness to risk your identity with a new risky initiative.

Many large companies have difficulty dealing with small, entrepreneurial organizations and are on the lookout for persons with experience in this regard. The message: Don't confine your search activity only to large successful institutions. The action and exposure are often greater in the entrepreneurial field.

Show up, be there. Use the Willy Sutton technique of focusing on banks because the money is there. Participate in as many selected events as reasonable where movers and shakers attend. The networking opportunities afford leads and exposure to possible invitations to contribute your experience and advice to those who need it.

Standard salesman practice of picking up the check with customers or prospects is a time-worn technique to build collateral with others. Carefully and subtly used, in a proper way and setting, this practice can encourage reciprocal hosting and increased exposure to those who may know of or influence an advisor search.

Look and act the part of a potential advisor. Avoid an unnatural approach to any such perception. But do not overlook the importance of demeanor and appearance expected of talented, experienced, professional advisors. There is no stereotypical image of a knowledgeable, even distinguished, advisor. But there is a befitting, deliberate, thoughtful, listening style.

As with upward influence and organizational politics, there are impression management techniques. These are sets of assertive tactics that have the purpose of gaining attention and/or approbation of an audience that controls significant rewards or acts as gatekeeper to desired networks.

Remember when Imelda Marcos arrived in New York in October 1988 to appear in court on charges of embezzlement. Imelda was dressed demurely by some standards, a floor-length Spanish evening dress of bright aquamarine silk, enormous butterfly sleeves, and "a flurry of jewelled ornament on the front." Consider the private aircraft that brought her, the $2,000-a-day suite at the Waldorf Towers, the twenty pieces of luggage, the traveling secretary, the nurse, the priest, the shoes, and more shoes. This display of "impression" management did not reflect her attorney's statement that since arriving in the United States, the Marcoses have been forced to live on borrowed funds.

There are also behaviors that can be employed to make oneself more attractive to others. These tactics depend on the climate of the occasion and may be assertive or nonassertive in nature. Also, they may be either premeditated or unintentional. Any manipulative nature of the behavior may be consciously or unconsciously recognized. Ulterior motives are always suspect.

Ingratiatory behavior of the positive variety takes different forms for different reasons and is obviously nondevious. Promoting oneself via an assertive strategy can involve, for example, sincere agreement with the target person(s) or a third person who interacts with the target. People who have similar attitudes and opinions tend to be attracted to one another. Another example: a focus on long-term goals, vision of the future avoids any defensive tactic of self-presentation. It can be a modest proactive assertion rather than reactive, defensive position.

In a networking strategy, the objective is to build outside contacts having common interests. A companion notion is building social collateral, or indirect support and reinforcement on a person-to-person basis. This is a means of gaining respect and consideration when advisory talent is needed. It takes years to achieve and is a consequence of the relationship rather than the target of the effort.

The strategies by which organizations secure resources from other organizations has become a major area of organizational research. Corporations coopt sources of uncertainty through such mechanisms as interlocking directorates, joint ventures, mergers and acquisitions, contract alliances, advisory boards, federations, cooperatives, syndicates, coalitions and various network linkages.

Some view financial interlocks or ties as mechanisms of "infiltration." For example, financial firms may demand a seat on the board of an unprofitable nonfinancial corporation to which they have extended loans. As an aspirant candidate for an advisory board, you have no such leverage. However, if you possess expertise sorely needed by a company in trouble (for example, expertise of a financial, technological, marketing, political, social, or environmental nature), your availability and interest in advising may be a positive influence, enhancing chances of being engaged on an advisory board if you have the proper contacts.

An advisory role may be initiated by the top management as a device to coopt outside expertise providing access to (1) capital or acquiring financial advice, or (2) various functional, political, social, or environmental advice. This cooptation may be provoked by expansion or contraction of the business in either a troubled, unstable, or stable state. The key to participating in a cooptation strategy is continual networking and sensitive marketing of your interest, competence, and availability through network connections of appropriate contacts.

Finally, ask yourself the following self-rating questions:

Are you a good listener?

Do you interrupt others?

Are you boring or ponderous to others?

Do you keep the floor too long and fail to yield to others?

Do you keep focused, or do you wander off on tangential issues and problems?

Are you tolerant of other persons' opinions?

Do you relate to others with humility and humor?

Are you aware of limitations in your knowledge and experience?

If the answers to most of these questions are affirmative, you have some attributes of a good advisor. These techniques and sensitivity skills can be learned and practiced. There are many self-improvement programs available to help enhance your advisor style and attitude. The key, of course, is to have the network contacts, directly or indirectly, to those in need of advisory services.

CULTURAL CHARACTERISTICS

Social cement or personal affinities with others is a pervasive force to reckon with when seeking an advisory relationship. Common cultural attributes smooth interpersonal affinity or valence between those who may wish to trust each other's perspectives and advice. When you understand the culture you are better able to forge a bond of trust and share understandings necessary for a two-way exchange of views and tentative responses to external stimuli. People feel comfortable with others who share the same faith, ethics, beliefs, attitudes, rituals, patterns of behavior, and customs. Thus, in seeking recognition as a potential advisor, perhaps the best target advisee is one where there is least likely to be a culture clash between your own culture and that of the target principals.

On the other hand, corporations seeking to do their business in a foreign land or domain are likely to want access to regional economic, political, and social knowhow and culture of the environment. Tapping the local environmental cultural conditions is essential for good business conduct. To find persons who can bridge the cultural gap that may exist is often the primary driving force seeking corporate advisors who can form a panel, council, or advisory board in the host country.

Some sophisticated nationals are often multicultural in their business and personal skills. They can provide the link with the guest company by acting as an advisory resource. An aspiring advisor must be conscious of the importance of cultural affinity between principals and not seek an advisory relationship where a culture clash is formidable or uncomfortable.

LEVERAGED BUY-IN

Much attention has been recently paid to the technique of employee leveraged buyouts (LBO) of corporations. Assets of the corporation are used as collateral for raising funds from a third source of financing. Seeking a personal relationship with the principals of a corporation selected as a potential target advisee can follow much the same technique, in a reverse sense, that of a leveraged buy-in (LBI).

An aspiring advisor may associate himself or herself with an organized group or network of professionals majoring their interests in affairs of relevance to the target advisee company. This association and identification may subtly enhance one's chances of being a recognizable resource to the target advisee company principals. For example, if a target advisee company is in a high technology field of business, the principals are usually active in the appropriate professional societies, trade associations, and various industry affairs. There they can learn and share experiences with others who are credible sources of information, technical and commercial opportunities, and development.

Being a fellow member of these groups can substantially increase network contacts and exposure to potential target advisee companies. Possible conflicts of interest and matters of confidentiality can be managed ethically. You develop the rapport with others that may lead to more formal or enduring relationship as a corporate advisor and thus achieve a leveraged buy-in to the advisee.

PEER POWER

Peer power is as powerful as position power in the business and professional worlds. Those seeking advisory relationships outside their base activity may employ peer power as an influence in seeking advisory invitations. Assuming positive personal and professional qualifications, belonging to and being active in professional organizations, learned societies, trade, political and social associations, are obvious arenas where peer relationship and introductions are most likely to benefit the search for a more formal advisory engagement.

The growth in interest in active networking makes this effort worth considering. Networking with peers, sharing and exchanging information and influence is a respectable and acceptable way of contributing to a project, program, or movement of mutual interest to others. Out of these relationships can come peer respect. Such standing is essential for a would-be advisor.

ETHICAL STANCE AND CENTRAL LIFE INTEREST

Your attraction to a potential advisee principal or organization has an ethical aura and dignity, and a positive identification with a central life interest that characterizes you as a potential advisor resource.

The ethical profile is a composite of your personal beliefs, articles of faith, attitudes (which are a pattern of your beliefs), value systems, morals and ethics. The ethical position is one in which you conduct yourself and your affairs in a manner that promotes human welfare. This is a dynamic attribute and adapts to the normative, social, and political mores of the times and surrounding culture. Deep down, however, ethical stance is determined by personal beliefs, attitudes, and morals. Thus, in positioning yourself in the "market" for advisory board membership, clarify in your own mind and behavior pattern just what you stand for with respect to ethical and value-laden issues of the day and venue.

Having a central life interest of relevance to the prospective advisee organization's principals is important. A company seeking counsel in management morale and motivation matters is unlikely to be attracted to a potential outside expert whose central life interest is transaction-oriented as, for example, a financially driven corporate raider and restructurer.

ADVISOR-POWER STRATEGIES

Achieving a position as a corporate advisor or counselor in other than a problem-solving, task-oriented consulting role may be viewed as an alternate approach to power. Advisor-power is derived from many sources, including personal expertise, reputation, integrity, ethics, and professional/social networks. Organization development (OD) practitioners devote much of their research to powerholders within organizations and the reconciling of power with development of effectiveness of human organizations, strategic consensus, and releasing power through leadership and collaboration. Relatively little research is available on development of a power base that is useful in the process of advisee search.

The perspective of advisor-power implies the creation of advisory relationships from a formal counseling, outside resource base of expertise. The contract is for the benefit of principals of a company seeking to retain a panel or board of professional advisors. Keys to creating advisor-power include the following approaches:

1. Building one's own power base (particularly one the target advisee does not have) in order to have access to those advisee principals in power at a target company.

2. Employing open and straightforward power strategies using alliances, coalitions, and networks with others who can influence principal power-holders of a target advisee firm in order to enhance the value of a formal advisory relationship.

3. Creating and presenting novel perspectives and realistic processes relevant to the critical issues and uncertainties faced by a target advisee company.

4. Understanding power in a target advisee organization with acknowledgment of the pervasive reality of political behavior and dynamics in the organization.

5. Leveraging one's individual position power including present and former titles, position descriptions, experiences, and track record with appropriate distinguished references and respected peer associations.

Scholars have categorized eight potential bases of such individual power under three broad types: (1) *Knowledge*—expert power, information power, and tradition power (corporate history); (2) *Personality*—charisma, reputation, and professional credibility; and (3) *Others' Support*—political access (ability to call on networks) and staff support power (tying in your power bases with the organizations's staff power bases).[1]

Of eighteen categories of "influence strategies" identified in 1986–87 studies of over 300 managers in the United States and United Kingdom, four or five categories may be considered applicable to an advisee-search strategy. In the top half-dozen most frequently used influence strategies, the following four are of possible use in seeking advisory roles: (1) formation of alliances and coalitions, (2) dealing directly with key decision makers, (3) using special information to convince others, and (4) focusing on needs of the target advisee.

This involves using social and professional networks and one's private contacts to obtain legitimately useful, valuable, and timely information not readily available to the advisee principals. Such information may be diagnostic, perceptive, innovative, predictive, or reflective in nature.

PRECIS: DIRECTORDOM AND ADVISORDOM

The separate states of being either a statutory director or an advisory director of a corporation are differentiated in chapters 3 and 4. Seeking statutory directorship or advisory directorship involves much the same process but not the same structure (or nonstructure), accountability, duties, or functions.

The nature of the invitation to enter directordom or advisordom varies. Directordom encompasses statutory accountability and personal ethics and judgment as prime attributes of the candidate. The second collective, advisordom, entails expert, professional, peer—not legal—accountability, plus personal ethics and judgment as distinctive attributes of a candidate advisor.

Both candidate roles are, for the most part, driven by the service ethic, rather than the competitive ethic. Servanthood as a statutory director or an advisory director implies performance of certain official duties or functions. From a legal viewpoint, servanthood includes any person employed by another and subject in his employment to his employer's direction and control, in other words, an agent who is subject to the direction and control of his principal.

In the case of a statutory director, the principal or "employer" is the share-holder(s). An advisory director is an agent of the contracting officer of the corporation, acting on behalf of the company, usually represented as the chief executive, chairperson, or a senior officer of the corporation.

An invitation to serve either a statutory or advisory role entails different duties, functions, obligations, accountability, liability, expectations and personal relationships. The selection criteria for the statutory and advisory director thus vary considerably as described in the referenced chapters. No wonder the approaches for advisee-search and director-search are both dissimilar and similar.

Similarities are that: (1) you are invited to join, the initiative being primarily that of the invitor; (2) individual characteristics such as experience, fitness, competence, diligence, judgment, integrity, intellect, ethics, reputation, personality, and certain sociodemographic factors pertain (education, social class, ethnic culture, family, and so on; (3) organizational characteristics dominate, such as behavior regulation appearing as social or corporate structure and norms. These pertain to respect for autonomy, control, stratification (hierarchy), flexibility (or inflexibility), effective synergy, stability, and participation with the group members. In addition, primary personal interactive networking with other principals within and without the organization is significant. These three sets of similarities cover many of the common characteristics of either statutory or advisory directors. Seeking an invitation to join either type collective involves qualifying on most of the value-laden, subjective criteria.

Dissimilarities in the approach to advisee-search and director-search include: (1) normally there is less formality involved by the contracting (invitee) source in the case of an invitation to be an advisor. Corporation law is relevant to directorship; commercial law normally deals with advisory services; (2) the advisee principal is not threatened by engaging advisors who can be discharged at the principal's will. Statutory directors serve at the pleasure of the shareowners and have obligation, among other things, to insure effective executive management. Hence, the formal invitation to participate contains different motivations, limitations, threats, and opportunities on the part of invitor and invitee; (3) public identification of appointment to an advisory board or council is not required. In some cases, the advisee principal may prefer to keep the invitation and service a private matter; (4) less compensation to the advisor and less cost to the advisee; (5) less time requirement and paperwork; (6) less formal meetings and more flexible schedules make an invitation to serve as an advisor less onerous an assignment than nomination to a statutory board. The subtle, often indirect, approach to a potential advisee principal can be less intimidating, more ingratiating on the part of the aspiring advisor; (7) no fixed patterns or standards apply to advisory boards or advisors; hence, the personal strategy in advisee-search is situation-specific. It is tailored to the perceived needs of the corporation or its principals, the style and personality of the target principals and the overlapping network contacts of the advisor and advisee. The key is careful timing and propriety of any direct or indirect signals by the aspiring advisor to the target principals.

The art of landing an advisory board engagement or statutory boardroom seat is a skill, acquired by experience, study and observation. Above all, your track record, reputation and networking are key characteristics.

The need for both statutory and advisory directors has been outlined in chapters 1 and 2. This career opportunity has not gone unnoticed by the executive recruiting firms. In the United States, more than one hundred top corporations used recruiters to fill board vacancies, according to *Business Week* of December 22, 1986. Spencer-Stuart is an international recruiting service organization like many other such organizations. Jack Lohnes, managing director of its board services, points out that he never uses unsolicited resumes as a source of candidates. Similar practice is common with many other recruiters. Catalyst, a New York recruiter dedicated to placing women executives, is an exception to this rule against using unsolicited resumes as a source of women directors.

The National Association of Corporate Directors (NACD), a Washington, D.C.–based, not-for-profit membership organization founded in 1977, has as its singular mission the concerns of the corporate boardroom. In addition to various educational services, the NACD has a Directors Register that helps companies find qualified candidates for board vacancies. Based on resume information provided by its members, NACD identifies to companies prospective directors in its files on a blind-match basis. While resume data are provided the Directors Register optionally by NACD members, no claim is made that the candidate will be optimum for numerous qualitative requirements involved in director nomination criteria.

The bottom line in a personal advisee-search strategy is that advisory directors have to be invited by the principal in a company. Overt solicitation of an advisor or statutory role is never de rigueur. Despite this, I have seen personal employment advertisements in the *International Herald Tribune* by an experienced Swiss national who should know better, advertising his desires to be engaged as either a director or advisor to international corporations. The *New Straits Times,* Singapore, had a similar "want ad" last December. The regional practice in seeking directorships varies widely around the globe.

Perhaps the ultimate situation for aspiring advisory directors is the apocryphal opportunity recently published by the fictional American Hemlockian Association (AHA). The advertisement portrayed in the Fall 1988 issue of *The Journal of Polymorphous Perversity* [2] announces the birth of a new spoof *Journal of Euthanasia: Theory, Research and Practice.* The listed board of directors of the association are all deceased. Possibly they took their duty of loyalty, and the directors' liability issues too seriously?

With the unusually high turnover (100 percent) among AHA board members, applicants are solicited. If the AHA had only an advisory board in place, perhaps this spurious governance crisis could have been better addressed. Advisory directors have no formal legal duty of loyalty to the corporation advised, albeit they should have faithful client allegiance to the company served to provide expert judgment. Nonfictional advisory boards can be an effective interim gap filler readily accessible to a chief executive or chairperson.

Figure A-1

Coming in Spring 1989...

The

Journal

of

Euthanasia:

Theory, Research, and Practice

BOARD OF DIRECTORS[1]

James C. Alt, M.D.
Deceased

Cynthia Block, M.D.
Deceased

Jay L. Fernly, Psy.D.
Deceased

Nigel R. Harrison, J.D.
Deceased

Stanly Smith, M.A.
Deceased

Ruth A. Stern, Ph.D.
Deceased

William Totwell, Th.D.
Deceased

Administrative Assistant

Mary Schneider

[1]Because of an unusually high turnover rate among board members, many positions on the Board of Directors are now open. Applicants should submit their applications ATTN: Mary Schneider, Administrative Assistant.

The American Hemlockian Association is pleased to announce the publication of **The Journal of Euthanasia: Theory, Research, and Practice**, the official periodical of the AHA. While the number of issues per volume is still undecided, each issue will present scholarly articles of singular clarity and focus on the theory, research, and practice of euthanasia. Members of the Board of Directors of the American Hemlockian Association, each a world renowned expert on the topic of euthanasia, will serve as editors of **The Journal of Euthanasia**. Submissions of highly relevant theoretical and practical articles relating to the topic of euthanasia are invited from the research and clinical community.

1-year subscriptions (domestic): $54.00
2-year subscriptions (domestic): $97.00

American Hemlockian Association
New Subscriptions Department
ATTN: Mary Schneider
The Hemlock Building
22345 Connecticut Avenue, N.W.
Washington, DC 20036

Source: Copyright 1988 Wry-Bred Press, Inc. Reprinted by permission of the copyright holder from the *Journal of Polymorphous Perversity.*

NOTES

1. Larry E. Greiner and Virginia E. Schein, *Power and Organization Development: Mobilizing Power to Implement Change* (Reading, Mass.: Addison-Wesley Publishing Co., 1988), pp. 27–32.

2. The *Journal* publishes humorous and satirical works in the fields of psychology, psychiatry, and the closely allied disciplines. The JPP is published by Wry-Bred Press, Inc., 10 Waterside Plaza, Suite 20B, New York, NY 10010, and has been called "a magazine for the Jung at heart" by the *New York Daily News,* and "a social scientist's answer to Mad Magazine" by the *Wall Street Journal.*

SELECTED BIBLIOGRAPHY AND REFERENCE READING LIST

Abbasi, Susan R., and Alfred R. Greenwood. "Energy Advisors: An Analysis of Federal Advisory Committees Dealing with Energy." U.S. Library of Congress. Environment and Natural Resources Policy Division. Washington, D.C., 1977.

"ACS Publications Choose Advisory Boards." *Chemical and Engineering News,* February 10, 1986, pp. 45–47.

"Advisor Board: A Personal Cabinet for Company Presidents." *Business Management* 26 (April 1964), pp. 44–49.

"Advisory Board Will Offer Views about Software to Ashton-Tate." *InfoWorld,* October 28, 1985, p. 11.

"Advisory Boards: Obtaining Peer Support and Counsel for Outside Advisors." *Small Business Report,* June 1988, pp. 56–59.

"Advisory Boards: Outside Advisors Provide the CEO with Peer Support." *Small Business Report* 10, 1 (January 1985), pp. 37–40.

"Advisory Committee; Outside View, Inside Management." *Journal of Accountancy* 120 (October 1965), pp. 86–87.

"Advisory Committees." *Small Business Report,* November 1979, p. 17.

"Advisory Committees." U.S. Federal Aviation Administration, Department of Transportation, Washington, D.C., January 26, 1973.

Advisory Council for Applied Research and Development Software. *A Vital Key to U.K. Competitiveness.* London: HMSO, December 8, 1987.

"Advisory Council Keyed to Newest Distributor Problems." *Industrial Distribution,* February 1986, pp. 54–55, 57.

"Advisory Councils: Precision Comes to Problem Solving." *Industrial Distribution* 65 (May 1975), pp. 43–46.

Alpert, G. "Consumer Advisory Boards and Investor-Owned Utilities: Rhetoric and Reality." *Public Utilities* 108 (August 27, 1981), pp. 19–22; and 108 (December 3, 1981), pp. 65–68.

"An Advisory Council to Back Up the Board." *Business Week,* November 12, 1979, pp. 131–37.

Amend, P. "Outside Advice: Who Says Boards Are Out?" *Inc.* 8 (June 1986), p. 105.

"Art of Landing a Board Room Seat." *Business Week,* December 22, 1986, p. 71.

Association of Governing Boards of Universities and Colleges. "The Board-Mentor Program." Washington, D.C.

Auerbach, Norman E., and William C. Turner. "Risks and Opportunities of Foreign Investment." *Chief Executive,* November 21, 1982, pp. 37–40.

Baker, H. K. "Making Advisory Boards Effective." *Burroughs Clearing House* 54 (May 1970), pp. 30–31.

"The Benefits of an International Advisory Board." *International Management,* June 1976.

Berenbeim, Ronald E. "Managing the International Company: Building a Global Perspective." Research Report No. 814. New York: the Conference Board, 1981, pp. 13–21.

Biles, William E. "Advisory Council Finds Research Opportunities." *Industrial Engineering,* April 1986, p. 20.

Brockinton, Langdon C. "CPI Retirees Go Back to Work." *Chemical Week,* April 2, 1986, pp. 17–19.

Buchan, P. Bruce. "Boards of Directors: Adversaries or Advisors." *California Management Review,* 24, 2 (Winter 1981), pp. 31–39.

Bull, George. "Role of the Non-Executive Director." *Director* 22 (December 1969), pp. 426–29.

"Buying Advice from the Top; Controls Corp. of America's Four-Man European Advisory Board." *Business Week,* March 5, 1966, pp. 139–40.

"The Case for Counsel to Outside Directors." *Harvard Business Review* 54 (July–August 1976), p. 125.

Charles, C. "The President's New Advisors: A Fable," *Personnel* 40 (November 1963), pp. 38–44.

"Cheap Brainpower in Washington—Boon or Boondoggle?" *U.S. News & World Report,* March 1, 1976, p. 63.

Cole, Jacquelyn M., and Maurice F. Cole. *Advisory Councils: A Theoretical and Practical Guide for Program Planners.* (Englewood Cliffs, N.J.: Prentice-Hall, 1982).

Cooper, G. H., and V. M. Jolivet. "Branch Advisory Boards, Useful or Superfluous?" *Burroughs Clearing House* 48 (October 1963), p. 45.

Councils, Committees & Boards: A Handbook of Advisory, Consultative, Executive and Similar Bodies in British Public Life, 5th ed. Beckenham, Kent, England: CBD Research Ltd., 1982.

Davids, L. E. "Advisory Directors: More than Window Dressing?" *Bankers Magazine* 153 (Summer 1970), pp. 64–68.

Dyer, W. Gibb, Jr. *Cultural Change in Family Firms: Anticipating and Managing Business and Family Transactions.* San Francisco: Jossey-Bass Publishers, 1986, ch. 2.

"Economic Advisors: Divided and Discounted," *Economist* 82 (March 13, 1982), p. 20.

Ellis, Susan J. "Rethinking Auxiliaries and Advisory Councils," *Nonprofit World,* July/August 1988, pp. 23–25.

"EPA Proposes Advisory-Group Rulemaking," *Electrical World* (June 1984), pp. 26–27.

Forbes, W. F., and A. H. Rosenblook. "Shield for Directors: The Outside Consultant," *Management Review* 66 (December 1977), pp. 26–28.

Fox, Harold W. "Advisory Board: Resource for Closely Held Companies." Federal Advisory Committees: Index to the Membership of Federal Advisory Committees Listed in the Fifth Annual Report of the President to the Congress Covering Calendar Year 1976.

Fox, Harold W. "Advisory Board: Resource for Closely Held Companies." *Michigan State University Business Topics* 27, 3 (Summer, 1979), pp. 26–30.

Fox, Harold W. "Quasi-boards: Guidance without Governance." *American Journal of Small Business* (Summer 1984), pp. 12–18.

Fox, Harold W. "Quasi-boards: Useful Small Business Confidants." *Harvard Business Review,* January–February 1982, pp. 158–65.

Friedman, J. J. "Sun Chemical's Shadow Cabinet (Advisory Management Committee, an Effective Way to Keep Middle Management from Getting Restless)." *Dun's Review and Modern Industry* 80 (December 1962), p. 35.

Gale, Robert L. "Lay Advisory Boards as an External Public Relations Tool." *Peabody Journal of Education,* April 1976, pp. 162–65.

Gleason, S. J. "Case for Advisory Boards." *Bankers Monthly* 82 (November 1965), pp. 48–51.

Gubernick, Lisa, and Laura Saunders. "Nobel Decorations: Investors Beware: The Presence of Star-Quality Scientists on 'Advisory Boards' of Start-Up Companies May Not Mean a Thing." *Forbes* 136 (August 1985), p. 86.

"Guidelines for Organizing a State or Local Agency Advisory Council." Monograph by U.S. Department of Agriculture, Food and Nutrition Service, 1981.

Hall, Peter. "The Big Board Takes a New Look." *Financial World,* May 28, 1985, p. 22.

Hand, Irving, and Charles Speers. "Role of Advisory Groups: Why Have an Advisory Group?" U.S. Environmental Protection Agency, Office of Water Program Operations, Washington, D.C., 1980.

"Hercules Inc. Forms 'Advisory Council of Outside Experts.'" *Wall Street Journal,* September 19, 1979.

Hill, Roy. "The Benefits of an International Advisory Board." *International Management,* June 1976, pp. 28–31.

"Hoffman Filters Out Potential Problems with a Representatives' Advisory Board." *Agency Sales Magazine,* November 1979, pp. 4–6.

"How a Science Board Keeps Gould on Track," *Business Week,* July 14, 1975, pp. 92–93.

"How a Small Bank Uses a Large Advisory Board." *Journal of ABA Banking* 73 (December 1981), p. 116.

Hussey, D. W. "Part-Time Executive Directors? The Paradoxical Answer by the Planners." *Director* 25 (October 1972), p. 76.

International Institute for Applied Systems Analyses (IIASA). *IIASA in Brief.* Laxenburg, Austria: Author, January 1986.

"In the 80's: Why Join an Advisory Council?" *Industrial Distributor* 72 (March 1982), pp. 63–65.

Juran, J. M., and J. Keith Louden. "Advisory Responsibilities." *The Corporate Director.* New York: American Management Association, 1966, pp. 112–29, 366–68.

Kenny, Roger M. "Helpful Guidance from International Advisory Boards." *Harvard Business Review,* March–April 1976, pp. 14–19, 156.

Kehrl, Howard H. "International Advisory Councils." *The Corporate Director,* November/December 1980, pp. 11–15.

Killian, Larita Jean Rouch. "A Comparative Analysis of Academic Governance at the Naval Postgraduate School (California)." Ed.D. dissertation, Stanford University, 1984.

Kirk, M. "Building an Advisory Board." *Venture* 6, 42 (October 1984).

Lear, Robert W. "Speaking Out: Nurturing Young CEOs." *The Chief Executive,* January/February 1988, p. 12.

Louden, J. Keith. "The Liability of Advisory Boards." *Directors and Boards,* Spring 1986, pp. 19–20.

Louden, J. Keith, and Jack Zusman. *The Director: A Professional's Guide to Effective Board Work.* New York: AMACOM, 1983, pp. 165–67.

"Making of a President's Panel." *Dun's Review* 93 (June 1969), p. 3.

Martin, John E. "Peer Directors Increase Board Effectiveness." *Directors & Boards,* Winter 1977, pp. 299–381.

Martin, John E. "The Board Advisory Council and Peer Directors." *Directors & Boards,* Fall 1976, pp. 44–49.

Matthews, Fred A. "Planned Giving Advisory Boards: Emerging Tactic." *Fund Raising Management* 16, 8 (1985), pp. 78–83.

Merritt, Giles. "Knights of the Roundtable: Can They Move Europe Forward Fast Enough?" *International Management,* July 1986, pp. 22–26.

Miller, William H. "CEO Sounding Boards, Where Can Top Executives Find Independent Perspectives on Their Business Problems?" *Industry Week,* July 13, 1987, pp. 47–49.

Mitchell, B. "Rockford's Remarkable Advisory Council (CETA programs)." *Worklife* 2 (Summer 1977), pp. 24–25.

Monsanto Company announcement, December 4, 1981, on "Advisory Directors."

Mueller, Robert K. *Board Compass: What It Means to Be a Director in a Changing World.* Lexington, Mass.: D. C. Heath and Company, 1978, ch. 12.

Mueller, Robert K. "The Care and Feeding of Advisory Boards." *The Journal of Business Strategy,* July/August 1988, pp. 21–24.

Mueller, Robert K. "Differential Directorship: Special Sensitivities and Roles for Serving the Family Business Board." *Family Business Review* 1, 3 (Fall 1988), pp. 239–47.

Mueller, Robert K. *The Incompleat Board: The Unfolding of Corporate Governance.* Lexington, Mass.: D. C. Heath and Company, 1981, ch. 20.

"Multi-Nationals: The Men Behind the Multi-Nationals." *International Management,* November 1983, pp. 21–26.

Newman, L. E. "Advice for Small Company Presidents." *Harvard Business Review* 37 (November 1959), pp. 69–76.

Nicolson, David. "Full-Time, Part-Time Director." *Director* 19 (November 1966), p. 254.

Nisker, Bernie. "Advisory Boards: A Low-Cost Way to Get High-Priced Counsel." *Canadian Business* 56, 11 (November 1983), pp. 115–16.

Otten, Alan. "Advisory Councils." Managers' Journal, *The Wall Street Journal,* June 16, 1980.

Oversight of the Federal Advisory Committee Act. June 21, 1984, Senate Hearing, Subcommittee on Information Management and Regulatory Affairs to Examine Implementation of the Federal Advisory Committee Act (FACA) of 1972 establishing procedures governing advisory committee establishment and use by federal departments and agencies of the president.

Pearson, Clifford. "Advisory Board Accentuates the Positives." *Corporate Design and Realty,* March 1987, pp. 38–41.

Perrin, H. F. Robert. "Advisory Boards—Their Tasks, Composition and Operation." Croydon, Surrey, England: SRI International, 1982.

Persinos, John F. "The Advice Squad: How Outside Boards Give CEOs What They Can't Get Anywhere Else." *INC.,* January 1986, pp. 80–84.

Putze, L. "Firm's Overseas Operations Guided by European Board." *Steel* 156 (May 10, 1965), p. 45.

Putze, Lou. "What a European Advisory Board Can Do for You." *Business Abroad* 92 (October 30, 1967), pp. 10–12.

"R&D Advisory Boards: A New Planning Touch." *Chemical Week,* January 21, 1981, p. 48.

Rock, Stuart. "The Wise Men Who Advise the World: International Advisory Boards Are Common Among U.S. Corporations but Only Beginning to Catch on in Britain." *Director* 42, 4 (November 1988), pp. 60–63.

Rohan, T. R. "The Brain Gain (technical committees of outside experts)." *Industry Week,* January 21, 1981, p. 48.

Sellers, Lindsay, ed. *Councils, Committees and Boards,* 6th ed. (Detroit: CBD Research Ltd., Gale, 1984).

"Setting Up International Advisory Councils." *Management Review* 73 (December 1984), p. 8–9.

Shell, R. "Advisory Boards: Making Time." *INC.* 7 (November 1985), p. 160.

Smith, R. Jeffrey. "Carter Reducing Plan Adds Pounds." *Science* 198 (December 2, 1977), p. 900.

Taravella, Steve. "Companies, Directors Grope for Answers to D&O Dilemma/Firms Find Different Solutions to Exodus of Outside Directors." *Business Insurance* 20, 4 (January 27, 1986), pp. 1, 62–63.

"Tenneco in Europe: The Essential Overseas Market." *Tenneco* 18, 4 (Winter 1984).

"Texas Instruments Names Panel of Six to Advise Its Board." *Wall Street Journal,* January 23, 1981.

"The Advisory Board." *Small Business Report,* May 1981, pp. 11–114.

Thompson, Hugh. "Are Boards Other than Trustees Needed?" *AGB Reports,* May/June 1984, pp. 27–34.

Tillman, Fred A. "Commentary on Legal Liability: Organizing the Advisory Council." *Family Business Review* 1, 3 (Fall 1988), pp. 287–88.

"Top Talent on Tap for Small Firms." *Steel* 148 (March 6, 1961), pp. 41–43.

Tucker, S. "Retired but Not Retiring." *Public Relations Journal* 40 (October 1984), pp. 16–18.

Turley, Paul W. "Advisory Committees. Federal Trade Commission: Government Investigations." Chicago Regional Office, FTC, August 2, 1979, pp. 275–80.

"The Network that Knows the World." *Directorship* 12, 3 (March 1987), pp. 2–3.

Turner, William C. "International Advisory Councils: What You Need to Know to Make Them Work." Spencer Stuart & Associates Special Report, 1984, pp. 7–19.

Turpin-Forster, Shela C. "Bank Directors and Advisors as Business Developers: A Selling Resource." American Bankers Association, Number 36 of the *Competitech* series, 1985.

Vance, Stanley C. *Corporate Leadership: Boards, Directors, and Strategy.* New York: McGraw-Hill Book Company, 1983, ch. 8.

Wells, William H. "Advisory Boards: Use Them or Lose Them." *ABA Banking Journal* 73 (April 1981), p. 65.

Wilson, Hillsman V. "A Tradition of Participative Management." *The President* 22, 4 (April 1986).

"Wisconsin Bank Forms Women's Advisory Councils." *Bank Mark* 19 (March 1987), p. 46.

Wright, John Donald. "A Development Board: How to Create 'Ties' for the Bank with Influential Young People." *The Effective Bank Director.* Reston, Va.: Reston Publishing Co., April 1985.

Zuckert, E. M., and J. H. Quinn, Jr. "Small Company Advisors: Substitute for Outside Directors." *Michigan Business Review* 26 (May 1974), pp. 18–23.

INDEX

About the Author

ROBERT K. MUELLER is a recognized expert on corporate governance. He has written thirteen books including: *Board Score: How to Judge Boardworthiness, Behind the Boardroom Door,* and *Corporate Networking: Building Channels for Information and Influence.* Mueller currently serves on three advisory boards and was Chairman of the Board at Arthur D. Little for ten years.